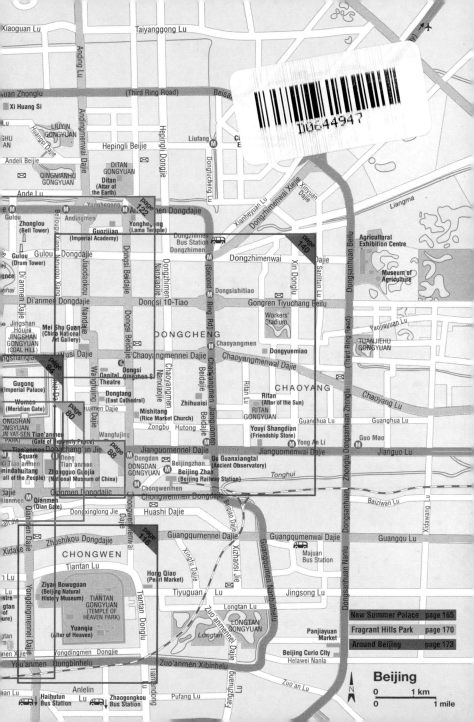

**INSIGHT** **CITY GUIDE**

# BEIJING

**Discovery**
**CHANNEL**

**APA PUBLICATIONS**
Part of the Langenscheidt Publishing Group

## ※ INSIGHT GUIDE
# BEIJING

*Editor*
**Tom Le Bas**
*Art Director*
**Klaus Geisler**
*Picture Editor*
**Hilary Genin**
*Cartography Editor*
**Zoë Goodwin**

### Distribution

*UK & Ireland*
**GeoCenter International Ltd**
The Viables Centre, Harrow Way
Basingstoke, Hants RG22 4BJ
Fax: (44) 1256-817988

*United States*
**Langenscheidt Publishers, Inc.**
46–35 54th Road, Maspeth, NY 11378
Fax: (1) 718 784-0640

*Canada*
**Thomas Allen & Son Ltd**
390 Steelcase Road East
Markham, Ontario L3R 1G2
Fax: (1) 905 475 6747

*Australia*
**Universal Publishers**
1 Waterloo Road
Macquarie Park, NSW 2113
Fax: (61) 2 9888 9074

*New Zealand*
**Hema Maps New Zealand Ltd (HNZ)**
Unit D, 24 Ra ORA Drive
East Tamaki, Auckland
Fax: (64) 9 273 6479

*Worldwide*
**Apa Publications GmbH & Co.
Verlag KG (Singapore branch)**
38 Joo Koon Road, Singapore 628990
Tel: (65) 6865-1600. Fax: (65) 6861-6438

### Printing

**Insight Print Services (Pte) Ltd**
38 Joo Koon Road, Singapore 628990
Tel: (65) 6865-1600. Fax: (65) 6861-6438

# ABOUT THIS BOOK

This guidebook combines the interests and enthusiasms of two of the world's best-known information providers: Insight Guides, whose titles have set the standard for visual travel guides since 1970, and Discovery Channel, the world's premier source of nonfiction television programming.

The editors of Insight Guides provide both practical advice and general understanding about a destination. Discovery Channel and its Web site, www.discovery.com, help millions of viewers explore their world from the comfort of their own home.

### How to use this book

The book is carefully structured both to convey an understanding of the city and its culture and to guide readers through its sights and activities:

◆ To understand Beijing today, you need to know something of its past. The first section covers the city's history and culture in lively, authoritative essays written by specialists.
◆ The main Places section provides a full run-down of all the attractions worth seeing. The main places of interest are coordinated by number with full-colour maps.
◆ A list of recommended restaurants is included at the end of each chapter in the Places section (with the exception of the Forbidden City and Further Afield chapters), and each can be located on the pull-out restaurant map.
◆ Photographic features illustrate various facets of the city, from its keep-fit activities and bicycles to the unique art form of Beijing Opera and picturesque labyrinth of *hutong*.

◆ The Travel Tips listings section provides all the practical information you will need, now divided into five easy-to-use sections: Transport, Accommodation, Activities (cultural, shopping, sports), an A to Z directory covering everything from budgeting to tour agents, and Language. The final section includes a short phrasebook and a list of recommended reading.

◆ A detailed street atlas is included at the back of the book, complete with a full index.

◆ Information can be located quickly by using the index printed on the back cover flap. The flaps are designed to serve as bookmarks.

◆ Photographs throughout the book are chosen not only to illustrate geography and buildings but also to convey the moods of the city and the life of its people.

## The contributors

This new edition of Insight: Beijing was co-ordinated by **Tom Le Bas** at Insight Guides' London office, who restructured the book into its practical and reader-friendly City Guide format. Assisting him in this task was **Sheila Melvin**, who also fully updated the text in the Places section and the Travel Tips, and contributed new essays on architecture and the Olympics. A writer who specialises in Chinese culture, Sheila first visited China as a backpacker in 1987 and has lived or travelled there regularly ever since. She and her husband, the conductor Jindong Cai, currently split their time between Beijing and California.

Past contributors whose work remains in this edition include **Bill Smith** and **Hilary Smith** (no relation), who between them rewrote much of the book for the 1999 edition. **Manfred Morgenstern** was the project editor for the first edition back in 1990, and wrote many of the original chapters. **Helmut Forster-Latsch** and his wife **Marie-Luise Forster-Latsch** contributed to several essays. **Marie-Luise Beppler-Lie** wrote the original chapters on Cuisine, Art and Crafts, Museums and Imperial Tombs, while **Elke Wandel** contributed the original chapters on the Summer Palaces. **Klaus Bodenstein** wrote the original Life in the Hutong text. Photographers for the guide include **Richard Nowitz**, **Catherine Karnow** and **Bodo Bondzio**.

This 2005 edition was proofread by **Neil Titman** and indexed by **Helen Peters**.

## CONTACTING THE EDITORS

We would appreciate it if readers would alert us to errors or outdated information by writing to:

**Insight Guides, P.O. Box 7910, London SE1 1WE, England. Fax: (44) 20 7403-0290. insight@apaguide.co.uk**

NO part of this book may be reproduced, stored in a retrieval system or transmitted in any form or means electronic, mechanical, photocopying, recording or otherwise, without prior written permission of *Apa Publications*. Brief text quotations with use of photographs are exempted for book review purposes only. Information has been obtained from sources believed to be reliable, but its accuracy and completeness, and the opinions based thereon, are not guaranteed.

**www.insightguides.com**

### Place names usage:

*For all places listed in this guide, rather than following a rigid system of English followed by the standard* pinyin *trans-literation in brackets, or the other way round, we have simply used the best-known and most appropriate name for tourist purposes. On the whole, this means English with* pinyin *in brackets, but there are many exceptions,*

*particularly for those temple names where the English is unwieldy. Thus Tiananmen Square (Tiananmen Guangchang), the Great Wall (Wanli Changcheng) and the Lama Temple (Yongheggong), but also Baiyunguan (Temple of the White Cloud) and Fayuansi (Temple of the Source of Buddhist Teaching).*

## Maps

## Travel Tips

### TRANSPORT

### ACCOMMODATION

### ACTIVITIES

### A–Z: PRACTICAL INFORMATION

### LANGUAGE

### FURTHER READING **237**

# THE BEST OF BEIJING

**Setting priorities, saving money, unique attractions... here, at a glance, are our recommendations, plus some tips and tricks even the locals won't always know**

## BEIJING'S MUST-SEE SIGHTS

- **The Forbidden City**. One of the world's most complete historical sights, this remarkable palace complex lies right at the heart of Beijing. *See pages 91–101.*
- **Tiananmen Square**. Beijing's gigantic central square is the largest urban space in the world, able to accommodate up to a million people. *See pages 79–82.*
- **The Temple of Heaven (Tiantan)**. Set in the midst of an attractive park, the collection of ancient buildings here is a superb legacy of imperial Beijing. *See pages 115–18.*
- **The Great Wall**. No matter which section of Wall you visit, the sheer drama of this incredible structure will take your breath away. *See pages 183–191.*
- **Summer Palace**. Visting the pavilions, temples, gardens and lakes of the Summer Palace (Yiheyuan) is akin to walking around in a classical Chinese painting. *See pages 162–7.*
- **Lama Temple**. The city's most important Buddhist temple, this is a thriving religious centre, full of interest. *See pages 129–131.*
- **Beihai Park**. A beautiful imperial playground, complete with historic buildings and picturesque lakes, now open to all. *See pages 121–5.*

LEFT: Brass lions keep guard at the Forbidden City.

**ABOVE:** Acrobatics has a 3,000-year history in China.

## ONLY IN BEIJING

- **Watch the flag ceremony in Tiananmen Square**. Daily at dawn and dusk, witness this solemn ritual at the northern end of the square. *See page 82.*
- **Enjoy an imperial banquet at Fangshan restaurant**. Beijing's most famous imperial restaurant was set up by chefs put out of work by the collapse of the Qing dynasty. *See pages 124, 134.*
- **Hike on the Great Wall**. To experience the true splendour of the Wall, try hiking along it. Simatai, Jinshanling and Huanghuacheng are the most rewarding sections. *See pages 188–190.*
- **See an acrobatics performance**. It may be aimed at tourists, and more kitsch than an "I climbed the Great Wall" T-shirt, but most people enjoy these extravagant shows. *See pages 67, 218.*
- **Shop for fake designer goods**. A Beijing speciality. Despite the pretend labels, many are of reasonable quality. *See pages 224–5.*

## BEST WALKS AND BIKE RIDES

- **The Forbidden City and Jingshan**. If you still have the stamina after a day spent exploring the Forbidden City, a climb to the top of Jingshan hill gives a splendid overview. *See pages 91–101 and 125–6.*
- **The back lakes area**. This attractive area north of Beihai Park is great for cycling. *See pages 126–9.*

- **Tiananmen and the Legation Quarter** A walk full of historical resonance, from the 1950s back to the colonial era. *See pages 79–89.*
- **Qianmen and the best of the *hutong*** Hire a bicycle and get lost in the maze of *hutong*. If you can, try to find your way to Dazhalan and Liulichang with their colourful shops. *See pages 105–8.*

**ABOVE:** Despite increased numbers of cars, Beijing is still one of the world's great cycling cities. Flat terrain and wide bicycle lanes help. **LEFT:** Street food is cheap and cheerful.

## BEST THINGS TO EAT

- **Peking Duck**. The city's signature dish.
- **Hot-pot**. Of Mongolian origin; combines fondue-style communal cooking with unlimited meat and vegetables.
- ***Jiaozi***, filled pasta parcels, and ***baozi***, steamed buns stuffed with mincemeat and vegetables, are found everywhere and are cheap and filling.
- **Imperial Cuisine**. Dine like an emperor in one of the city's imperial restaurants.
- **Sichuanese and Hunanese**. Delicious spicy food from China's south and southwest.

**BELOW:** Karaoke nightclub in Chaoyang District in eastern Beijing. The city's nightlife scene is thriving, with a wide range of late night venues catering to all tastes.

## EATING OUT & NIGHTLIFE AREAS

- **Sanlitun**. In the northeast of the city between the Second and Third Ring Roads, Sanlitun Lu and the streets leading off it form the hub of a large proportion of Beijing's nightlife.
- **Jianguomenwai to the Workers Stadium**. South of Sanlitun, this part of Chaoyang District is well supplied with restaurants and bars. Further east, the **Chaoyang Park** area is a new nightlife zone.
- **Back lakes**. Lots of bars and restaurants, now extending eastwards towards the Bell and Drum towers.
- **Weigongcun and Wudaokou**. In the northwestern Haidian District around the universities.

## BEST SHOPPING

- **Wangfujing**. Beijing's most prestigious shopping street is now part-pedestriansed. The vast Oriental Plaza shopping mall at its southern end has food courts and countless retail outlets. *See pages 140, 222.*
- **Panjiayuan Market (Ghost Market)**. The best place to find all kinds of Chinoiserie; silk cushion covers,

wonderful old antique mah jong sets and gramaphones, scroll paintings, ornaments and a huge assortment of odds and ends. Beijing Curio City, just to the south, is good for antiques. *See pages 119, 224.*
- **Hongqiao Market**. Just outside the eastern gate of the Temple of Heaven, Hongqiao is famous for its pearls. It is also an excellent place to look for bargain silk

**RIGHT:** Posing for the camera in Qing-dynasty attire.

items, more general clothing and footwear, as well as some interesting antiques. *See pages 119, 224.*
- **Dazhalan** and **Liulichang**. In the atmospheric *hutong* south of Qianmen, these two old streets are lined with interesting shops. The mock Qing-dynasty buildings that line Liulichang are some of the best places to find unusual souvenirs. *See pages 106–7. 222–3.*
- **Beijing Friendship Store**. A reliable bet for all kinds of items from silk to toys, this department store was for years the only place in the city where foreigners could purchase Western goods. *See pages 145, 223.*

**ABOVE:** masks for sale at Panjiayuan Market in southeastern Beijing.
**LEFT:** there is plenty for children to do and see in the city.

## BEIJING FOR FAMILIES

These attractions are popular with children, though not all will suit every age group.

- **Boating in Beihai Park**. Paddle around to your heart's content in the beautiful surroundings of Beihai park. Pedal boats are also available on Qianhai Lake. *See page 121.*
- **Beijing Aquarium**. Part of the Beijing Zoo complex in the northwest of the city, always popular with children. Dolphin shows daily. **The Blue Zoo Aquarium** by the south gate of the Workers' Stadium is also good. *See pages 154, 226.*
- **Fundazzle**. For those with young children, this former Olympic-

size indoor swimming pool has been converted into a massive play-land in which kids can climb through tunnels, slide down slides, or plunge into the former diving pool now full of plastic balls. *See page 226.*
- **The Sony Explora Science Center** in Oriental Plaza is full of interactive exhibits and gadgets. *See pages 141, 226.*
- **The Chinese Science and Technology Museum** in the north of the city features a variety of hands-on activities and displays that appeal to kids. *See page 226.*

## AMAZING BEIJING

- **The Dongyue Daoist temple** is packed full of deities for every occasion. Visit the Department for Bestowing Material Happiness, or, if you are feeling victimised, try the Department for Controlling Bullying and Cheating. *See pages 143–4.*
- **The Golden Resources Shopping Mall**, the largest shopping centre in the world, opened in October 2004 in northwest Beijing. It has 230 escalators and over 1,000 shops.
- **Tiananmen Square** is the world's roomiest public square, covering some 170,000 sq. metres (1.83 million sq. ft), with space to accommodate more than 1 million people.

- **There are more than** 10 million bicycles in Beijing, almost one for every man, woman and child in the city.
- **The Great Wall** can be seen from orbit, as can other large man-made objects, but cannot be seen from the moon. However, in a blow to national pride, a sighting eluded the first Chinese astronaut, Yang Liwei, from his orbital position. Some questioned Yang's eyesight and demanded that future astronauts receive specific training to spot the Wall, while others suggested it be illuminated at night to make it easier to spot from space.

**ABOVE:** Jinggouyyuan Fortress, on the Great Wall near Badaling, a vital link in protecting the city from the northern steppes.
**LEFT:** Worshipping at Baitasi (White Pagoda Temple), one of the main Buddhist centres in Beijing.

## SURVIVAL TIPS

**Street Vendors**. As a tourist visiting Beijing, you are likely to be approached by countless people trying to sell you something, be it a copy of Mao's Little Red Book or a pirated DVD. After a while it can become tiresome, but on the whole vendors are not too persistent and a polite "no thanks" is usually accepted.

**Taxi Hire**. Taxis are cheap in Beijing, and metres are always installed. Consider hiring a taxi for a day's sightseeing outside the city. Bargain hard and agree the fare before you set off – it shouldn't be too expensive, and will give you control and flexibility to do what you want.

**Safety**. Beijing is a safe city in terms of crime, but you should still take the usual precautions against pickpockets on crowded buses and subways. Be cautious when crossing the street – cars don't always respect traffic signals, and in any case are permitted to turn right on a red light. The best advice is to go with the flow of other pedestrians. The same applies if you hire a bicycle – just follow the locals.

**Health**. Avoid any street food that you haven't seen cooked in front of you. It's worth carrying a set of chopsticks around with you. Most Chinese restaurants use disposable chopsticks, but some re-use them and don't clean them properly. If in doubt, you can always use your own set.

**Tipping** is not expected in China.

# CITY ON THE RISE

**Laid out according to ancient geomantic principles, modern Beijing is a dynamic and increasingly sophisticated city**

**B**eijing is a city of opposites and extremes – it captivates and confuses, excites and exasperates, all in equal measure. As the capital of the People's Republic, it is both the seat of the world's largest communist bureaucracy and the source of the policy changes that have turned China into an economic powerhouse. Its walled compounds and towering ministries are full of bureaucrats who technically legislate in the name of Marx and Mao, while the streets outside are a riot of speeding cars, flashing neon and cellphone-wielding citizens whose aspirations and lifestyles are increasingly akin to those of London or New York. Beijing may lack the futuristic glow of Shanghai – it remains altogether a grittier place than its southern rival – but nonetheless the changes in the past few years are remarkable.

Repression and freedom exist side by side in Beijing. Open political dissent is not tolerated. But politics is a favourite subject of Beijingers, who like nothing better than a witty joke at the expense of their leaders or the communist system. Barely veiled political critiques abound on the capital's stages and in its growing number of art galleries. Cultural and intellectual life flourishes – if it's not overtly political, seemingly anything goes, whether it's lambasting official economic policy in a government-owned newspaper, or staging an art exhibition that uses human body parts as material. The government that controls everything in theory in reality cannot even get residents of its own capital to follow traffic laws or pay taxes.

Beijing's contradictory nature is perhaps best apparent to the visitor in the jarring juxtaposition of ancient and new, Chinese and foreign, communist and capitalist – the Starbucks outlet in the Forbidden City, the souvenir vendors behind Mao's Mausoleum, the ultra-modern French-designed opera house adjacent to the staid Soviet-influenced Great Hall of the People.

Beijing is in the midst of reinventing itself as it prepares to host the 2008 summer Olympics. The games are widely seen as an unparalleled opportunity to sell the world its own – and China's – past greatness and future potential. Fabulous new buildings and venues are being built while fabulous old ones are getting facelifts. Everything from the subway system to the air quality to the English-speaking level is being improved. Beijing is a city on the up – one can only hope that respect for the past will survive into the future as it realises its Olympic dreams.                  ❏

**PRECEDING PAGES:** at the Hall of Prayer for Good Harvests, Temple of Heaven; the view across Tiananmen Square from Tiananmen Gate.
**LEFT:** marble ramp to the Hall of Supreme Harmony in the Forbidden City.

# FROM ANCIENT TIMES TO 1949

**Once a frontier town at the edge of fertile lowlands, Beijing served as the capital of imperial dynasties for more than 1,000 years**

The geographical position of Beijing has been one of the leading factors in its eventful history. Lying at the northern edge of empire – where the very different cultures of the settled Chinese farmers and the nomads of the steppes collided – the city became the prey of each victorious faction in turn, a fact reflected by the many changes to its name throughout the centuries.

Evidence of human settlement in the area goes back half a million years or so with the discovery of Peking Man *(Sinanthropus pekinensis; see page 175)*. This find, in Zhoukoudian, 50 km (30 miles) southwest of Beijing, revealed that Peking Man belonged to a people who walked upright, were already using stone tools and who knew how to light fires.

Around 3000 BC, neolithic villages were established in the area of modern Beijing, inhabited by people familiar with agriculture and the domestication of animals. There is to this day dispute as to the existence of the first dynasty recorded in Chinese historical writings, the Xia dynasty (21st to 16th centuries BC). The dynasty's legendary Yellow Emperor, Huangdi, is thought to have ruled between 2490 and 2413 BC and to have fought battles against the tribal leader Chiyo here, in the "Wilderness of the Prefecture of Zhou". It is presumed that Zhu-luo, to the west of Beijing, was the earliest settlement in this area. It was here that Huangdi's successor, Yao, is said to have founded a capital named Youdou, the "City of Calm".

Throughout Beijing's prehistory, the hills to the north, northeast and northwest served as a natural frontier for the people who settled here and who traded with the nomadic tribes living beyond the passes of Gubeikou and Naku. These northern hill tribes also had close ties with the people who occupied the Central Plain, which stretched along the Yellow River to the south and southwest of Beijing. The important role of trading post promoted the settlement's rise to become the ancient city of Ji. During the Warring States period (475–221 BC), the count of the state of Yan annexed this area and made Ji his central city. In the 3rd century BC, the first emperor of the Qin dynasty and of China,

**LEFT:** Emperor Kangxi practising calligraphy.
**RIGHT:** the imperial bodyguard.

Qin Shi Huangdi, made the city an administrative centre of the Guangyang Command, one of 36 prefectures of the unified, centrally organised feudal empire. With the construction of the Great Wall during his reign (221–210 BC), Ji became a strategically important trade and military centre, a position it retained for approximately 1,000 years, until the end of the Tang dynasty. During this time, it was often the subject of wars and conflict.

## Beijing, the imperial city

At the beginning of the Tang dynasty, Ji was not that different from the other great cities of feudal China. But by the end of the dynasty,

In relation to today's Beijing, Yanjing lay roughly in the western part of the city. The temple of Fayuansi was in the southeastern corner of the old walls, the Forbidden City lay to the southwest and the markets were in the northeast corner. Each of the city's four quarters was surrounded by massive walls.

In the early part of the 12th century, the Nüzhen, another nomadic tribe from the northeast, vanquished the reigning Liao dynasty and replaced it with the Jin dynasty. In 1153, they moved their capital from Huiningfu (in the modern province of Liaoning) to Yanjing, and renamed it Zhongdu, "Central Capital". New buildings were constructed, and the Jin moved

the Great Wall had lost much of its protective function, leaving it more vulnerable to attack from the north.

The city became an imperial seat when the Khitan conquered northern China and founded the Liao dynasty in AD 936. The Khitan renamed Ji "Yanjing", meaning "Southern Capital" (it was also known as Nanjing – not to be confused with the city of the same name in east-central China, to which the Ming later decamped). As the southern centre of the nomad empire, this area became a point of support and departure for many expeditions of non-Chinese peoples – Khitan, Nüzhen and Mongols – on their way to the south.

the centre of their capital into the area to the south of today's Guanganmen Gate. But it only lasted a few decades: in 1215, Mongol cavalry occupied Zhongdu and the city was completely destroyed by fire.

## The Great Khan's capital

It was not until 1279 that Kublai Khan made Zhongdu the capital of the new Yuan dynasty. He completely rebuilt the city and gave it the Chinese name of Dadu, meaning "Great Capital". In the West, it was mostly known by its Mongol name, Khanbaliq or Khambaluk. Marco Polo praised this city of the Great Khan in his journals:

"There are in Khanbaliq unbelievable numbers of people and houses, it is impossible to count them. The houses and villas outside the walls are at least as beautiful as those within, except, of course, for the imperial buildings… Nowhere in the world are such rare and precious goods traded as in Khanbaliq… jewels, pearls and other precious items… "

The building of Dadu continued until 1293, while Kublai Khan ruled the empire. The centre of the city at that time was moved to the vicinity of the northeast lakes. In the south, Dadu reached the line of today's Chang'an Boulevard, with the observatory marking the southeast corner. In the north, it reached as far

1368, Beijing became Chinese once more and was renamed Beiping ("Northern Peace"). Zhu Yuanzhang, founder of the Ming dynasty, at first made the more modern Nanjing, hundreds of miles to the south, his capital and gave Beiping to one of his sons as a fief. When the latter succeeded to the throne in 1403, taking the ruling name of Yongle, he moved the country's capital back up to Beijing.

At first the city was made smaller. The outer city wall was demolished and rebuilt more towards the south, between today's Deshengmen Gate and Andingmen Gate. One can still see remains of the demolished northern wall of Dadu outside the Deshengmen. Local people

as the present Lama Temple, which was at that time the site of the trade quarters by the Bell and Drum Towers. In 1293, the Tonghua Canal was completed, linking the capital with the Grand Canal and making it possible to bring grain from the south into the city by boat. The population was about 500,000.

## Emperor Yongle's city

Beijing's role as capital city continued during the Ming and Qing dynasties. With the conquest of Mongol Dadu by Ming troops in

call it the Earth Wall, since only a broken row of hillocks remains. From 1406 to 1420, the new Beijing was built, with the Imperial Palace that still exists today at its centre.

Most ancient buildings in today's inner city date back to this time. Like Kublai Khan, the Ming emperors followed the square pattern dictated by the old rules. The main axis ran southwards and the city was completely enclosed by walls with three gates on each side. Civil engineers dug moats and canals, planned Beijing's extensive road network and, in 1553, completed a massive city wall to protect their thriving capital. The ground plan resembled a chessboard, with a network of north–south and

**LEFT:** Kublai Khan and the Ming emperors Hongwu and Wanli. **ABOVE:** an early view of the Forbidden City.

east–west streets, at the heart of which nestled the Forbidden City, surrounded by high red walls. To the south, starting from today's Qianmen, an Inner City was built.

Yongle's decision to make Beijing his capital may seem surprising, as the city's northerly position brought with it the permanent danger of attack by the Mongols or other nomadic tribes (which did indeed follow in the 16th and 17th centuries). In all probability, it was an expression of his drive for expansion. Under his rule, the imperial boundaries were pushed north as far as the river Amur (the present-day border with Russia). Moving the capital to the edge of the steppe zone could also be viewed

as a sign that the Ming dynasty planned to restore the pre-eminence of the Chinese empire in Asia, the foundations of which had been laid by the Mongols. This ambition later became the hallmark of the entire Qing dynasty.

The Ming also undertook China's greatest ever public-works project: the "10,000 Li" Great Wall, which linked or reinforced several older walls. Yet this costly project ultimately failed to save their empire. In 1644, Li Zicheng led a peasants' revolt, conquered the city of Beijing and toppled the Ming dynasty. A mere 43 days later, Manchu troops defeated Li's army and marched into Beijing, making it their capital.

## The Manchu rulers

The Manchu did not change the orientation of the city. They declared the northern part of the city, also known as the Tartar City, their domain, in which only Manchu could live, while the Ming Inner City to the south was renamed the Chinese City. The new Qing dynasty left their mark on the architecture of the Forbidden City, but did not change the basic structure.

Though the Qing emperors continued to observe the Confucian rites of their predecessors, they also brought their own language and customs with them. Chinese and Mongolian were both used in official documents. Tibetan Buddhism, which had flourished among the northern tribes since the Mongols promoted it in the 12th and 13th centuries, was the main Manchu religion. The Qing brought the fifth Dalai Lama from Lhasa to Beijing in 1651 to oversee the introduction of Tibetan Buddhism (Lamaism) to the capital. The White Dagoba (stupa) in Beihai Park commemorates the Dalai Lama's visit; the Lama Temple (Yonghegong) and the temples at the imperial 'resort' of Chengde are other legacies of the Qing emperors' religious faith.

## Foreign influence

At around this time, the outside world began to make inroads into China. In 1601, the Italian Jesuit Matteo Ricci arrived in Beijing, followed in 1622 by Johann Adam Schall von Bell (1592–1666), who in 1650 received permission to build the first Catholic church in the city (Nantang, or Southern Cathedral, *see page 108*). Jesuit missionaries quickly won influence at court because of their astronomical and other scientific knowledge.

By the beginning of the 19th century, at the time when the Qing empire was at its peak, Beijing had a population of 700,000, including a small foreign community. But signs of decay were beginning to surface – due to corruption within the imperial household, and the gradual wresting of power away from the centre by warlords and princes. Revolts increased and secret societies sprang up everywhere, rapidly gaining influence. Xenophobia grew with the rise in Han nationalism. The first persecutions of Jesuits and the destruction of churches took place. Emperor

Qianlong, still self-confident, supposedly told the ambassador of the British queen that the Middle Kingdom had no need of "barbarian" products, for the Middle Kingdom produced all that it required. And yet the time of humiliation for Beijing and for all of China was just around the corner, with the advance of foreign colonial powers from the time of the First Opium War (1840–2) onwards.

At the end of the Second Opium War (1858–60), the emperor was forced to flee from the Western armies, who went on to destroy part of the city, including Yuanmingyuan, the Old Summer Palace (the ruins can still be seen today, *see page 159*), and plundered Beijing's treasuries. The emperor was obliged to grant concessions to the foreign powers. Extra territorial areas were granted and the diplomatic quarter in the southeast part of the imperial city was put at the disposal of the foreigners, which became the Legation Quarter *(see page 87)*. Many Chinese, however, were unwilling to accept this humiliation, and hostility gradually increased. During the 1880s and 1890s a programme of Chinese "self-reliance", supported by the powerless Emperor Guangxu, was instituted. It centred on the construction of railways, docks and other infrastructural projects that had hitherto been built and controlled by foreigners. The programme met with opposition from the imperial court, and after China's defeat in the Sino-Japanese war of 1894–5 it effectively collapsed. All this added momentum to the demands of extremist groups, and slogans such as "Drive the barbarians from our country!" were to be heard everywhere.

Two years later, in 1900, followers of a secret society named the Society for Peace and Justice – known in the West as the Boxers – rebelled. For two months, partly supported by imperial troops, they besieged the foreign embassies. Western countries quickly sent forces to Beijing. The Empress Dowager Cixi fled to Xi'an, and the Boxer Rebellion was crushed. A foreign newspaper based in Beijing reported: "The capital of the emperors was partly destroyed, partly burned down. All that

was left was a dead city. The streets were choked with the bodies of Chinese, many charred or eaten by stray dogs."

Once again, the increasingly weak Manchu regime had to pay great sums in reparations, while the foreigners received further privileges. As Beijing continued to decay, the imperial court carried on in the same old way, cut off from reality, bound up as it was in luxury, corruption and intrigue.

## End of empire

In October 1910, an advisory council met for the first time in Beijing. By then the middle-class Xinhai revolution, led by Dr Sun Yat-

sen, had become a real threat to the Manchu imperial house. The prince regent recalled the Imperial Marshal, Yuan Shikai, the strongman of Cixi, dismissed earlier in 1909. He was appointed supreme commander and head of the government. However, Yuan Shikai wanted to prepare a change of dynasty in the traditional style. He avoided confrontation with the republican forces in the south, elected himself president of the National Assembly in November 1911, and the next month forced the child emperor Pu Yi to abdicate, effectively sealing the fate of the Qing dynasty.

The long rule of the Sons of Heaven was over. Chinese men could finally cut off their

---

**LEFT:** massive rebuilding of the Great Wall failed to save the Ming dynasty. **RIGHT:** Chinese and German troops in battle during the Boxer Rebellion in 1900.

hated pigtails – the external symbol of servitude imposed by the Manchu. But the city continued to decay and social problems became more acute. Yuan Shikai failed in his attempt to defeat the republicans – who had organised themselves as the Guomindang (Kuomintang), the National People's Party, led by Sun Yat-sen. Yuan died in 1916 and the dynasty was overthrown, but the social and political problems remained unsolved. Beijing stagnated in a half-feudal state.

Warlords struggled for control, dashing any hopes of unity and peace. The north and Beijing, which remained the nominal capital of the republic after 1911, were badly affected by these battles. Social and political problems became more acute, and the misery of the poor was indescribable.

Expansionist foreign powers remained greedy for profit and influence in China. In the Treaty of Versailles of 1919, the former German concessions – Qingdao and the adjacent Jiaozhou Bay – were not returned to China but given to Japan. This deeply wounded national pride. More than 300,000 young Chinese, mostly students and intellectuals, demonstrated in Beijing on 4 May 1919 to demand national independence and territorial integrity. A manifesto passed at the demonstration ended with the words: "China's territory

## PU YI, THE LAST EMPEROR

Pu Yi was one of the tragic figures of 20th-century China. Born into the imperial family in 1906, he acceded to the throne aged two, but was forced to abdicate just four years later, although he continued living in the Forbidden City for another twelve years until a military coup forced him to move to Tianjin. During China's uncertain 1920s, he wavered between different ideas and considered emigration, but later hoped to persuade warlords to unite in restoring the throne. The growth of anti-Qing sentiments in Tianjin forced Pu Yi to take refuge in the Japanese legation, which led, in 1932, to his appointment as "chief executive" of Japanese-occupied Manchuria, and "emperor"

status two years later. After liberation by Soviet troops he was captured and imprisoned in Siberia, where he was allowed to live in relative comfort. Pu Yi was then sent back to China in 1950, and spent ten years in Fushun War Criminals Prison, where he was "re-educated" in revolutionary ideology. After his release, he lived as an ordinary citizen of Beijing until his death in 1967. China's last emperor ended his days an apparently zealous communist: in a strong echo of George Orwell's *Nineteen Eighty Four*, Pu Yi's response to being awarded a special pardon by the Party was: "Before I had heard this to the end I burst into tears. My motherland had made me into a man."

may be conquered, but it cannot be given to foreign powers. The Chinese people may be slaughtered, but they will not surrender. Our country is in the process of being destroyed. Brothers, defend yourselves against this!"

As a result of this May Fourth Movement – considered a turning point in modern Chinese history – the Chinese workers' movement grew. Trade unions and the Communist Party came into existence, the latter soon becoming active in Beijing. At that time, the party's future leader, Mao Zedong, was a librarian at Beijing University. In the 1920s, Guomindang and Communist Party forces still fought side by side against the warlords in the north. But after the right wing of the Guomindang gained the upper hand in 1928, the Communist Party was banned. Chiang Kai-shek, the Guomindang leader, moved his capital to Nanjing.

Beijing in the 1920s was a vibrant yet poor and chaotic city, with a street life of fortune-tellers, opera troupes, nightclub singers, foreign businessmen and adventurers. Modernity was slowly creeping in; the network of streets was extended, water pipes were laid, hospitals were established and banks opened branches.

Yet the outside world influenced Beijing far less than it did Shanghai, an open treaty port with foreign concessions ruled by foreigners and in which foreign law applied, almost like a colony: the official languages here were French or English and the people making the laws were foreign. Beijing was still China, far less hospitable in terms of living or business conditions for foreigners.

## The Japanese and World War II

The years leading up to World War II were overshadowed by the threat of the Japanese. Already, in 1931, Japan had occupied northeast China, which they named Manchuria. In 1935, huge anti-Japanese demonstrations marched through the streets of Beijing. Following the 1934–6 Long March from the south, surviving Communist troops regrouped in Shaanxi Province, to the southwest of Beijing. The Guomindang, responding to popular pressure, made a new alliance with the Communists, this time to fight against Japan.

A confrontation choreographed by the Japanese in 1937 on the Marco Polo Bridge, on the western outskirts of Beijing, served the Japanese as a pretext for occupying Beijing and then all of China.

Life became worse for the people of Beijing during World War II, a time when the foreigners remained "neutral" and the Japanese secret police controlled everything. By 1939, Japan had seized all of eastern China and the Guomindang had retreated west to Chongqing in Sichuan Province. The US began supplying the Guomindang troops, hoping that they would oust the Japanese and, later, the Communists – still at that time

fighting alongside the Guomindang against the common enemy. In 1941, an attack on Communist troops by a rogue Guomindang unit split the alliance, although both sides continued separate action against the Japanese.

Towards the end of the war, Communist guerrillas were operating in the hills around Beijing, but after the Japanese surrender the Guomindang took control of the city, supported by the Americans. However, by 1948 their position was weakening daily, as the Communists gained support across the Chinese countryside, and eventually in 1949 the People's Liberation Army marched victoriously into the city. ❑

**FAR LEFT:** Pu Yi as a young child. **LEFT:** Sun Yat-sen. **RIGHT:** a depiction of the Long March.

# COMMUNISM AND MODERN TIMES

### After decades of turmoil which reached its nadir during the brutal Cultural Revolution, the Deng era brought bold economic reforms. The ensuing economic growth continues to accelerate, with implications for China's world role

On 31 January 1949, Beijing was taken without a struggle. On 1 October, Mao Zedong proclaimed the foundation of the People's Republic of China from Tiananmen, the Gate of Heavenly Peace. Just like the emperors before them, the Communists moved their centre of power into part of the Forbidden City, to Zhongnanhai, west of the Imperial Palace.

All government bodies were based in Beijing. Important schools and colleges moved here, and new factories were built. The city, which had just 1.2 million inhabitants in 1949, grew through the incorporation of eight rural districts of Hebei Province in 1958. Urban reshaping began in the 1950s. The slum areas were cleared, new buildings erected and the streets widened. Despite pleas by planning experts, Mao insisted on demolishing Beijing's ancient city walls. Grey and dusty Beijing was to become a green city within the decade.

As the centre of political power, the capital led several fierce ideological campaigns in the 1950s. During the Korean War (1950–3), it rallied support for its North Korean allies against "US imperialists". In 1956, Mao issued his infamous edict, "Let a hundred flowers bloom, let a hundred schools of thought contend." It sounded too good to be true, and sure enough – whatever the original intent – the Hundred Flowers movement soon became a vehicle for flushing out dissenting voices. Many of those who heeded Mao's call

found themselves purged or arrested. At least 300,000 intellectuals, most of them committed communists, were labelled "rightists" or "capitalist roaders" and sent to remote labour camps for "re-education". Many were from Beijing; some would never return.

Khrushchev's 1956 condemnation of Stalin shocked the Chinese leadership. When the Soviet premier later criticised Mao, shock turned to anger, and a full-scale diplomatic rift. In July 1960, all remaining Soviet experts left China. Beijing residents were largely unaffected by the focus of Khrushchev's concern, the Great Leap Forward. Party secrecy also ensured ignorance of the mass famine in

---

**LEFT:** revolutionary imagery.
**RIGHT:** the PLA marches into Beijing in 1949.

the countryside. From 1958 to 1961 over 30 million people starved to death, mainly due to misguided Great Leap policies. In the middle of this rural catastrophe, in 1959 the capital celebrated the 10th anniversary of communist rule with a huge rally and ten major construction projects, including the Great Hall of the People and the huge museums which flank Tiananmen Square.

## Redder than red

As if the traumas of the Hundred Flowers and the Great Leap movements were not enough, in 1965 the first rumblings of the Cultural Revolution began with the launch of a campaign,

exhorting the people, in typically lyrical fashion, to "Hand over the Khrushchevs sleeping next to Mao". Defence minister Lin Biao henceforth orchestrated the rise of Mao to godlike status. Images of the Great Helmsman decorated Beijing's public buildings and homes, and everyone wore Mao badges. Red Guard groups mushroomed across the capital. Encouraged by Mao, students abandoned their lessons and persecuted their teachers and other authority figures. They took over factories and offices to pursue "class struggle". Some even fought pitched battles with other groups to prove ideological supremacy. The Red Guards also ransacked many of Beijing's ancient cultural sites, and searched

### MELTDOWN MANIA

Beijingers did not starve to death during the Great Leap Forward, but they were expected to participate by doing "more, cheaper, better, faster". To meet ludicrous steel-production goals, families melted down pots and pans in backyard furnaces. The city's Central Philharmonic Orchestra, eager to demonstrate its patriotism by "producing" more, doubled its annual number of performances from 40 to 80. In the near-hysterical atmosphere, it was soon decided that this was not ambitious enough, and the number was doubled again, to 160; and then again, to 320; and again, to 640; they finally settled on the nice round number of 1,200 concerts a year.

homes for "bourgeois" or "feudal" items. Mao's wife, Jiang Qing, and supporters of her Gang of Four, used Beihai Park throughout the Cultural Revolution as a private domain.

In 1968, a million Red Guards marched into Tiananmen Square, while Mao waved encouragingly from Tiananmen Gate. Yet even the instigators realised the Red Guard movement was growing dangerously chaotic. As a solution, in 1968, the idea of sending educated urban youngsters to "learn from the peasants" was born. Young Beijingers were sent away with little idea of when they might return, though most came back in the mid-1970s as the fire of the Cultural Revolution was quelled.

At the end of the 1960s a new fear gripped Beijing, as soldiers and civilians hurriedly built a vast network of tunnels and air-raid shelters, preparing for possible war with the Soviet Union. The "Underground City" still exists to this day and can be visited, *see page 108)*. The two powers had skirmished along China's northeast border, and Mao was convinced the Soviets planned an invasion.

War was avoided, but the internal struggles continued. In 1971 the heir apparent, Lin Biao, died in a plane crash, allegedly while fleeing China after a failed coup attempt. But Lin's death merely left the way clear for a second faction to manipulate the Mao personality cult. The Gang of Four hijacked Mao's "Criticise Lin Biao and Confucius" campaign, launched in 1973. Zhou Enlai, probably China's most popular premier, became "Confucius" and was criticised, but remained in office.

US president Richard Nixon made a historic visit to Beijing in 1972, marking the beginning of the end of China's international isolation. But it did not signal the end of the Cultural Revolution, which would last another four years, until the momentous events of 1976.

## Signs of change

In early April 1976, during the week of the Qingming Festival when the Chinese remember their dead, the silent rage of the people found expression in a massive demonstration. Dissatisfaction had increased because of food rationing and the poor quality of goods available. Support and trust in the leadership, even in Mao, had evaporated.

The people of Beijing gathered by the thousands for several days in Tiananmen Square, to pay homage to the recently dead President Zhou Enlai, and to protest against Mao and the radical leaders of the Cultural Revolution. The first demands for modernisation and democracy were heard, signalling the end of the Cultural Revolution. In response to the unrest, a new face was presented to the Chinese people: Hua Guofeng, who was named First Vice-Chairman, second only to Mao.

The Chinese, great believers in omens and portents, have always viewed natural disasters as signs from heaven of great changes to come. In July 1976, a massive earthquake destroyed the city of Tangshan, to the east of Beijing, and claimed hundreds of thousands of victims. In imperial times this would have been interpreted as a sign that a change of dynasty was imminent.

Just a few weeks later, a comparable change came about. Mao Zedong, the Great Helmsman who had led China out of feudal servitude, died on 9 September 1976. Everywhere machines stood still, shops closed and people gathered on the streets. The television showed

pictures of mourners weeping. But an astute observer would have concluded that the Chinese were shocked less by the death itself than by the uncertainty of what the future, after Mao Zedong, would bring.

First came the toppling of the Gang of Four, in October 1976. Hua had the four radical leaders, one of whom was Mao's widow Jiang Qing, arrested during a party meeting. They were convicted of creating and directing the Cultural Revolution. Jiang Qing died in prison.

By spring 1977, the new Chairman Hua's portrait was prominently displayed in the capital. A large poster showed him at the deathbed of the Great Helmsman. Attributed

**LEFT:** fanatical Red Guards wave Mao's "Little Red Book". **RIGHT:** despite the government line that Mao was "30 per cent wrong", the Great Helmsman remains an iconic presence in China.

# Maomorabilia

Away from Tiananmen Gate, the most likely place you will see the image of Mao Zedong is in one of the city's curio markets. In a recycling of an icon that has endured for over 40 years, the vast sea of kitsch created during the 1960s and early 1970s in his honour has, in recent years, become at least semi-fashionable.

Mao, of course, attained Messianic status during the mayhem of the Cultural Revolution which began in 1966, a time when his likeness appeared on some two billion pictures

and three billion badges, when Red Guards waved his "Little Red Book" during huge rallies; more than 350 million were printed between 1964 and 1966, and translations into all major languages followed. The arms of waving Red Guards became the hands of Cultural Revolution alarm clocks, while double-image Mao medallions, rubber stamps, resin busts and ceramic ornaments all fuelled the personality cult.

Despite the huge volume produced, some items have become valuable collectors' pieces, especially original postage stamps, paintings and posters. A few Cultural Revolution paintings have sold for more than $1 million. Many badges were thrown away or used as scrap metal, but Beijing's leading collector has reputedly salvaged more than 100,000.

You may also find ornaments or pictures showing a young soldier wearing a fur-lined hat with earflaps. This is Lei Feng, adopted by Mao as a model of selfless devotion. Lei Feng fixed engines in temperatures of −30°C (−22°F); he worked a 12-hour day but still helped his colleagues; and he gave away much of his meagre pay and rations to those in greater need. Schoolchildren are still taught to follow his example.

Look out, too, for reproduction and original ceramics depicting gun-toting young women dressed in pale blue short suits. The Red Detachment of Women was one of seven model stage works allowed by Mao's wife Jiang Qing, a former film actress and self-appointed cultural arbiter.

In the 1980s and 1990s, many artists reworked styles and images from the Cultural Revolution, with varying degrees of irony, including one portrait of Whitney Houston with the Chairman. Advertising campaigns and pop-music videos also recycle Cultural Revolution pictures and slogans. And Beijing has several restaurants with Cultural Revolution and "Mao hometown" themes.

The cult of Deng Xiaoping has partly continued the Mao trend. Souvenir stalls sell Deng watches, musical lighters, T-shirts, and pendants for car windscreens. But for some people, Deng will always be second best. For them, Mao remains the greatest hero of the 20th century, if not China's entire history. Most people accept the government line that, despite his grave errors, Mao was 70 per cent right. Others, however, especially people whose family members died or were imprisoned, find the nostalgia strange, sick even. They hold Mao responsible for 30 million deaths from famine after the Great Leap Forward, and more deaths and persecutions in the Cultural Revolution.

The Hongqiao, Panjiayuan and Beijing Curio City markets are good places to look, particularly for more interesting items. ❑

**LEFT:** Mao kitsch is easy to find in city markets.

to Mao, the caption read: "With you in charge, my heart is at ease." Hua, however, remained in power only a short time. A veteran of the revolution was waiting in the wings, one who had twice disappeared into obscurity during the intra-party struggles: former vice-premier Deng Xiaoping, who emerged as China's leader in late 1978.

From 1978 to 1980, Beijing was the scene of countless demonstrations by dissatisfied Chinese from all over the country. Most were young students who courageously joined the Democracy Wall movement in spring 1979. On the wall by Xidan market, *dazibao* (big character posters) reappeared. These were familiar from the Cultural Revolution years but were significantly different in their content. Officials were accused of corruption, and individuals demanded justice for past wrongs. One concise wall poster asked: "Who knows the representative of my district, who is supposed to represent me in the People's Congress?" Space for name, address and telephone number were left pointedly blank, a plain reference to the fact that National People's Congress (NPC) members in China were selected by the higher echelons of the Communist party and in practice no elections took place.

Students at the Xidan wall sold journals that they had produced themselves. It was through these journals that many city dwellers learned for the first time of the mass poverty in the countryside. Petitions were handed in daily, putting considerable pressure on the Party, and while many of the leaders of these demonstrations were arrested, some of their ideas became official government policy.

## Opening the doors

In 1982, a new Constitution came into being. An open-door policy to foreign countries was one important step in the modernisation programme designed to quadruple China's economic power by the year 2000. Soon, the first free markets arrived, seen at many major crossroads. In contrast to the state-run shops, they were able to offer fresh fruit and vegetables. For years, independent work and private trade had been condemned. Now cooks,

cobblers, hairdressers, tailors and carpenters simply started to work for themselves.

The city seemed to have awoken from a long sleep, and the pace was hectic. People enjoyed the new beginning. The time of forced participation in political events and campaigns was over and interest in politics faded away. New horizons opened for the young, and never before had they been known to study so eagerly. Careers as scientists, engineers and technicians, study trips abroad, and freedom and prosperity beckoned.

Television showed pictures from abroad and spread, intentionally or subliminally, the message of the blessings of consumerism.

Suddenly the three "luxury goods" – a bicycle, clock and radio – were no longer enough. The department stores filled up with refrigerators, washing machines, television sets and expensive imported goods. Fashion shows and magazines, as well as pop singers and film stars, awoke the desire of women and men to look attractive and different. In contemporary literature, young lovers no longer vowed to fight to the death for the revolution and their homeland. Instead, they would study hard and help with the modernisation of their country.

All of this reform, however, was not without controversy. After Deng Xiaoping's protégé Hu Yaobang became general secretary

**RIGHT:** during the 1980s, Deng Xiaoping's policies increasingly opened China to Western influence.

of the Party and Zhao Ziyang became premier, opposition grew in conservative circles, especially in the army. At the end of 1983, a campaign began against "spiritual pollution". Many serious criminals were publicly executed as a deterrent, but the fight was mainly against intellectuals and artists, and against fashions such as long hair and Western music, which were being steadily imported from Hong Kong.

For some, economic freedom was not enough. At the end of 1986, student protests that began in Hefei reached their peak in Shanghai, where they ended peacefully. This led to conservatives pressuring party secretary

of mourning. Students initially proceeded with caution, coming out to demonstrate only in the small hours of the night and returning to their campuses by morning. But by the time of Hu's funeral a week later, they had become far more daring, making demands on the government and occupying Tiananmen Square.

The protests soon spread across the rest of China. Beijing remained the epicentre, however, and many adventurous students jumped aboard trains – generally allowed to ride for free by sympathetic workers – and travelled to the capital to join the demonstrators. The government's willingness to allow the protests to continue astonished many and gave them

Hu Yaobang to retire, as he had sympathised with the students' calls for greater democracy and curbs on corruption. Zhao Ziyang, who was regarded as a relative liberal, succeeded Hu, and in 1988 Li Peng took over from Zhao as premier.

### Pro-democracy demonstrations

The discontent that had been mounting as the 1980s wore on found an outlet in April 1989 with the death of former Party secretary Hu Yaobang. Since Hu had previously shown sympathy for students and their needs, his death was both a cause of sorrow and a perfect pretext for protests veiled as demonstrations

hope, but was in actuality a sign of a leadership deeply divided over how to handle the situation. Finally, in mid-May, the moderates led by Zhao Ziyang lost the battle and martial law was declared in Beijing on 19 May. Zhao visited the Tiananmen protesters at 4am and sobbed as he said, "We have come too late." His political career was over, and it was only a matter of time until the protests would be forcibly ended.

The end duly arrived on 4 June, when Deng Xiaoping sent in the People's Liberation Army "to end the counter-revolutionary rebellion". The soldiers turned their tanks and guns on the students and on the many citizens of Beijing who supported them. Estimates of the number of people killed range from the hundreds to the thousands. The Chinese government has never given a full account of what happened.

In the weeks and months that followed, Beijing and much of the nation remained in a state of shock. Foreigners left China en masse and the economy spluttered as foreign investment dwindled. Jiang Zemin, who as Party secretary of Shanghai had handled the protests there with relative aplomb while also demonstrating his loyalty to Beijing, was named to replace Zhao Ziyang as general secretary.

provide the spark for a burst of economic development and reassured foreign investors, who began increasing the number and size of their investments in China.

With economic development back on track, Deng retired from all his official positions (except that as head of the Chinese Bridge Players' Association) in 1993, although he remained important behind the scenes. When he died in 1997, the unofficial position of "core" of the Communist Party leadership passed to Jiang Zemin. Later that year, the Hong Kong handover and a visit to the United States gave Jiang two opportunities to show his new stature to people in China and abroad. He

Deng Xiaoping had severely damaged his reputation as an open-minded reformer, but, if he had proven himself willing to resist political change at all costs, he was still determined to continue with his pragmatic policies of economic reform and opening to the outside world. To make this clear, he travelled to several special economic zones in the south and to Shanghai in 1992, using every opportunity to explicitly reaffirm the Party's commitment to continued economic reform. This helped to

**LEFT:** street scene from the mid-1970s.
**ABOVE:** Deng Xiaoping led China into the modern era.
**RIGHT:** modern architecture in eastern Beijing.

### BUILDING BEIJING

During the 1970s, Beijing still seemed very much the Forbidden City to the handful of foreigners staying there. There was practically no tourism whatsoever until 1977. The most modern landmarks were still the "Ten Great Buildings" completed in 1959 to mark the tenth anniversary of the PRC. In stark contrast, tiny brick houses lined many streets, built as refuges after the Tangshan earthquake. There was no hurry to demolish these one-room homes, since Beijing still needed the additional living space. For years, almost no new homes were built, although the population had increased explosively. The first skyscrapers, however, appeared as early as 1977.

# Preparing for the Olympics

The Olympic Games to be held in Beijing in 2008 is unarguably one of the most important events in the city's modern history. Determined to stage the best-ever Olympics, the Chinese government has essentially decided to reinvent its own capital by improving everything from the air quality to the people themselves. To underscore its intentions, it has issued the Beijing Olympic Action Plan which reads something like a list of New Year's resolutions penned by a drunken optimist, but is

actually a blueprint of how the government will use the games as a catalyst to modernise Beijing and give it a new image.

One of the plan's top priorities is to significantly improve the city's environment. To increase air quality, it will reduce the role of coal in supplying power, implement strict vehicle emissions standards, and even move 200 polluting factories outside the Fourth Ring Road. Capital Steel – one of the city's biggest polluters – will reduce its production by 2 million tons. Trees and grass will be planted in an effort to reduce particle pollution, as well as improve the city's appearance; the plan calls for 45 per cent

of the city to be "green" by 2007. This new greenery will include 50 tree-planted areas in downtown Beijing, with trees along all major roadsides, and a major new park in the Olympic Green. Water is a major problem in semi-arid Beijing, and plans call for increasing the use of recycled water, reducing the exploitation of underground water resources, and raising conservation awareness among residents. Planners wax euphoric about the impact they hope their environmental improvement projects will have, writing that by 2008 Beijing will be a city of "green hills, clear water, grass-covered ground, and blue sky."

Getting around this urban oasis should also be much easier, since plans call for the construction of 148 kilometres (93 miles) of new rail transport, including four new subway lines and a fast train from Dongzhimen to the airport. The Fifth and Sixth Ring Roads will be in use by 2008, and hundreds of roadways and streets within the city proper will be upgraded or expanded. Parking lots will be constructed for all the vehicles plying these new roads, and "a social environment favourable for traffic regulation enforcement will be established and the citizens' consciousness of observing traffic regulations will be raised." To make sure all these drivers don't get lost, the plan even calls for giving supplementary names to Beijing streets and redoing its utterly confusing system of numbering.

On the cultural front, plans call for the expansion and renovation of major museums, the renovation and restoration of such historical relics as the Ming dynasty city wall, and the preservation of some old city neighbourhoods. And, as if this weren't ambitious enough, the "general quality" of Beijing citizens is also scheduled for an upgrade. By 2008, if the planners prevail, the city will be peopled by polite, honest, friendly, thrifty and moral people who also speak English. Although a name change for the capital is not in the plan, it may be in order if all these goals are achieved – Utopia, perhaps? ❑

**LEFT:** an artist's impression of how the Olympic Stadium will look.

continued to push for greater economic development and worked to strengthen China's international standing, aided by Premier Zhu Rongji.

The PRC celebrated its 50th anniversary in 1999 and that same year enshrined "Deng Xiaoping Thought" in the Constitution, thereby giving Deng's theories a status equal to Mao's. Collections of his writings and speeches were published and his sayings were promoted, including the catchy "To get rich is glorious", and "It doesn't matter if the cat is black or white, as long as it catches the mice." Despite 1989, Deng's position as the pragmatic, courageous and far-seeing architect of China's economic reform remains intact.

finally admitted. This was important not only because of the trading privileges it brought, but also because it cemented China's status in the global community.

Jiang's desire to improve China's diplomatic status in general, and its relations with the US in particular, encountered several serious obstacles. In the spring of 1999, thousands of practitioners of a martial art known as Falun Gong surrounded the Zhongnanhai leadership compound in a silent protest against the treatment their members had received in Tianjin. Jiang, his fellow leaders and the world in general were shocked that so many protesters could appear from nowhere and surround the

## Jiang Zemin's tenure

Jiang Zemin did not share the war-hero status of Deng Xiaoping, and his oversized glasses and tendency to show off awkwardly by speaking poor English, reciting poetry or singing songs made him an easy butt of jokes. In the early years of his tenure, many expected him to be a flash in the pan and even compared him to Hua Guofeng, Mao's ill-fated successor. But Jiang proved smarter than his critics. His determination to join the World Trade Organisation paid off, and in 2001 China was

**ABOVE:** Beijing beat off tough competition to host the 2008 Olympic Games.

leadership compound without anyone stopping them – or even noticing them until it was too late. Subsequent investigations revealed that the movement had tens of thousands of followers across the country, including high-level members of the Party. Jiang was smart enough not to call in the army, but he did unleash a crackdown in which the movement was banned and many of its followers arrested, drawing international criticism. Falun Gong members outside China continue to protest against the movement's repression.

During the Kosovo war of 1999, the accidental bombing of the Chinese embassy in Belgrade by a US NATO plane sent US–China relations into a tailspin and brought student protesters onto the streets. This time, however, the protests were an eerie mirror-image of those of 1989, with students demonising America and its values instead of glorifying them – and the Chinese government permitting, even encouraging, their activities. In April of 2001, another diplomatic incident occurred when a US spy plane collided with a Chinese fighter jet over the South China Sea. The Chinese pilot died, but the Americans survived after landing on Hainan Island, where they were immediately detained by the Chinese and released only after 11 days of intense public propaganda and private negotiations.

Afghanistan and then in Iraq. Tensions over North Korea's suspected nuclear weapon programme also benefited China, which found itself sought after as a vital intermediary in negotiations with its hermetic neighbour. In 2004 the US–China relationship was on its best footing since before the events of 1989.

In the last few years of his tenure, Jiang Zemin began to put forward a new theory called the "Three Represents". The basic idea of this theory is that the Communist Party must strive to represent the requirements of China's "advanced productive forces", "advanced culture", and the fundamental interests of the overwhelming majority of the

These and other less public disagreements made the road ahead look rocky for US–China relations. However, the shocking tragedy of the September 2001 terrorist attacks in New York proved a turning point for relations, and indeed, for China's international diplomatic position. As the US and other Western nations focused their attention on fighting terrorists, China suddenly became a needed ally rather than a convenient target for governments and politicians who wanted to show their support for human rights. The Chinese government – ever mindful of its own simmering separatist problems in Xinjiang and Tibet – remained largely silent as the US went to war first in

Chinese people. Even to someone versed in the opaque language of the Communist bureaucracy, the theory is virtually unintelligible, and it was at first the subject of much muttered ridicule from those who had to study it. However, Jiang's underlying purpose in espousing the Three Represents was of great importance: to allow capitalists and private entrepreneurs to join the Communist Party and to guarantee them the same basic rights and protections as everyone else. Despite opposition from hard-line Communists, the Three Represents was added to both the Party and State constitutions and may prove to be Jiang's most important legacy.

## The new leadership

Jiang Zemin relinquished his position as Communist Party secretary in 2002, as state president in 2003, and as head of the Central Military Commission in 2004. He was replaced in all three positions by Hu Jintao, a native of Anhui Province who studied engineering at Beijing's prestigious Tsinghua University. Hu is by all accounts an able and affable manager, who rose quickly through the ranks of the Communist Party based on his own merit and hard work.

Hu had something of a baptism by fire when the SARS epidemic broke out almost as soon as he assumed office. Institutionalised obfuscation significantly worsened the problem, but once Hu recognised that the cover-up was nearly as dangerous as the disease, he fired those who had lied and opened China up to international disease experts. His background has given him a deep understanding of the problems in rural areas, and he has adopted a somewhat more populist governing approach than his predecessor. His premier, Wen Jiabao, also has a strong interest in rural affairs and is a well-liked populist; he is still remembered by many for having accompanied Zhao Ziyang on his visit to the students in Tiananmen Square in May of 1989.

In the first years of their leadership, Hu and Wen have channelled much of their energy into redressing the ever-growing gap between rural and urban income. They have also laid aside the Deng-era rhetoric that emphasised getting rich in favour of a less-used Deng-era catchphrase related to building a *xiaokang* society – a more egalitarian and socially responsible community in which wealth is more evenly distributed. The target is a per capita GDP of US$3,000 by 2020.

## Looking ahead

Problems and potential pitfalls are easy to see when one considers China's future prospects. Modernisation has brought a huge gap between rich and poor, urban and rural. Unemployment is a growing problem. Vast numbers of rural residents and migrant workers have virtually no access to medical care. The number of school-age children attending school has actually begun to decline, largely because many parents cannot afford the required fees.

Corruption remains a seemingly incurable disease despite a long-running campaign to end it. The banking industry is beset by bad loans to state-owned enterprises, most of which remain inefficient and unprofitable. Calls for greater political participation are growing louder at the village level and from among the rising urban middle class and private entrepreneurs. The environment is in a bad way; air quality may have improved a little in Beijing but it is still a very polluted city. Environmental degradation has contributed to such problems

as water shortages, flooding and desertification. And, always there on the horizon, is the possibility of armed conflict with Taiwan.

If all these issues sound overwhelming, perhaps the most important thing to remember is that China has consistently confounded its critics. Even as pessimists point out problems of every variety, the economy grows steadily and strongly, foreign investment pours in, the general standard of living rises inexorably. Newspaper columnists prosper by imagining terrible scenarios of social chaos, war and upheaval, but it is far more likely that China will continue muddling through its manifold problems and steadily achieving its goals. ❑

**FAR LEFT:** one of Beijing's *nouveaux riches.* **LEFT:** the massive road-building programme is struggling to cope with the increase in traffic. **RIGHT:** Hu Jintao.

# Decisive Dates

## Early History

*c.*3000 BC Neolithic villages are established in the area around present-day Beijing.
*c.*700 BC Trading between the Chinese, Koreans, Mongols and northern tribes starts to take place around the site of the modern city.
475–221 BC Warring States period. Rise of the city of Ji, the forerunner of Beijing.
221 BC Qin Shi Huangdi unifies China to found the first imperial dynasty, and creates the Great Wall. Beijing (still known as Ji) becomes the administrative centre of Guangyang prefecture.

206 BC Han dynasty founded; capital in Chang'an.
165 BC Civil service examinations instituted.
2nd century AD Trade between China and Asia/Europe thrives. The first Buddhist temples are founded in China. Beijing (Ji) develops into a strategic garrison town between the warring kingdoms of northern China, and the lands of the Mongols and other nomads.
220 Abdication of the last Han emperor. Wei, Jin, and Northern and Southern dynasties divide China.
581 After nearly four centuries of division, the Sui dynasty reunifies China.
589–610 Repairs of early parts of the Great Wall. Construction of a system of Grand Canals linking northern and southern China.
618 Tang dynasty proclaimed. Government increasingly bureaucratised.

## Mongol Dynasties (916–1368)

907–960 Fall of Tang dynasty. Five Dynasties and Ten Kingdoms partition China. Beijing, (called Yanjing or Nanjing), becomes the southern capital of the new Khitan (Mongol) empire under the Liao dynasty.
1040 Development of neo-Confucianism, which continues through the 11th and 12th centuries.
1125 The Nüzhen, another Mongol tribe, overthrow the Liao to begin the Jin dynasty.
1153 Beijing (Zhongdu) is the Nüzhen capital.
1215 Genghis Khan destroys the city.
1267 Kublai Khan starts construction of Khanbaliq, known in Chinese as Dadu (Great Capital), using Confucian ideals. An imperial palace is built in today's Beihai Park.
1279 Mongol armies rout the Song court to establish the Yuan dynasty, reinstating Beijing (Khanbaliq/Dadu) as capital. Trade along the Silk Road flourishes.
1293 City rebuilding completed. Tonghua Canal links the city with the Grand Canal.

## Ming Dynasty (1368–1644)

1368 Han Chinese overthrow the Mongols. Ming dynasty is founded. Dadu is renamed Beiping ("Northern Peace") and the capital is moved south to Nanjing.
1403 Beiping reinstated as capital of the empire by the emperor Yongle.
1406–20 During Yongle's reign the city is rebuilt around the new Imperial Palace and its basic layout is established.
1553 Macau becomes a Portuguese trading port and the first European settlement in China. Completion of Beijing's city wall.
15th, 16th and 17th centuries Rebuilding of the Great Wall to make the "10,000 Li" Wall.

## Qing Dynasty (1644–1911)

1644 The Manchu, a non-Han Chinese people from Manchuria, seize Beijing, to initiate the Qing dynasty.
1661–1722 Reign of Emperor Kangxi.
1736–95 Reign of Emperor Qianlong.
1800 First edict prohibiting the importation and local production of opium.

**1838** All trade in opium banned. The following year, the Qing court terminates all trade between England and China.

**1840–2** First Opium War.

**1842** Treaty of Nanjing signed. More Chinese ports are forced to open to foreign trade, and Hong Kong island is surrendered to Great Britain "in perpetuity".

**1851–64** The Taiping Rebellion.

**1858–60** Second Opium War. Treaty of Tianjin signed, opening more ports to foreigners.

**1894–5** China is defeated by Japan in the Sino-Japanese War.

**1900** The Boxer Rebellion.

**1911** Republican Revolution: Sun Yat-sen is chosen president, but soon steps down. Abdication of the last emperor, Pu Yi.

## Post-Imperial China

**1912–16** Yuan Shikai takes over as president. Several provinces proclaim independence. After Yuan dies, the warlord period ensues.

**1919** On 4 May in Beijing, a large demonstration demands the restoration of China's sovereignty, thus beginning a Nationalist movement.

**1921** Founding of the Communist Party in Shanghai.

**1925** Sun Yat-sen dies.

**1934–6** The Long March: Communists forced to abandon their stronghold in southern China. Only 30,000 of the original 100,000 who began the march arrive at the northern base in Yan'an.

**1937** The Marco Polo Bridge Incident prompts Communists and Nationalists to unite to fight the Japanese.

**1945** Japan defeated in World War II; full-scale civil war ensues in China.

## People's Republic of China

**1949** Mao Zedong declares People's Republic in Beijing on 1 October; Nationalist army flees to Taiwan.

**1950–3** Chinese troops support North Korea.

**1957–9** Tiananmen Square and "Ten Great Buildings" built for the tenth anniversary of Communist Party rule.

**1958–61** Mass famine kills over 30 million.

**LEFT:** watercolour of old China.
**RIGHT:** SARS caused panic in Beijing in 2003.

**1960** Split between China and Soviet Union.

**1965–6** Beginning of the Cultural Revolution.

**1972** President Richard Nixon visits China.

**1976** Zhou Enlai (Jan) and Mao Zedong (Sept) die. Tangshan earthquake kills 242,000, mainly in Hebei Province east of Beijing.

**1978** Deng Xiaoping becomes leader, instituting a policy of economic reform and openness to the West.

**1979** The US formally recognises China. Democracy Wall movement crushed.

**1989** Pro-democracy demonstrations in Tiananmen Square brought to an end by a brutal military crackdown on 4 June.

**1992** Deng restarts economic reforms.

**1997** Deng Xiaoping dies. Hong Kong reverts to Chinese sovereignty on 1 July.

**1999** PRC's 50th anniversary is marked with old-style military parades.

**2001** Beijing is named host city of the 2008 Olympic Games. China joins the World Trade Organization after a 15-year quest.

**2002** The Party's 16th congress ends with significant changes to the constitution. Jiang Zemin replaced as president by Hu Jintao.

**2003** An outbreak of the SARS virus brings panic to Beijing, with schools closed.

**2004** In an effort to restrain the speeding economy, interest rates are raised for the first time in 10 years. ❑

# PEOPLE

Beijingers, with their distinctive burr, love to talk.
And the economic and social changes of recent years
have certainly given them plenty to talk about...

Stereotyping Chinese from other parts of the country is a favourite pastime in China. As residents of the nation's capital, Beijingers are a favourite target and, indeed, are not above playing the game themselves. It is perhaps unsurprising that the traits Beijing residents like to ascribe to themselves are somewhat different from those that non-Beijingers tend to ascribe to them.

Indeed, if you ask a Beijing resident to describe his fellow citizens, he is likely to tell you that they are generous, affable, loyal, hard-working and patriotic people, who love to talk, especially about politics. But if you ask someone from outside Beijing, he is more likely to describe a typical Beijinger as someone who is arrogant, eager to get rich but unwilling to do hard or menial work, and full of talk but short on action. If the person you ask happens to be Shanghainese, he is likely simply to sniff and say that Beijingers are *tu*, which roughly translates as "country bumpkins."

Stereotypes aside, the reality is that it gets harder to define a typical Beijinger with each passing year, as the economy booms and the city evolves at breakneck speed. Like most big capital cities, Beijing attracts leading entrepreneurs, actors, singers, models, bureaucrats, politicians, generals, scientists, and sports stars. It also attracts poor rural residents from around the nation, who come to the capital to take on the myriad tasks that many Beijing residents no

longer care to do. There are nowadays so many poor migrants working as construction workers, household servants, nannies, waitresses, janitors and refuse collectors, that public and private life in Beijing would virtually cease to function if they all went home.

## Daily life

Contrary to stereotype, most people work hard. The cellphones carried by all but the city's poorest, oldest and youngest residents are generally used for business communications rather than chit-chat. Because so much of their time is devoted to work, most white-collar workers – and even some labourers – hire others to care

**PRECEDING PAGES:** relaxing in the park. **LEFT:** living standards have improved beyond all recognition for most people. **RIGHT:** Beijingers face a bright future.

for their children and do their cleaning and cooking. It is even common for couples to board their toddlers at live-in nursery schools and take them home only on weekends.

The material rewards of all this hard work are everywhere to be seen. Just over a million Beijing residents now own a car, more than in either Shanghai or Guangzhou, and well over half own their own homes. Goods that were once seen as luxuries – telephones, air-conditioning, refrigerators, stereos – are now considered necessities. Holidaying in other parts of China or even overseas is increasingly popular, and some of the city's wealthiest residents even own second homes.

Though people may have less free time than they once did, they have more money to spend on it, so leisure-time activities are booming. Watching television and pirated DVDs, eating out and shopping are the main leisure pursuits for most Beijingers. Wangfujing is the capital's premier promenading street, but diners and window-shoppers can be found in any corner of the city at almost any time of day. Countless small karaoke venues, bars and discos form the backbone of Beijing's nightlife, although older and wealthier people tend to visit huge cabaret-style nightclubs and restaurants. Exercise is increasingly trendy, with health clubs, yoga centres and even rock-

## NOT-SO-LITTLE EMPERORS

Since the one-child policy was introduced in 1979, a single child often has a monopoly over two parents and four doting grandparents. Boys, seen as inheritors of the family line, are spoilt more. Memories of hard times, and the desire to get the most out of one offspring, mean many parents believe bigger is better. Obesity has become common among urban children puffed up by Western fast food and countless brands of snacks and sweets.

In return for all the attention, the "little emperors" face increasing pressure to succeed in their exams. Yet sympathy is in short supply: "Many of them are selfish, lazy, arrogant and uncaring", wrote *China Daily*.

climbing walls springing up around the city. Education is also a prime leisure-time activity, especially learning English. "Crazy English", in which students are told to shout out the words, has caught on after promotion at evangelist-style rallies.

Because old habits die hard – and many Beijingers still live in cramped, sub-standard accommodation – much leisure activity still takes place on the city's busy streets and in its narrow *hutong*. Walk around a major intersection and you will see families flying kites over the road, boys kicking a football around on the grass verges and elderly people chatting on bridges. On summer evenings, along the pavements and under the bridges sit barbers, bicycle repairers, fruit and vegetable vendors, neighbourhood committee wardens and fortune-tellers. *Qi gong* practitioners and *Yang Ge* dancers use whatever space remains. And there, keeping order among the motley procession of pedestrians, cyclists, drivers and passengers, are the ever-watchful eyes of authority; the police, flag-waving traffic wardens, and bicycle and car park attendants.

## The generation gap

Unsurprisingly, there is also a downside to the fast-changing lifestyle that prosperity has brought to Beijing. High-rise apartments with

cause of death among people aged 15–34.

If families have more money and freedom, they also seem to feel more pressure. The one-child policy to which most city dwellers are subject causes parents to place inordinate hopes on their single children, or "little emperors" *(see panel, opposite)*. Many kids are expected not only to excel at school, but also at extra-curricular study courses, languages and music lessons. Children who used to run around in the street are now confined to high-rises where they watch TV, play video games or do homework while their parents work. This increasingly sedentary lifestyle – supplemented with junk food – has led to an obesity rate of nearly 20 per

private baths and kitchens are more comfortable than crumbling low-rises with shared facilities, but they are also isolating. Older people, in particular, find it hard to adjust. While some gather to chat in the front entrances of their shiny new buildings or do tai chi together in the early morning, others succumb to loneliness and despair. The young and seemingly successful are not immune to such feelings either – China's suicide rate is 2.3 times the world average, and it is the leading

cent among Beijing children. Those with no siblings sometimes find it hard to play with others and are often considered to be somewhat spoiled, and are often stressed by the time they become teenagers. Indeed, between 16 and 25 per cent of college students are believed to be suffering from some sort of mental disorder, and the media has recently begun to write of the "psychological plague" on college campuses.

The institution of marriage has also come under considerable pressure. A negative side-effect of China's increasing freedom is the huge rise in prostitution. Prostitutes generally work in massage parlours, hairdressers' salons, bars, clubs and hotels, and can be a

**FAR LEFT:** a "little emperor" at a fashion show.
**LEFT:** promoting family planning. **ABOVE:** Western styles influence the young… **RIGHT:** … if not the old.

regular part of a business trip or an evening with work colleagues. Extra-marital affairs are commonplace and are a major contributor to the city's escalating divorce rate. Extra-marital sex also contributes to the increasing rate of STD infection and even HIV, although the latter is still low compared to rates elsewhere in China and in other major cities around the world. In a belated bow to reality, the Beijing government in late 2004 launched a large-scale campaign to promote condom use. This includes the installation of thousands of condom-vending machines near universities, entertainment spots and construction sites around the city. With Beijing's rising divorce

rates, second and third marriages are common. Couples marry later and have children later – or not at all – and young people often live together before marriage. More people are opting to remain single and the number of women who choose to become single mothers is slowly starting to grow.

## Migrants and minorities

Beijing has roughly 3 million migrant workers, who play crucial roles in the city's economy and even in the private lives of its residents. Most are men who clean toilets, transport waste on heavy tricycle carts, un-block drains and canals or construct roads,

## TOO MANY PEOPLE, TOO FEW SURNAMES

When Genghis Khan was asked how he would conquer northern China, it is said that he replied, "I will kill everybody called Wang, Li, Zhang, and Liu. The rest will be no problem." With well over a billion people, it is natural to assume that China would have a surplus of surnames to go around. Yet of the 12,000 surnames that once existed in China, today there remain just 3,000. Nearly a third of the population shares just five family names. In fact, nearly 90 per cent of Chinese use just 100 surnames (hence the phrase "old hundred names" which refers to the masses), with 90 million sharing the name Li, by default the world's most common surname. In the US, by

comparison, there are only 2.4 million people with the name Smith, the most common family name in the English-speaking world.

Much of the problem began centuries ago, when non-Han Chinese, seeking to blend into the dominant culture, abandoned their own surnames and adopted common names of the Han. In modern China, with its vast population, literally thousands of people can share the same full name, leading to numerous frustrating cases of mistaken identity. The possibility of a bureaucratic meltdown over the confusion of a limited number of names is not far-fetched.

housing and shopping centres. Some sell fruit and vegetables, often sleeping under make-shift stalls in summer. Many women find live-in jobs as waitresses, beauty-shop workers, nannies or servants.

But migrant workers do not receive much of a welcome. Much of Beijing's "disorder" – from unplanned births to crime and pollution – is blamed on them, and they have few rights or privileges. Until the outbreak of SARS, those employed by construction firms were often crammed into dorms that slept 100 people; now the regulation is that there must be no more than 14 to a room. Although they are paid much less than a Beijing resident would be for the same

Beijing. Parents who cannot afford these fees must send their children to illegal, makeshift schools run by other migrant parents – 30 per cent of the 240,000 school-age migrant children in Beijing attend such substandard facilities. Faced with such a choice, many choose to leave their children back home to be raised by grandparents or other relatives,

Beijing's minority population consists of both migrants and permanent residents. The most visible are the Tibetan merchants, with their long hair and flowing sheepskin robes who sell jewellery and religious items. Otherwise, the Hui Muslims are the capital's most obvious minority. Beijing has several

job, they frequently have trouble collecting any money at all – a regulation passed by the city in 2004 requires that migrant construction workers be paid once a month, instead of once a year. Few have insurance or access to health care, and most must rely on the goodwill of their employers if they are injured on the job.

While many migrants are young and single, some have children and for them life is partic-ularly difficult. Hefty surcharges are levied on migrant children who attend public school in

mosques and Islamic cultural centres, as well as Muslim districts like Niu Jie, with its ancient mosque *(see page 109)*. Hui women wear headscarves, and men usually wear white skullcaps similar to those worn in Muslim countries. The men often grow beards, but otherwise resemble China's Han majority. The capital's other main Muslim group, Uighurs from Xinjiang in the far west of China, look more Turkish than Chinese.

Beijing's increasing worldliness is bol-stered by its ever-growing number of foreign residents, both Western and Asian, who are particularly in evidence in the Chaoyang District in the east of the city. ❏

**LEFT:** a billboard promotes the one-child policy.
**ABOVE:** in the run-up to 2008, construction is a major employer. **RIGHT:** the downside of the new economy.

# LIFE IN THE HUTONG

**The heart of Beijing lies behind its modern facade, in the tranquil *hutong*, narrow alleys that have been the hub of the city's street life for 700 years**

Since the time of Genghis Khan, Beijingers have built single-storey homes with tiled roofs, facing into a central courtyard and protected by high walls. They are set within a labyrinth of crumbling grey alleyways, some dating back many centuries. These are the *hutong* (the word itself is of Mongolian origin), the heart of traditional Beijing and one of its most alluring sights.

There are two main areas of *hutong* in Beijing: the tight knot of streets that lies immediately south of Qianmen Gate, and the attractive area around the Bell and Drum towers and back lakes to the north of the Forbidden City. Strolling or cycling around these areas is an experience not to be missed, giving a glimpse of the city as it used to be. Tiny workshops dimly lit by a single bare bulb, street vendors selling steamed *baozi*, snot-nosed children, old men carrying their songbirds in bamboo cages, coal smoke and bicycles – all form part of this vaguely Dickensian scene. For those who bemoan the increasingly standard-ised, interna-tional facade of modern Beijing, these alleyways provide instant succour. See them before they disappear.

**ABOVE:** Family members wrap up against the Beijing winter to dine together in an old courtyard. Privacy, security and a close-knit sense of community are some of the upsides of life in a *hutong*. To many residents, these benefits make up for the prevalence of substandard housing and often grimy living conditions.

**ABOVE:** Chinese chess (*wei ch'i*) contends with backgammon for the right to be called the oldest game still played in its original form.
**LEFT:** A *siheyuan* courtyard from above. The characteristic tiled roofs slope down to a private quadrangle, often filled with flowers and trees – usually apricot, walnut or pomegranate. Each courtyard is closed off with wooden gates, on which characters are carved for good fortune.

## A DISAPPEARING WAY OF LIFE

As Beijing continues to modernise, the *hutong* are under threat. The least salubrious were cleared in the 1950s to make way for apartment blocks, but sizeable areas of courtyard houses remained until the late 1980s. As in the West, housing policies have wavered between wholesale redevelopment and sensitive renovation. Now *siheyuan* (courtyard houses) and *hutong* are bearing the brunt of the drive to create a modern metropolis of mirrored-glass skyscrapers and ivy-clad flyovers.

It is easy for outsiders to be sentimental about the destruction of old buildings, but the fact is that many *hutong* dwellings are cramped and squalid. Some are comprised of just one or two small rooms, functioning as combined kitchens, living rooms, bedrooms and washrooms. The families use a public toilet in the alley, not pleasant at the best of times, let alone in the freezing winter months. A 15th-floor apartment with all modern conveniences naturally holds great appeal.

Yet some families prefer to stay put, fearing exile to distant suburbs with poor infrastructure. Others believe *hutong* should be preserved for their historical value. In a country where government control normally restricts public debate to the most trivial issues, the fate of the *hutong* has prompted academics to write articles stressing the importance of the alleys to Beijing's cultural heritage and residents to petition officials and courts. Nearly two-thirds of the 1,330 *hutong* that existed in Beijing in the mid-1950s have gone. Though the demolition continues, the ongoing debate seems likely to guarantee that some, at least, will survive.

**BELOW:** Behind protective walls, inside the courtyards of the *hutong*, is another world. Assorted jumble collects in doorways, pot plants catch the sun's angled rays, and caged songbirds hang from the eaves. The secret to a sweet voice, so they say, is frequent baths and a diet of cornmeal and ground peanuts.

**BELOW:** Starting from the north end of Beihai Park, organised tours will expose visitors to the history and culture that lies behind these ancient and curious structures. They take you to the *hutong* around Qianhai and Houhai lakes, often acknowledged as Beijing's most picturesque area.

# RELIGION

Daoism, Buddhism and Confucianism are slowly regaining popularity, after the Cultural Revolution abruptly halted one of the world's richest spiritual traditions

Although only one major religion, Daoism, actually originated in China, the nation has absorbed all the world's major faiths over the centuries and is now home to millions of Buddhists, Muslims and Christians. The practices and doctrines of all these religions have been sinified in varying degrees, with Buddhism having been so significantly assimilated that it is now common to speak of "Chinese Buddhism" as one form of the religion. Indeed, the Chinese approach to all religion has historically been so syncretic that it is somewhat difficult to isolate religious practices – a Daoist temple might have a statue of Confucius or Buddha, while a portrait of the Virgin Mary might be hard to distinguish from a rendering of Guanyin, the Buddhist goddess of mercy.

New gods are readily adopted into local religious practice; peasants in some parts of the country now pray for good harvests before statues of Mao Zedong. The confusing nature of Chinese religious belief leads some foreigners to belittle it. But religion in China is for real, and it is growing – among newly affluent urbanites as well as rural peasants.

## Ancestor worship

The ancestor worship of the Chinese is based on the belief that a person has two souls. One is created at the time of conception. After death, its strength dwindles, although it remains in the grave with the corpse and lives on the sacrificial offerings, until it eventually leads a shadow existence by the Yellow Springs in the underworld. However, if no more sacrifices are offered, it will return to earth as an ill-willed spirit and cause damage.

The second soul emerges at birth. During its heavenly voyage after death, it is threatened by evil forces, and is dependent upon the sacrifices and prayers of living descendants. If the sacrifices cease, then this soul, too, turns into an evil spirit. But if the descendants continue to make sacrificial offerings and maintain the grave, the deceased may offer help and protection.

Originally, formal ceremonies of ancestor worship were exclusive to the king, but around 500 BC peasants began to honour their

LEFT: the Jade Emperor, a Daoist deity appropriated by popular religion. RIGHT: ancestor worship.

ancestors. At first, people believed the soul of the ancestor would search for a human substitute, usually the grandson of the honoured ancestor. About 2,000 years ago, genealogical tables were introduced as homes for the soul during sacrificial acts. Until then, the king and noblemen had used human sacrifices for ancestral worship. Today they offer their ancestors sacrifices of food, for example, during the Qingming Festival.

## Popular beliefs

The original popular Chinese religion focused on the worship of natural forces. Later on, people began to worship the Jade Emperor, a

doctrines, only Confucianism and Daoism had gained wide acceptance. Buddhism, China's other major religion, arrived from India in the 1st century AD, though it remained small-scale for several more centuries.

## Daoism

Two of the central concepts of Daoism are *dao* and *wuwei*. *Dao* means the way or path, but also means method or principle. *Wuwei* is sometimes simply defined as passivity, or "swimming with the stream". The concept of *de* (virtue) is closely linked to this, not in the sense of moral honesty, but as a virtue that manifests itself in daily life when *dao* is put

figure from Daoism; from the 14th century onwards the Jade Emperor became the most important god in popular religion. Guanyin, the goddess of mercy, originated in Mahayana (Great Wheel) Buddhism. There were also earth deities, and every town, large or small, worshipped its own town god. Demons of illness, spirits of the house and even the god of latrines had to be remembered. The deities of streams and rivers were considered particularly dangerous and unpredictable.

Until the founding of the Qin empire in 221 BC, China was divided into many small states, with a variety of contending schools of philosophical thought. From these myriad

into practice. The forces of *yin* and *yang* determine the course of events in the world. The masculine, brightness, activity and heaven are considered *yang* forces; the feminine, weak, dark and passive elements of life are *yin*.

In popular religion, Laozi is seen as the founder of Daoism, although people today still argue about his historical existence. He was born, it is said, in a village in Henan Province in 604 BC into a distinguished family (among the colourful myths is one that relates how his mother was pregnant with him for 72 years and that he was delivered into the world through her left armpit). For a time, he held the office of archivist in the then capital, Luoyang. But he later retreated into solitude and died in his village in 517 BC.

The classic work of Daoism is the *Daodejing*. It now seems certain that more than one author wrote this work. The earliest, and most significant, followers of Laozi were Liezi and Zhuangzi. Liezi (5th century BC) was concerned with the relativity of experiences, and he strived to comprehend the *dao* with the help of meditation. Zhuangzi (4th century BC) is especially famous for his poetic allegories. The abstract concepts of Daoism did not attract ordinary people, but by the Han period (206 BC–AD 220) there were signs of a popular and religious Daoism. As Buddhism also became more popular, it borrowed ideas from Daoism, and vice versa, to the point where one might speak of a fusion between the two.

Religious Daoism developed in various directions and schools. The ascetics either lived in monasteries or retreated to the mountains and devoted all their time to meditation. Daoist priests had important functions as medicine men and interpreters of oracles. They carried out exorcism and funeral rites, and read mass for the dead or for sacrificial offerings. Many of these practices drew on ancient shamanism.

Baiyunguan Temple (The Temple of the White Cloud) in southwestern Beijing is an important, and thriving, Daoist centre *(see page 111)*.

## Confucian influence

For Confucius, too, *dao* and *de* are central concepts. For more than 2,000 years, the ideas of Confucius (551–479 BC) have been an important part of Chinese culture, which in turn influenced neighbouring lands such as Korea and Japan. It is debatable whether Confucianism is a religion in the strictest sense, including as it does strong elements of social theory and philosophy. Confucius himself was worshipped as a deity, although he was only officially made equal to the heavenly god by an imperial edict in 1906.

Confucius – or Kong Fuzi (Master Kong) – came from an impoverished family of the nobility who lived in the state of Lu (near Qufu in western Shandong Province). Having failed

to gain office with one of the feudal lords, he became an itinerant scholar, preaching his ideas and gaining a modest following – although it wasn't until centuries after his death that his ideas really caught on. Confucius significantly reinterpreted the idea of the *junzi*, a nobleman, to that of a noble man, whose life is morally sound and who is, therefore, legitimately entitled to reign. Humanity *(ren)* was a central concept, based on fraternity and love of children. A ruler would only be successful if he could govern according to these principles.

Confucius defined the social positions and hierarchies very precisely. Only if and when every member of society takes full responsi-

bility for his or her position will society as a whole function smoothly. Family and social ties – and hierarchy – were considered fundamental: between father and son (filial piety), man and woman (female subservience), older brother and younger brother, friend and friend, and ruler and subordinate.

Confucianism has had many incarnations. After the Han-dynasty emperors adopted it, it became a religion of law and order, which ensured popularity with subsequent dynasties. It became the official state religion and the basis of all state examinations, a determining factor for Chinese officialdom until the 20th century. Mao tried to annihilate Confucianism – and all

**LEFT:** the Forest Ghosts and Spirits Altar at the Daoist Dongyue Temple. **RIGHT:** a Daoist monk.

religion – in the Cultural Revolution, but non-religious Confucianism is slowly finding favour with a new breed of pragmatists who value the ancient religion's emphasis on order and social hierarchy. The Confucius Temple (Kong Miao) in northeastern Beijing is a centre for religious Confucianism *(see page 132)*.

## Buddhism

The Chinese initially encountered Buddhism at the beginning of the 1st century AD, when merchants and monks came to China over the Silk Road. The type of Buddhism that is prevalent in China today is the Mahayana (Great Wheel) school, which – as opposed to

Hinayana (Small Wheel) – promises all creatures redemption through the Bodhisattva (redemption deities).

Two aspects were particularly attractive to the Chinese: the teachings of karma provided a better explanation for individual misfortune, and there was a hopeful promise for existence after death. Nevertheless, there was considerable opposition to Buddhism, which contrasted sharply with Confucian ethics and ancestor worship.

Buddhism was most influential during the Tang dynasty (618–907). Several emperors officially supported the religion; the Tang empress Wu Zetian, in particular, surrounded herself with Buddhist advisors. However, following Wu Zetian's abdication in 705, anti-Buddhist sentiment again began to grow. Some critics faulted it on nationalist grounds, noting that Buddha was "of barbarian origin" and could not even speak Chinese. Others saw it as an economic drain, pointing out the huge number of monasteries that were exempt from taxes, the hundreds of thousands of monks and nuns who did not plant or weave, and the large amounts of precious metal that were used to make statues. The emperor Wuzong further came under the influence of Daoists who viewed Buddhism as a a competitive threat, and in 845 launched a massive suppression of the "insignificant Western religion", in which more than 40,000 temples and 4,600 monasteries were destroyed and more than 250,000 monks and nuns returned to the laity.

Wuzong died the following year and the suppression was quickly ended, but the blow it had struck was one from which the religion would never fully recover.

Even so, ten Chinese schools of Buddhism emerged, eight of which were essentially philosophical in nature and did not influence popular religion. Only two schools have remained influential: Chan (School of Meditation or Zen Buddhism) and Pure Land (Amitabha), a form of Mahayana Buddhism that has dominated in China since the 14th century.

The masters of Chan considered meditation to be the only path to knowledge, although this did not have to consist of silent contemplation. Instead, it could be found through total absorption in one's normal activity. This school was based at the Shaolin Temple in Henan Province, now more famous for its martial arts. The most important method was a dialogue with the master, who asked subtle and paradoxical questions, to which he expected equally paradoxical answers.

In Mahayana Buddhism, worship focused on the Bodhisattva Avalokiteshvara. Since the 7th century AD, the ascetic Bodhisattva has been a popular female figure in China. She is called Guanyin, a motherly goddess of mercy who represents a central deity for the ordinary people. Guanyin means "the one who listens to complaints." The centre of religious attention in the Amitabha school is the Sakyamuni Buddha, the founder of Buddhism. In Chinese monasteries, Sakyamuni greets the faithful as a laughing Buddha in the entrance hall.

In the 7th century AD, Buddhism was introduced into Tibet from India. With the influence of the monk Padmasambhava, Tibetan Buddhism (Lamaism) incorporated shamanist beliefs and rituals from the indigenous Bön religion. One of Beijing's most popular sights, the Lama Temple (Yonghegong; *see page 129)* is a reminder of the historic links between Beijing, Mongolia and Tibet.

## The arrival of Islam

Islam probably reached China in the 7th century via the Silk Road, as well as by sea to the southeast coast. During the Yuan dynasty (1279–1368), it finally became permanently established, while territorial expansion of the empire into central Asia brought more Muslims into the empire.

Muslims have perhaps suffered more persecution than other religious groups in China, partly because their faith is still considered "foreign", unlike Daoism and Buddhism. In the 18th century, slaughtering animals according to Islamic rites was forbidden, and the building of new mosques and pilgrimages to Mecca were not allowed, while marriages between Chinese and Muslims were illegal.

After another round of persecution during the Cultural Revolution, Chinese Islam has been allowed to revive. Today, ten of the 56 recognised nationalities in China profess themselves to Islam, a total of nearly 20 million people. Many live in the far northwest and speak non-Chinese languages – the Uighurs, Kirghiz and Kazakhs – but more than half are Han Chinese, known as Hui, and have the distinction of being the only minority group recognised solely on the basis of religion, and the only one whose members do not share a common language. The Hui are represented in nearly every part of China and are the largest urban minority, with 200,000 living in Beijing alone. Thanks to more enlightened policies and, some say, the Chinese government's need for oil from Muslim countries, Chinese Muslims are allowed to worship freely, to celebrate traditional festivals, and even to make pilgrimages to Mecca.

---

**LEFT:** a statue of Laozi, founder of Daoism.
**RIGHT:** lighting incense at a Buddhist temple.

## Christianity

Christianity was first brought to China by the Nestorians in AD 635, who, in spite of persecutions, managed to spread the word to all regions of the empire. Around the mid-14th century, initial contacts were made between China and the Roman Catholic Church, and during the Ming period, Catholic missionaries began to be very active in China. The Italian Matteo Ricci was one of the leading Jesuit missionaries to China. When he died, there were about 2,000 to 3,000 Chinese Christians.

The Jesuits used their knowledge of Western sciences to forge links with Chinese scholars, but other Catholic Orders were more dogmatic

and caused tensions. At the onset of the 19th century, the Protestants began their missionary activities. By 1948, there were some 3 million Catholics and 1 million Protestants in China.

The Vatican's vigorous anti-communist stance after World War II resulted in the Chinese government proclaiming that the Catholic Church in China should no longer consider itself accountable to Rome. To this day, the pope recognises only the Taiwan government. Yet relations are slowly improving. China now has over 10 million Protestants and 4 million Catholics worshipping in state-sanctioned churches, and many more Christians who attend independent (illegal) house churches. ❏

# FOOD AND DRINK

**Eating out is one of the main pleasures in a city that not only offers its own specialities but also acts as a melting pot for cuisine from all over China. A fast-growing number of other Asian and Western restaurants have added variety, and everything is pleasingly affordable**

**B**eijing cuisine has traditionally existed in two largely separate forms; the imperial food of the royal court and the home-style cooking enjoyed by the ordinary citizen.

Over the centuries, the finest chefs were attracted to the imperial court, and the best among them could count on being given the rank of minister. In the palace kitchens, cooks created dishes that belonged at the pinnacle of world cuisine, dishes made from rare ingredients and prepared with great culinary skill. This is where dishes that belong to every sophisticated Chinese kitchen originated: Peking Duck, Phoenix in the Nest, Mandarin Fish, Lotus Prawns, Mu Shu Pork and Thousand Layer Cake, among others.

In contrast, the traditional cuisine of the capital's workers, peasants and soldiers was simple, with plenty of onions and garlic. The variety of vegetables available further south in China was lacking – in winter, it was common to see nothing but cabbages filling the markets. Improved transportation and the widespread use of greenhouses means that today's residents can get pretty much anything they need, albeit at a higher price.

Beijing's modern cuisine is a mixture of these two traditions, allied to influences from across the country. The main meal of a family of four usually consists of rice, noodles or steamed bread, soup and three or four freshly prepared hot dishes. Many families will eat three cooked meals a day, which makes for a

lot of domestic work; many working people – especially those on lower incomes – eat in workplace canteens.

"Food first, then morals", wrote the dramatist Bertolt Brecht, a maxim particularly appropriate to China. During its long history, it has suffered repeated famines. Even today, the problem of an adequate food supply is by no means solved, despite the generous supply of goods in Beijing's stores and markets.

The great importance of eating in China is expressed in everyday speech. A common greeting is "*Chiguolema?*" or "*Chifanlema?*" (Have you eaten?). The government constantly reminds its critics that China feeds 22 per cent

**LEFT:** imperial-style cuisine.
**RIGHT:** fried grasshoppers are not to everyone's taste.

of the world's population on just 7 per cent of its arable land. Much of China's land is unsuitable for agriculture, which explains why in fertile areas every square metre is used for growing something edible, even in spaces barely large enough for a single head of cabbage. Pasture or fallow land is rarely seen.

## Eating in Beijing

Western palates generally have little difficulty adjusting to and thoroughly enjoying Chinese cooking – and there are few better places than Beijing for sampling it. The most famous local dish is unquestionably Peking Duck *(see below)*, but many other culinary styles and

Hot-pot, sometimes called Mongolian hot-pot – although Mongolians claim it originated in Korea – is another speciality. This combines fondue-style cooking – usually in a communal hot-pot – with unlimited meat and vegetables. A newer challenger has also caught on: Sichuan "yin-yang" hot-pot, divided into two compartments. Beware the fiery *yang* half.

"Thousand-year-old" eggs *(pidan)* remain one of Beijing's most popular appetisers. These are duck eggs that have been packed raw into a mass of mud, chalk and ammonia and left for two weeks or so – not a thousand years. When fully preserved, the egg white turns a transparent, dark-greenish black and the yolk

specialities have found fame here. Traditional Beijing haute cuisine is said to reflect two styles of cooking: imperial, which is based on Qing dynasty palace dishes; and Tan, named after the Tan family, a synthesis of salty northern cuisine with sweeter southern cuisine.

For northern China's *laobaixing* (ordinary people; literally, "old hundred names"), the most common specialities are *jiaozi* (meat- and vegetable-filled pasta parcels), *baozi* (steamed buns stuffed with mincemeat and vegetables), noodles, cornbread and pancakes – rice is not grown in the harsh climate of the north. Stir-fried and boiled dishes often feature cabbage and potatoes.

turns milky yellow-green. The eggs are then cut into wedges, sprinkled with soy sauce and sesame oil, and served with pickled ginger. To many Westerners the taste is an acquired one, but nonetheless worth trying at least once.

## The city's signature dish

A prerequisite for true Peking Duck is a special kind of duck bred in and around Beijing, which is force-fed for about six months before it is slaughtered. Preparing the duck so that it

**ABOVE:** the art of making noodles. **RIGHT:** Peking Duck involves elaborate preparation. **FAR RIGHT:** Beijing has plenty of fast-food joints – Chinese as well as Western.

has the perfect, world-renowned melt-in-the-mouth crispness requires great skill. After slaughter, plucking and cleaning, air is carefully blown through a hole in the neck, so that the skin is loosened from the flesh. This process helps to make the skin as crisp as possible after roasting. The duck is then painted with a mixture of honey, water and vinegar and hung up to dry for three days. Afterwards, still hanging, it is slowly grilled in a special oven.

Equally important to the Peking Duck experience are the dishes served alongside it: very thin pancakes, little sesame-seed rolls, spring onions and *haixian* (or *hoisin*) sauce, a sweetish bean sauce flavoured with garlic and spices.

An authentic meal of Peking Duck begins with a selection of appetisers, most of which derive from various parts of the duck: fried liver, deep-fried heart with coriander, intestines, boiled tongues and the webbed skin of the feet cut very finely – in Chinese cooking, little is wasted. Next, the cook brings the roast duck to the table and cuts it into bite-sized pieces of skin and meat. Take one of the pancakes, use the chopped spring onion to spread *haixian* sauce on it and put a piece of duck over the spring onion. Then roll the whole thing up and eat it using your fingers.

It is this combination that provides the highest gastronomic pleasure and makes the

### TIPS ON ETIQUETTE

If you are invited into someone's home to eat, it is usual to bring a gift – alcohol, cigarettes, or small presents typical of your home country. The Chinese are not judgemental when it comes to how you eat. No one will think less of you if you cannot use chopsticks or if you don't know where to put your bones – just do as others are doing, or what comes naturally to you. On the other hand, you may be pressured to eat more than you want to, or to taste foods that you may not really desire. Here, too, it is important to hold your ground politely. If the thought of eating something doesn't appeal, then don't eat it – profess an allergy, explain that you pre-

fer something else, or just tell the truth. If you are full, say so. If your hosts continue to pressure you, just take a tiny bite.

Take care of your neighbours at the table, serving them some of the food, especially from dishes that they cannot reach easily. Remember also not to pick out the best pieces on each dish, but to take food from the side of the dish closest to you.

At the meal, the host will drink toasts to the guests. "Ganbei!" (empty cup) means you should empty your glass in one shot, and turning your glass upside down shows that you have followed this instruction.

often rather fatty meat digestible. For the final course, you will be served a soup made of the remains of the duck – mostly bones.

Full duck banquets don't come cheap; in fact, they are too expensive for most Chinese families, and reserved for special occasions. There are a number of cheaper duck restaurants in Beijing, but sadly many have become pure mass-production centres.

## Gastronomic melting pot

Beijing has assimilated food from many Chinese regions into its *jia chang cai* (home-style dishes). These are the standard dishes you will find in restaurants and homes.

Sichuan, Guangdong (Canton), Dongbei (the northeast), Shanghai, Shandong and Hunan are some of the regions that continue to influence typical Beijing menus. Milder Sichuan dishes, such as *Mala Doufu* (spicy tofu) and Gongbao Chicken (with chilli and peanuts), can be found in most large restaurants. Sizzling rice-crust, called *guoba*, also originated in Sichuan.

Apart from the dishes that have already joined the ranks of the city's *jia chang cai*, Beijing has many restaurants specialising in cuisine from different regions of China, especially the spicy cuisine of Sichuan and Hunan, and the stir-fries and rice dishes from Guang-

### CHOPSTICKS

Chopsticks, or *kuaizi*, date back thousands of years. Although bone, ivory, gold, jade and steel have all been used, most chopsticks are now made of wood, and thrown away after each meal. The main production area, the northeast, produces around 75 billion pairs a year from 68 million cubic metres of birch wood – enough to build a chopstick Great Wall every five years.

Once a luxury, disposable chopsticks are found in most restaurants (except, ironically, the more expensive places). This is primarily for reasons of hygiene; greasy chopsticks have in the past helped spread epidemics of hepatitis and other diseases.

dong in the deep south, universally known as "Chinese" to the rest of the world. You can eat lean, grilled mutton and beef at restaurants run by China's Korean and Uighur minorities. The Uighurs, from Xinjiang in China's far northwest, make flatbreads and kebabs similar to those found in the Middle East. Hand-cut, stir-fried pasta pieces served in spicy tomato sauce, called *chaopian'r*, are another Xinjiang speciality. Restaurants run by Dai (from Yunnan), Mongolian and Tibetan people offer further tastes of China's remote frontiers.

Thanks to the number of Chinese travelling abroad and the number of Westerners coming to China, there are now also a large number of

Western restaurants in Beijing. Some of these are fast-food joints familiar the world over, such as McDonald's, KFC (there are over 100 branches of each in the city, as well as Chinese imitations) and Pizza Hut, which are favoured by young Chinese. Others are more sophisticated – it is possible to find quite good French, Italian, Middle Eastern and many other types of international cuisine around the city. Indeed, the government is planning to establish a Western-style food training centre so the city will be equipped to feed foreign visitors during the 2008 Olympics.

To balance this culinary invasion, "Old Beijing" fast food and the lively dining style common before 1949 have made something of a comeback. Traditionally dressed waiters shout across the restaurant, announcing those coming and going. Diners order a range of dishes, which are whisked through the restaurant and clattered down. Noodles, usually eaten with a thick sesame- and soy-based sauce, are standard fare.

Countless snack restaurants, some open 24 hours, offer a relaxed atmosphere in which you can try much more than noodles. You will also find an endless choice of snacks like red-bean porridge, sesame cakes, *jiaozi*, *baozi*, *hundun* (wonton, like *jiaozi* soup), and *guotie* (fried *jiaozi* "pot stickers"). Many department stores and shopping malls, such as Oriental Plaza, Parkson and Sun Dongan Plaza, feature food courts serving snacks from around China.

For a quick breakfast try *jidan guan bing* (egg pancakes), sold at roadside stalls. Or sample *youtiao*, deep-fried bread sticks (like doughnuts) usually eaten with hot *dou jiang* (soy milk). They are a delicious traditional start to the day and the ideal fuel for a hard morning exploring all that the city has to offer. They go well with a glass of *dou jiang*, a soybean drink served hot or cold.

Street food is also worth seeking out at other times of day. Look out for *xianer bing*, meat-filled pancakes, wonton soup, *jiaozi* and *baozi*. The Dong'anmen Night Market *(see page 143)* just off Wangfujing is a good place to try regional specialities, such as skewers of

spiced meat *(kaorou chuaner)*, but there are street-food vendors on many street corners all over town (less so around Tiananmen Square).

## A liking for liquor

Alcohol is often an integral part of a Chinese meal. A warning to take care is not unwarranted here, as Chinese men often drink very strong grain liquor. The expensive *Maotai*, named after its place of origin, is famous, as is *Wuliangye* from Sichuan. *Erguotou*, the most popular Beijing brand, gives you 56 per cent alcohol by volume for just a few *kuai*. Spirits are usually found in every restaurant and home, and are in special abundance at any type of offi-

cial gathering. Many wealthy Beijing businesspeople now prefer *Remy Martin XO* or similar luxury brandies. In property, construction and many other industries, bottles of brandy are used as small gifts to oil networks of *guanxi* (connections), especially among officials.

Sweet liqueurs, more popular in the south of China, are also drunk, as is beer *(pijiu)*, which is a standard mealtime drink – Chinese beer (Tsingtao is the leading brand) is generally good. Several Sino-French joint ventures produce passable, inexpensive wines. Dragon Seal, Dynasty and Changyo are among the better brands. Mineral water *(kuangquan shui)* and soft drinks are universally available. ❏

**LEFT:** multi-course banquet at a Peking Duck restaurant. **ABOVE:** street food at Dong'anmen Market.

# THE ARTS

**Silk, jade and cloisonné epitomise China's rich artistic heritage, yet the Chinese consider painting and calligraphy as their highest art forms. Performance arts include classical music and spectacular acrobatics, as well as Beijing Opera**

The arts have long played a crucial role in Chinese society, culture and government. In Confucian China, for instance, music was believed to reflect the state of society, and a proper gentleman was someone who could write beautiful calligraphy, play an instrument and craft a poem. The Communists viewed art as an important propaganda tool and devoted many resources to creating a new, proletarian art that would help win people over to their viewpoint.

To this day, the government is the nation's biggest arts patron, supporting hundreds of opera companies, orchestras, drama troupes and art schools, as well as untold numbers of writers, poets, composers and musicians. Chinese leaders still believe that they must demonstrate proficiency at music, poetry and calligraphy; Jiang Zemin, for instance, played the piano and published his poetry and calligraphy on the front page of the *People's Daily*.

Beijing is the most important arts centre in China and – somewhat surprisingly – is also artistically freer than many other cities. Artists find it easy to hide between the cracks of its many bureaucracies, or to play one ministry off against another in order to get approval for an avant-garde exhibition or performance. The city's artistic hardware is currently getting a major upgrade with museum renovations and the new National Theatre *(see page 83)*, so it is likely that the arts themselves will flourish even more in the next few years.

**LEFT:** hard at work at the Beijing Mosaic Factory.
**RIGHT:** brush painting.

## VISUAL ARTS AND CRAFTS
### Brush painting

Writing and painting have always enjoyed an intimate association due to the original pictographic nature of the Chinese script. This is evident from the customary incorporation of written words, such as a poem or the name of the artist, into most Chinese paintings.

In China, painting comprises various different disciplines: calligraphy; monochromatic and coloured work in ink on fabric or paper; mural reproductions such as woodblock prints; and other related techniques, such as embroideries and woven pictures; and purely decorative paintings.

Because of their close connection, painting skills are learned in much the same way as writing: through copying old masters or textbooks. A painter is considered a master of his art only when the necessary brushstrokes for a bird, a chrysanthemum or a waterfall can flow effortlessly from his hand. The strong emphasis placed on perfection quickly leads to specialisation by painters on specific subjects. In this way, for instance, Xu Beihong (1895–1953) became known as the painter of horses, just as Qi Bai-Shi (1862–1957) was famous for his shrimps. Many of Xu's best works are displayed at the Xu Beihong Memorial Hall *(see page 152)*.

One of the most favoured painting forms in China is landscape painting. Notable characteristics of this form are perspectives that draw the viewer into the picture, plain surfaces (unpainted empty spaces) that add a feeling of depth, and the harmonious relationship between man and nature, with man depicted as a small, almost vanishing, figure in nature.

Chinese brush painting and calligraphy are generally mounted on a hanging scroll. In days gone by, the scroll was rolled up, stored away, and brought out on special occasions to be slowly unfurled, revealing only parts of a scene, subtly drawing the observer into the picture. Thus, the picture was handled while

### THE FOUR TREASURES OF THE STUDY

Writing and painting materials are referred to in China as the Four Treasures of the Study, consisting of the brush, ink stick, rubbing stone and paper. Such tools have long been held in high esteem by Chinese poets, scholars and painters; there are reliable records which show that brush and ink were being used as early as the 1st century BC, during the Han period. Chinese ink was only taken up in Europe as a distinct kind of paint in the 17th century. The attractive shops along Liulichang *(see page 107)* are the best places in Beijing to buy traditional brushes, paper, ink sticks, rubbing stones and other artists' materials.

being scrutinised. With horizontal scrolls, always unrolled little by little, the hands were in constant movement. The same applies to the two other formats for classical painting – the fan that needed unfolding and the album leaf that needed pages turned. The idea was to create a bond between picture and observer, whereas Western painting on panel or canvas imposes a rational distance. In keeping with this, a landscape painting often has a path or bridge in the foreground to draw the viewer in.

Oil painting was introduced by Jesuit missionaries, along with such Western painting techniques as the use of perspective. It never caught on, except as an export product, until the communist era, when it became a popular medium for producing socialist-realist art. Many of China's best-known contemporary painters also work in oil paints.

Contemporary art is big in Beijing, visible at private galleries and at performance-art exhibitions. The Beijing suburbs are home to several colonies of artists from around the country, although the life of these colonies tends to be short-lived, since they are usually torn down by real-estate developers or abandoned by artists who have grown rich from selling their paintings to foreigners. The contemporary art scene has moved rapidly through styles, including pop art and a horrific mid-

mulberry trees and keeping silkworms. For centuries, silk held the place of currency: civil servants and officers as well as foreign envoys were frequently paid or presented with bales of silk. The precious material was transported to the Middle East and the Roman empire via the famous Silk Road.

The Chinese maintained a monopoly on silk until about 200 BC, when the secret of its manufacture became known in Korea and Japan. In the West – in this case the Byzantine empire – such knowledge was acquired only in the 6th century AD. The Chinese had prohibited the export of silkworm eggs and the dissemination of knowledge of their cultiva-

1990s focus on "body art", which involved the use of corpses and body pieces as art materials. In recent years, the trend is toward installations, film and video. The first Beijing International Art Biennale was held in 2003.

## Silk

The cultivation of the silkworm is said to go back to the 3rd millennium BC. Legend has it that the wife of the mythical Yellow Emperor Huangdi began the tradition of planting

tion, but a monk is said to have succeeded in smuggling some silkworm eggs to the West.

Today's centres of silk production are areas in the east of China around Hangzhou, Suzhou and Wuxi. Hangzhou has the largest silk industry, while Suzhou has the finest embroidery.

## Porcelain

The Chinese invented porcelain in the 7th century AD, a thousand years before Europeans. The most widespread original form was celadon, a product of a blending of iron oxide with the glaze that resulted, during firing, in a characteristic green tone. *Sancai* ceramics,

**FAR LEFT:** modern brushes. **LEFT:** calligraphy for sale in a Liulichang shop. **ABOVE AND RIGHT:** examples of the classic Chinese painting style.

ceramics with three-colour glazes from the Tang dynasty, became world-famous, while the Song period celadons – ranging in colour from pale or moss green, pale blue or pale grey to brown tones – were also technically excellent.

As early as the Yuan period, a technique from Persia was used for underglaze painting in cobalt blue to distinctive effect. These days, wares decorated in such a way are generically known as Ming porcelain. Common themes seen throughout the subsequent Ming period were figures, landscapes and theatrical scenes. At the beginning of the Qing dynasty, blue-and-white porcelain *(hua qing)* attained its highest level of quality.

in China, a clear emerald-green stone is valued most highly – but there are also red, yellow and lavender jades.

In jade-carving workshops there are as many as thirty kinds of jade in use. The most famous are those in Qingtian (Zhejiang Province), Shoushan (Fujian Province) and Luoyang (Hunan Province). Masters of jade work include Zhou Shouhai, from the jade-carving establishment in Shanghai, and Wang Shusen in Beijing, the latter specialising in Buddhist figurines. In government shops, jade can be trusted to be genuine. On the open market and in private shops, however, caution is advised. Genuine jade always feels cool and

From the 14th century, Jingdezhen in Jiangxi Province has been the centre of porcelain manufacture, although today relatively inexpensive porcelain can be bought throughout China. Antique pieces are hard to come by because, in order to protect the country's valuable heritage, the government prohibits the sale of articles predating the First Opium War of the 19th century.

### Jade, China's cherished stone

With its soft sheen and rich nuances of colour, the Chinese have valued jade since antiquity; but it became widely popular only in the 18th century. Colours vary from white to green –

cannot be scratched with a knife. Quality depends on the feel of the stone, its colour, transparency, pattern and other factors. If in doubt, consult a reputable expert.

### Lacquerware

The glossy sheen of lacquerware is not only attractive to the eye but is also appealing to the touch. It is made by coating an object, such as a bowl or vase, with extremely fine layers of a lacquer that comes from the milky sap of the lacquer tree *(rhus verniciflua)*, which grows in central and southern China. If soot or vinegar-soaked iron filings are added to the lacquer, it will dry into a black colour; cinnabar turns it red. The colour combination of red and black, first thought to have been applied in the 2nd century BC, is still considered a classic.

The carved lacquer technique, which began in the Tang dynasty, when large lacquerware Buddhist sculptures were produced, reached its highest peak during the Ming and Qing periods. The core, often of wood or tin, is coated with mostly red layers of lacquer. When the outermost coat has dried, decorative carving is applied, with the knife penetrating generally to the lowest layer so that the design stands out from the background in relief. Today, lacquerware is mainly produced in Beijing, Fuzhou and Yangzhou; best-known is the

the rods are filled with enamel paste and fired in the kiln, usually four or five times. Finally, metal surfaces not already covered with enamel are gilded. Cloisonné jewellery and ornaments are available all over Beijing.

## THE PERFORMING ARTS

*For Beijing Opera, see pages 68–9.*

### Classical music

Western classical music came to China by way of Western missionaries, and was eventually adopted by Chinese reformers who believed it would help to improve the morals and behaviour of their fellow citizens. Even the

Beijing work, which goes back to the imperial courts of the Ming and Qing dynasties.

### Cloisonné

The cloisonné technique, a way of decorating metal objects with enamel, reached China from Persia in the 8th century AD, was lost and then rediscovered in the 13th century. In cloisonné, metal rods are soldered to the body of the metal object. These form the outlines of the ornamentation, while the spaces between

**FAR LEFT:** porcelain from the Qing dynasty.
**LEFT:** carving in nephrite jade. **ABOVE:** jade Buddha.
**RIGHT:** creating a cloisonné jar.

Communists saw its usefulness as a diplomatic tool and founded a symphony orchestra at their revolutionary base at Yan'an. During the Cultural Revolution, Western music was banned, but Western instruments were introduced into all the "model operas", several of which were created and performed around the nation. The upshot of all this is that classical music is now deeply rooted in China's cities. Beijing has two major orchestras – the China National Symphony Orchestra and the China Philharmonic – and more than half a dozen others that perform less regularly. It is also home to the Central Conservatory of Music, which was founded in the early 1950s at Zhou

Enlai's behest, and is arguably the best conservatory in the country. The Beijing International Music Festival held every October has grown into a major international event with scores of top-notch performers from around the world.

Western opera was first introduced to China through foreigners resident in Shanghai in the 1920s and 1930s, but its more formal introduction came via Soviet advisers during the 1950s. Beijing has a major opera company and many conservatory students study opera, but the cost of staging productions is so prohibitive that there is no formal opera season – a situation that will hopefully change once the National Grand Theatre is up and running.

modern and progressive because it differed from traditional Chinese drama – which was always sung and accompanied by music – and because it frequently dealt with social issues. It soon caught on among young people in the main cities, who flocked to see productions of plays like Ibsen's *A Doll's House* (Mao Zedong's wife, Jiang Qing, even performed the role of Nora in her younger years). Chinese writers soon became involved, and the works of such playwrights as Guo Morou, Cao Yu and Lao She have become classics.

Spoken drama enjoys an especially large and faithful audience in Beijing, whose people are known for their love of conversation.

The influence of Western-style symphonic music has been so strong in China that during the 1950s orchestras of traditional Chinese instruments were created. Because these were not intended to be played in huge ensembles, many technical changes had to be made and new instruments invented. Purists still scoff at the whole idea, but Beijing's China National Traditional Orchestra is here to stay. For a list of classical music venues *see page 219.*

The Beijing People's Art Theatre is the nation's most illustrious drama company, performing to full houses in the Capital Theatre on Wangfujing. It has a tight-knit group of actors who perform both Chinese and foreign plays and whose acting style is instantly recognisable. The China National Drama Company was created only recently and has quickly carved out a role for itself and also attracts large audiences. For a list of theatres *see page 219.*

## Theatre

Spoken drama was first introduced to China by Chinese students studying in Japan around the turn of the 20th century. It was seen as

## Dance

Dance has been a part of ordinary people's entertainment in China since antiquity. It played a key role at the imperial court during the cosmopolitan Tang dynasty – some scholars believe that foot-binding first developed because fashionable women began to imitate the way Tang court dancers wrapped their feet (a practice that did little to help the development of dance for the next millennium and more). Most of China's 55 official minority groups have strong folk-dance traditions, and dance has also traditionally formed a regular part of rural entertainment for Han Chinese, especially at the Spring Festival (Chinese New Year). However, institutionalised, formal performances are a relatively modern phenomenon, and Beijing has played a key role in their development.

group. It was the ex-PLA dancer Jin Xing who founded Beijing's first modern dance company in 1995. For a list of venues *see page 219.*

## Acrobatics

Acrobatics has a history in China of close to 3,000 years. The art form spread along the Silk Road and was for many centuries highly popular entertainment. Its star began to fade as early as the 13th century, when early forms of Chinese opera started to develop, but it remained popular in rural areas. The Cultural Revolution era saw something of a comeback for acrobatics, since leftist revolutionaries considered it to be a respectable "proletarian" art

China's first ballet company, the Central Ballet of China, was founded in Beijing in 1959 with the help of Soviet experts. It performs both Western and Chinese repertoires, including a "model opera" from the Cultural Revolution, *The Red Detachment of Women.* The Central Song and Dance Ensemble performs dance of all kinds from around the world, while the Central Nationalities Song and Dance Ensemble focuses on the dances of China's ethnic minorities. The People's Liberation Army Song and Dance Ensemble is also a top-notch dance

**LEFT AND ABOVE:** acrobatics shows tend to include all kinds of balancing acts.

form, and today there are about 80 professional acrobatics troupes in China. Beijing's troupe is one of the best, and the city is also home to an acrobatics school that trains young acrobats from around the world. The acrobatics performances generally staged in Beijing are intended to impress foreign tourists (and of course collect their money) and they serve this purpose – once. After that, it is sad to say, these performances staged day after day are hard to view as anything more than highly skilled acrobats performing kitsch. Beijing residents themselves rarely go to see acrobatics, unless out of duty to a guest from afar. For details on where to see performances *see page 218.* ❏

# BEIJING OPERA

**The emphasis in Beijing Opera is on Confucian ethics and morality: goodness is upheld and evil is punished**

Although Chinese theatre in the form of skits, vaudeville, puppet shows and shadow plays has existed for over 1,000 years, formal music-drama has its origins in the 13th-century Yuan dynasty. This evolved into more than 300 different styles of Chinese Opera, but today the highly stylised Beijing *(jingxi)* variety – dating from the 1800s – is by far the most popular.

Beijing Opera is a composite of different expressive art forms: literature, song, dialogue, mime and acrobatics (disciplines normally separated in Western theatre). Plots are based on historical stories or folklore with which audiences are already familiar. The main division is between *wenxi* (civilian plays), and *wuxi* (military dramas), but there are also comedies and skits.

*Wenxi* pieces are more like Western drama, and describe daily life. The *wuxi*, on the other hand, consist mainly of fights, and tell of historical wars and battles, making great use of acrobatics. Many operas draw upon popular legends, folk or fairy tales, or classical literature; tales such as *The Three Kingdoms*, *The Dream of the Red Chamber*, or *Journey to the West* are much better known in China than their equivalent literary classics in the West.

In the old days, permanent theatres were a rarity, even in Beijing. As a result, opera was performed on the streets and in the market places – a sign of its popularity with ordinary people. It was a useful way for them to learn about life outside the narrow circle of their own day-to-day existence.

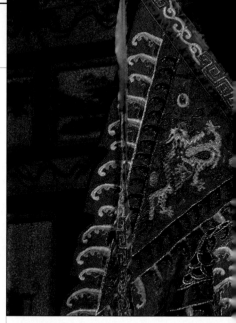

**ABOVE:** Whether in soliloquys, spoken verse, songs or dialogue, the words used in any Beijing Opera performance are almost always colloquial. The opera was meant from the start to be watched by the common people. Audiences are usually noisy but appreciative.

**ABOVE:** Although Beijing Opera is the best-known style of Chinese Opera, there are many variants of local folk opera performed across China, including *kunqu* and *pingju*, *bangzi xi* and *chaozhou*.

**LEFT:** It is not uncommon for musicians and assistants to remain on stage throughout the entire performance; when not acting, they wait in the shadows to help with prop changes.

## THE ART FORM OF OPERA TRAINING

Beijing Opera is considered one of the most convention-alised forms of theatre to be found anywhere in the world, requiring years of training to master.

Actors often undergo seven years of training as children, after which they are selected for specific roles such as the male, female, warrior or clown. Before the 1930s, all the roles were required to be played by men.

Mastery of singing, of course, is essential for the male and female roles, while clowns are often required to demonstrate acrobatic prowess. All actors must hone the fine body movements that are the opera's style. An actor's training includes learning how to apply the elaborate make-up that serves to identify each character.

**BELOW:** To get the most out of Beijing Opera, it helps to know something of its conventions. Changes in time and place are evoked through speech, action and ritualised use of props. Walking in a circle symbolises a journey, while circling the stage with a whip indicates riding a horse.

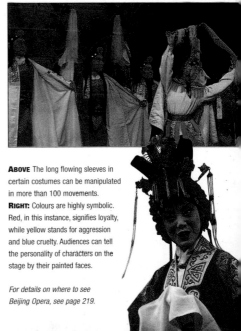

**ABOVE** The long flowing sleeves in certain costumes can be manipulated in more than 100 movements.
**RIGHT:** Colours are highly symbolic. Red, in this instance, signifies loyalty, while yellow stands for aggression and blue cruelty. Audiences can tell the personality of characters on the stage by their painted faces.

*For details on where to see Beijing Opera, see page 219.*

# PLACES

A detailed guide to the city, with the principal sites
clearly cross-referenced by number to the maps

In traditional Chinese thought, the world was not imagined as the flat, circular disk of the Ptolemaic system familiar in the West, but as a square. A city, too – and especially a capital city – was supposed to be square, a reflection of the cosmic order; in no other city in China was this basic idea realised as completely as in Beijing. Screened from the north by a semicircle of hills, the city lies on a plain which opens out to the south. In an analogy to this position, all important buildings are built to face south, thus protecting them from the harmful *yin* influences of the north – be they the vicious Siberian winter winds or enemies from the steppes. A line from north to south divides the city into eastern and western halves, with a series of buildings laid out as mirror images to their equivalents on the opposite side of the city. These northern and southern approaches converge at the Forbidden City, which the meridian line bisects, passing through the Hall of Supreme Harmony and, within it, the Dragon Throne – facing south, of course.

The central part of Beijing is like that of no other metropolis. At its heart is a giant open-air museum, the Forbidden City. Adjacent to the south is the world's largest public square, Tiananmen, with its gargantuan communist buildings, monuments and historical gravitas. These are the places most visitors want to see first, but there is plenty more on offer in all directions.

Immediately south from Tiananmen Square is an area of narrow *hutong* alleyways full of interest; this is where Qing officials would visit the tea and opera houses, baths and brothels, restaurants and bazaars. Further south is the glorious Temple of Heaven, surrounded by its pleasant park. To the east are the shiny modern shopping centres centred around Wangfujing, and further east the business and expat district of Chaoyang, full of gleaming skyscrapers and hotels, as well as a wide variety of restaurants and bars. To the west and north is beautiful Beihai Park and the attractive back lakes area, full of atmospheric old *hutong*, and plenty of bars and cafés. Throughout, the increasingly modern cityscape is dotted with Buddhist, Daoist, and Lamaist shrines, and a scattering of mosques and churches.

Within easy reach of the city itself are some of China's most exciting sights, becoming all the more accessible each year via the improving road and suburban rail networks. No visit to Beijing is complete without a trip out to the Great Wall. The Summer Palaces, old and new, are now practically within the city suburbs. Further afield are the magnificent Imperial Resort at Chengde and the old treaty port of Tianjin, where many handsome 19th-century houses built by foreign merchants still stand. ❑

**PRECEDING PAGES:** the intricately carved ceiling in the Hall of Prayer for Good Harvests; a summer storm over Tiananmen. **LEFT:** model city at the Beijing City Planning Museum.

Yiheyuan
(Summer Palace),
Beijing Daxue
(Beijing University)

Dazhongsi
(Temple of
the Great Bell)

Xueyan Lu

Beisanhuan Zhonglu

SHUANGXIU
GONGYUAN

Suzhou Dajie

Haidian Lu

Beisanhuan Xilu

M Dazhongsi

Xihumen Beidajie (Second Ring Road)

Xinjiekouwai Dajie

Deshengmenwai Dajie

Weigongcun Lu

Xueyuan Nanlu

Xueyuan Nanlu

Baishiqiao Lu

Suojafen Lu

Deshengmen
Bus Station

Xisanhuan Beilu

Deshen
Former
of Song C

Xiangshan
(Fragrant Hills)

Gaolianqqiao Lu

Jishuitan

M

Banjing Lu

Wutasi
(Temple of Five Pagodas)

Sidaokou Lu

Deshengmen Xidajie Xu Beihong
Memorial Hall

Xihai

Beixinxun Beilu

Wanshousi

Zhongguo Guojia
Tushuguan
(National Library)

Xizhimen
Railway Station

Xitang
(West Cathedral)

Jishui

Deshengmennei Dajie

Ho

ZIZHUYUAN GONGYUAN
(PURPLE BAMBOO PARK)

Beijing
Dongwuyuan
(Beijing Zoo)

Beijing Zhanlanguan
(Beijing Exhibition
Centre)

Xizhimennei Dajie

Mei
Lanfang
Memorial

Di'a

Zizhuyuan Lu

Xizhimenwai Dajie

M Xizhimen

Chegongzhuang Xidajie

Chegongzhuang Dajie

Sanlihe Lu

Ping'anli Xidajie

Gangwashitang
(Earthenware & Brick Market
Church

Xisi Beidajie

Beitang
(North
Cathedral)

Xishiku Dajie

Fushi Lu

Fucheng Lu

Baiwanzhuang Jie

XICHENG

Chengongzhuang
M

Baitasi
(Temple of the
White Pagoda)

Baitasi

Wenjin

Zhong

Fuchengmenwai Dajie

Former Residence
of Lu Xun

Fuchengmennei Dajie

Guangjisi
(Temple of
Universal Rescue)

Xidan Beidajie

Xiuangchenga

Fuyou Jie

YUYUANTAN GONGYUAN

Yuyuan

Yuetan Beijie

M Fuchengmen

Nanlishi Lu

Taipingqiao Dajie

Picai Hutong

(SONG QINGLING CHILDREN'S
SCIENCE PARK)

Sanlihe Lu

Yuetan Nanjie

Sanlihe Donglu

YUETAN
GONGYUAN
(ALTAR OF THE
MOON PARK)

Minzu
Wenhuagong

Xinh

China
Millennium
Monument

Nanlishilu

M Fuximen

Xicha

Fuxing Lu

M Fuxing Lu

Xidan

Zh

Gongzhufen

Jungshibowuguan

Muxidi

Fuxingmennei Dajie

Guojia Da
(China
Grand
Hepingl

Yangfandianxi Lu

Yangfandian Lu

Baiyun Lu

Baiyuanguan
(Temple of the
White Cloud)

Nantang
(South Cathedral)

Xisanhuan Zhonglu

Changchunjie

M Xuanwumen Xidajie

Xuanwumen

M

Lianhuachi Donglu

Xuanwumenwai Dajie

Beijing Xi Zhan
(West Railway Station)

Tianning Si
(Temple of Heavenly
Tranquillity)

Huaibaishu Jie
XUANWU
ART GARDEN

Baoguo Si
(Baoguo Temple)

Guang'anmennei Dajie

Luomashi Da

Lianhua
(Lotus Pond)

Lianhuachi Xilu

Guang'anmennei

Nanxiange Jie

Niu Jie

Niu Jie Qingzhensi
(Ox Street Mosque)

Guang'an Lu

Guang'anmen Nanbinhelu

Guang'anmenwai Lu

Fayuansi
(Temple of the Source of
Buddhist Teaching)

Liu Li Qiao
Bus Station

Maliandao Lu

Zaolingian Jie

Guang'ammen
Railway Station

Guang'anmenwai Nanjie

WANSHOU
GONGYUAN

Xisanhuannan Lu

XUANWUMEN

Baizhifang Xijie

Baizhifang
Dongjie

TAORAN
GONGYI
(HAPPY PA
PARK

Lize Qiao
Bus Station

Sanluju Lu

Liucun Lu

Caiyuan Jie

DAGUANYUAN
(GRAND VIEW
GARDEN)

You'anmen

Yongdin
Railw
Stati

Fengtai Beilu

Fengtai Beilu

You'anmen Xibinhelu

You'anmen
Dajie

Liangshui

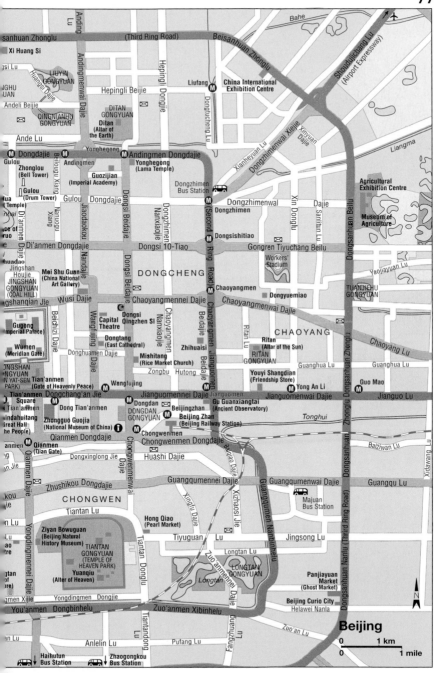

# TIANANMEN SQUARE
# AND SURROUNDINGS

**The giant open space at the heart of Beijing, where imperial and communist monuments meet as nowhere else, reflects China's tumultuous history**

**T**iananmen Square ❶ (Tiananmen Guangchang) is the symbolic centre and political heart of Beijing, and it is to this immense plaza – said to be the world's largest public square – that most first-time visitors to the Chinese capital are initially drawn. This is the place where classical heritage and revolutionary symbolism meet head on. Imperial gateways, representing the feudal centuries of the Middle Kingdom, face the monuments and museums erected by the Communist regime that flank the square. Overlooking all is the iconic Tiananmen Gate, with its Mao portrait, entrance to the Forbidden City.

## At the centre of things

For many Westerners, the words "Tiananmen Square" have become synonymous with the democracy demonstrations of 1989 and their brutal suppression. For most Chinese the square is a place that conjures up a broader range of images, both joyous and dark. Since the end of imperial times it has been at the heart of Chinese politics, both for dissent and (stage-managed) celebration. It was here, on land once occupied by imperial office buildings, that May Fourth protesters gathered in the spring of 1919 to demand that their government

reform itself and the nation. Thirty years later, on 1 October 1949, hundreds of thousands of cheering soldiers and citizens gathered in the square to hear Mao Zedong proclaim the founding of the People's Republic from atop Tiananmen Gate with the words, "The Chinese people have stood up!" In the late 1950s the square was quadrupled in size and paved with concrete so that it could accommodate up to a million people. This enlarged space then became the site of near-hysterical

Map on page 80

**LEFT:** carved *huabiao* pillars outside Tiananmen Gate symbolise dialogue between emperors and their subjects.
**BELOW:** kite-flying in Tiananmen Square.

*The Mao Mausoleum in the middle of the square continues to pack in the crowds.*

gatherings of Red Guards when the Cultural Revolution broke out in the mid-1960s. The end of the Cultural Revolution was foretold a decade later when the citizens of Beijing flocked to the square in April of 1976 to leave paper flowers and poems in memory of Zhou Enlai, whose death in January they felt had been too lightly acknowledged.

In the late 1990s, Tiananmen Square was again renovated, this time in readiness for the October 1999 celebrations of the PRC's 50th anniversary. This involved it being closed to the public for almost a year

– a time which conveniently encompassed the 10th anniversary of 4 June 1989. The cement blocks were replaced with granite slabs – which could bear the weight of armoured vehicles without a scratch.

Every Chinese visitor to Beijing makes a visit here a top priority, along with the obligatory photograph. On a day-to-day basis, it functions as a kind of concrete park, albeit one with an unusually high security presence. Kite-flying is a favourite hobby, and local kite-flying veterans are eager to share advice with novices.

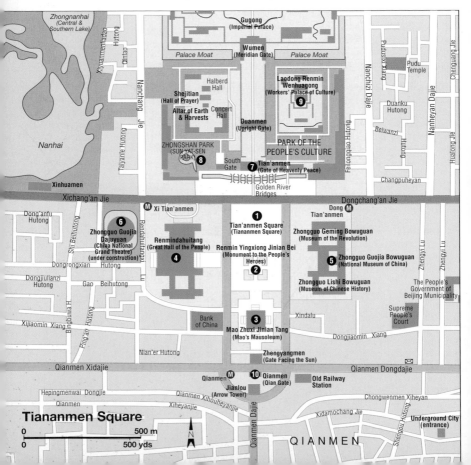

**Tiananmen Square**

In the middle of Tiananmen Square is the **Monument to the People's Heroes** ❷ (Renmin Yinxiong Jinianbei), an obelisk dedicated in 1958 to the remembrance of soldiers who fell in the Revolution. It stands on a double pedestal, and at a height of 37 metres (123 ft) is 4 metres (14 ft) taller than the Tiananmen Gate. The lower part of the base is ornamented with bas-reliefs portraying the stages of Chinese revolutionary history, from the first Opium War (1840–42) to the founding of the People's Republic.

To the south, in front of Zhengyangmen Gate, is the **Mao Mausoleum** ❸ (Mao Zhuxi Jiniantang; open Tues–Sun, 8.30– 11.30am; also 2–4pm on Tues and Thurs Sept–May; free, but small fee for compulsory bag deposit across the street). After the death of Mao Zedong in 1976, political circumstances dictated the building of an everlasting memorial to the leader of the Revolution, founder of the state and Party chairman. In contrast, President Zhou Enlai, who died in the same year, had his ashes scattered to the winds. Mao's body was embalmed – by Vietnamese experts, it is said – and placed on display here. The mausoleum was built in only nine months in 1978 and also contains rooms commemorating other state and Party leaders. It was renovated in 1999 for the 50th anniversary of the PRC. Nowadays, some Chinese regard the monument as an unfortunate reminder of the personality cult of Mao.

There are massive group sculptures by the front and rear entrances to the mausoleum, depicting the people's common struggle for socialism – typical examples of the style of socialist realism. The body of Mao lies in state in a crystal coffin in the Central Hall of Rest. He is dressed in the typical blue suit and covered with the flag of the Communist Party. In the southern hall beyond, calligraphy by Mao himself can be seen, bearing the title "Reply to Comrade Guo Moruo". The mausoleum was visited by countless Chinese in the months after it was opened, with people queuing patiently across Tiananmen

Map on page 80

Be sure to store bags and cameras in the facility provided before queuing to enter the mausoleum or you'll be turned away. Once inside, it is advisable to maintain a respectful demeanour, speak quietly and look fast – visitors are herded past Mao's corpse by brusque soldiers who brook no lingering.

**BELOW:** The Monument to the People's Heroes is a fine example of socialist-realist art.

*The Tiananmen flag ceremonies – raising at dawn and lowering at dusk – attract large crowds, and are precisely timed to accord with the sunrise or sunset.*

Square. These days it is rather less frequented, although it can still be busy. Mao's status in 21st-century China is odd – he is at once the father of the nation and the man who, in the official words of the Party, got it "30 per cent wrong"; still revered as something like a god by many, yet removed from public display throughout the land – the famous portrait at Tiananmen *(see page 84)* being the one exception. The rapid rise of the Mao memorabilia phenomenon *(see page 28)* further muddies the waters.

## Communist behemoths

Tiananmen Square is flanked by vast Soviet-style edifices dating from the days of close relations between the two countries in the 1950s. The **Great Hall of the People ❹** (Renmindahuitang; open daily except when in session, 8.30am–3pm; entrance fee; bag deposit compulsory), on the west side of the square, is the largest of these behemoths. The National People's Assembly, the Chinese parliament, meets in the 50,000-square-metre (19,300-sq-ft)

building. Various official departments are also housed here, as is a banquet hall that seats 5,000. In addition, the hall is used to receive political delegations from abroad and to hold concerts by major visiting orchestras, though the acoustics are abysmal. There isn't much specific to see, but walking around the dimly lit, cavernous halls with their red carpets and polished wooden floors certainly gives a feel of the Party spirit.

On the eastern side of Tiananmen Square, directly opposite the Great Hall of the People, is the **National Museum of China ❺** (Zhongguo Guojia Bowuguan; open daily 8:30am–4:30pm; Nov–Feb 9am–4pm; July and Aug 8am–6pm; entrance fee), created in 2003 by merging the Museum of the Chinese Revolution and the Museum of Chinese History. The two-winged four-storey hulk, constructed at great speed for the celebrations of the PRC's 10th anniversary in 1959, is undergoing major renovation work that will extend its length 70 metres (76 yards) to the east and more than double its current 65,000-square-

metre (25,000-sq-ft) area, as well as enclosing the courtyard. The renovation will involve closures of various galleries until their scheduled completion in October of 2007; a varied programme of temporary exhibitions will run through this period. At the time of going to press, the **Museum of the Chinese Revolution** (Zhongguo Geming Bowuguan) was closed. When it reopens it will chronicle the history of the Communist Party in China, the revolutionary civil wars and the campaign of resistance against the Japanese. During the Cultural Revolution, the displays had to be constantly readjusted to fit in with whatever was the current campaign (rather like the Ministry of Truth in George Orwell's *Nineteen Eighty Four*), but recently the aim has been to provide an objective record, albeit a governmentally approved one.

The southern section of the museum houses the **Museum of Chinese History** (Zhongguo Lishi Bowuguan), opened in 1926, but with limited displays in late 2004 due to the ongoing renovation work. Many of the pieces on display were

donated from private collections in China and elsewhere in the world. Among them is a valuable blue-glazed lamp from the Southern Dynasties period (AD 420–589), Tang figures and an embroidered silk portrait of the Celestial Kings. Ancient bronzes, jade pieces and bones, and ceramics from the Tang and Song dynasties are also on show. In addition, the museum features Chinese discoveries such as printing, gunpowder, the compass and paper manufacture.

## National Grand Theatre

Behind (to the west of) the Great Hall of the People is the **China National Grand Theatre ❻ (Zhongguo Guojia Dajuyuan)**, a striking titanium and glass dome surrounded by water that is scheduled to open in late 2005. Land for the structure was set aside by Premier Zhou in the late 1950s, but the vagaries of politics and the inability to agree on a design caused the project to be delayed for four decades. The decision to finally proceed in the late 1990s only led to

*The large auditorium in the middle of the Great Hall of the People.*

**BELOW:** Tiananmen Square and the Great Hall of the People.

*The long-awaited, controversial China National Grand Theatre is the first unorthodox modern building in central Beijing.*

more controversy – there were objections to the budget, to the idea of putting multiple theatres under one roof, and to the exclusion of foreign architects from the bidding process. When no Chinese design was deemed suitable, a second round of bidding was held that included designs by foreigners. The choice of French architect Paul Andreu's design – which supporters likened to a water pearl and detractors to a duck egg – caused an uproar, with critics complaining that it was "un-Chinese" and utterly incompatible with its surroundings. This is true in a way, as it is the city's first unconventional modern building. Construction delays and the 2004 roof collapse at the Andreu-designed Paris Charles de Gaulle airport – which killed two Chinese tourists – have led to yet more arguments, but the criticism is likely to fade once the much-needed theatre is finally functioning. The "Eggshell", as the National Theatre has been dubbed, will have four theatres, including an opera hall seating 2,416, and a similarly large music hall.

## Tiananmen Gate

At the northern end of Tiananmen Square, across the 38-metre (125-ft) wide Chang'an Jie, seven marble bridges lead across a small moat to **Tiananmen Gate ❼** (Gate of Heavenly Peace; open 8.30am–5pm; free to pass through, entrance fee to ascend). The first structure here, the Guomen (Gate of the Empire), was built out of wood in 1417. When this was damaged by fire in 1465 it was rebuilt in stone. In 1651, the gate was rebuilt again after destruction by Manchu troops and renamed Tiananmen. The side gates were demolished in 1912 to open up the square. This was the meeting place of the divided city, where the levels of traditional pyramid of authority – the city to the south of Qianmen, the Imperial City and the Imperial Palace (or Purple City, the actual Forbidden City) – touched.

When the emperors left the Forbidden City to celebrate the New Year rites at the Temple of Heaven, they made their first offerings at Tiananmen Gate. On important occasions, imperial decrees were

## Mao's Portrait

As Mao's body lies in its mausoleum, his seemingly ageless likeness looks down from the Tiananmen Gate. The gigantic portrait of the leader measures 6 metres by 4.5 metres (20 ft by 15 ft) and weighs nearly 1.5 tons. It is cleaned every year before Labour Day (1 May) and replaced before National Day (1 October), when Mao is joined by the founder of the Republic, Sun Yat-sen. The portrait first appeared at the founding of the New China in 1949 and was originally hung only for these two occasions, but it became a permanent fixture during the Cultural Revolution – though a black-and-white picture briefly replaced it after Mao's death in 1976.

Ge Xiaoguang, the latest of four artists who have maintained the image, has painted 19 giant portraits of the Great Helmsman. Each one takes about two weeks. The paintings are reinforced with plastic and fibreglass and have to be lifted into place by crane. Used portraits are apparently kept in case of demonstrations like those in 1989, when paint bombs added a touch of Jackson Pollock to Ge's work. Ge, incidentally, became a minor celebrity after he appeared on TV in 1994. As an employee of the Beijing Art Company, he receives no extra payment for his special assignment.

Map on page 80

lowered from the gate in a gilded box. The civil servants, kneeling, were to receive them, copy them, and then distribute them all over the country. Thus it was in a decidedly imperial manner that Mao Zedong proclaimed the People's Republic of China from this spot on 1 October 1949, and in the same way received the adulation of millions of Red Guards during the Cultural Revolution.

Tiananmen Gate has become the symbol of Beijing, and, indeed, of the whole of the People's Republic. It is the only public building still to display the portrait of Mao on the outside. To the left of this portrait is a sign in Chinese characters: "Long live the People's Republic of China." The sign on the right says, "Long live the great unity of all the peoples of the world."

There are five passages through the massive gate walls. The central one follows the imperial route and was reserved for the emperor; today it is open to all. Subjects are said to have put up petitions to the emperor, along with suggestions for improvements, on the carved marble pillars *(huabiao)* in front of the gate. On the other side of the passageway is a large courtyard full of souvenir and drinks vendors and parading soldiers. The ticket office for the **viewing platform** above the Mao portrait on Tiananmen Gate is on the left (open daily 8am–4.30pm; entrance fee; bag deposit compulsory).

Continue north through the **Upright Gate** (Duanmen) to reach the ticket office for the Imperial Palace. The Palace complex itself is entered through the Meridian Gate (Wumen; *see page 95*).

### North of the Gate

To the left of the promenade leading from Tiananmen Gate to the Meridian Gate, and separated from the

Imperial Palace by a wall and a moat, **Zhongshan Park ❽** (Sun Yat-sen Park; open daily, summer 6am–8pm, winter 6.30am–5pm; entrance fee) is a fine example of the fusion of imperial architecture and garden design. Over 1,000 years ago this was the site of the Temple of the Wealth of the Land, but the ancient cypresses are all that remain from that time. The park was named after Sun Yat-sen following his death.

From the main entrance to the park in the south, the path first goes through a white **marble arch**. In 1900, the German ambassador Baron von Ketteler was shot dead on Hatamen Street (modern day Chongwenmen), on his way to the Chinese Foreign Ministry by one of the rebellious Boxers. In reparation, the imperial family were required to build a triumphal arch on the spot, with the inscription: "In memory of the virtuous von Ketteler." However, after 1919, Germany no longer existed as an imperialist power, and the arch was moved to its present position and inscribed: "Justice will prevail." In 1953, it was reinscribed again, this

*Lush grass and flower beds flank Tiananmen Gate.*

**BELOW:** kite-flying is a popular pastime in Tiananmen Square.

*An army of workers keep Tiananmen Square spotlessly clean at all times.*

**BELOW:** seven marble bridges lead across the Golden Water River to Tiananmen Gate.

time by poet Guo Moruo *(see page 127)*, and reads: "Defend peace."

Further north, in the centre of the park, is a great square area, where in 1421 the Ming **Altar of Earth and Harvests** stood. The altar's shape is a reminder of the old Chinese concept of the earth as a square. Twice a year, in the grey light of dawn, the Ming and Qing emperors brought their offerings here in the hope of obtaining divine support for a good harvest. During the sacrifice, the altar was covered with five different types of coloured earth, and these colours can still be seen today, repeated in the tiles that cover the low surrounding walls.

The symbolism of the five colours is thought to stand for the five points of the compass (north, south, east, west and centre). To the north of the altar is the **Zhongshan Hall** (formerly called the Shejitian, or Hall of Prayer), built of wood, a typical example of Beijing's classical architecture. Also inside the park is a modern concert hall, which puts on concerts by Western and Chinese orchestras.

To the east, on the other side of the promenade between Tiananmen and Meridian gates, is the **Workers' Palace of Culture** ❾ (Laodong Renmin Wenhuagong; open daily, summer 6am–8pm, winter 6.30am–5pm; entrance fee) – the grounds of which are used for temporary exhibitions and cultural events. In the centre of the complex is a venerable temple dating from the 15th and 16th centuries – the **Temple of the Imperial Ancestors** (Taimiao). Five times a year the wooden ancestor tablets, upon which the names of the dead forefathers of the imperial family were recorded, were taken from the central hall in which they were kept to the southern hall, where the emperor paid his respects to his forefathers.

The veneration of ancestors is one of the oldest practices in the Chinese spiritual tradition, hingeing on the belief that the well-being of the dead is dependent on the offerings and veneration of the living. The dead, in turn, are thought to be able to influence the fate of the living *(see page 49)*. The imperial ancestors received

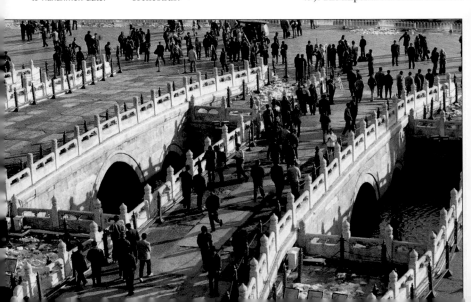

extraordinary honours and respect, of course, as they were believed to be responsible for the well-being of the whole country. The Taimiao was thus one of the country's most important ritual sites.

After 1949, the temple complex was restored and equipped for its new life as a workers' college and pleasure garden. Now, the "sacred halls" are used for leisure activities, further education courses and occasional high-profile performances billed by promoters as "Forbidden City" concerts.

## Qianmen Gate

At the southern end of Tiananmen Square, **Qianmen** ❿ (Front Gate) was once the outer, southern entrance into the old Inner (Chinese) City from the Outer (Tartar) City, and dates from 1421 during the reign of Yongle. The gate is in fact comprised of two separate structures; the stone **Jianlou** (Arrow Tower), which burned down in 1900 and was reconstructed in 1903; and the main gate, the wooden **Zhengyangmen** (Gate Facing the Sun), just to the north,

also damaged in 1900 and reconstructed, to which the city wall was connected. The gates are free to walk through, but a ticket is required if you want to ascend (both open daily 8.30am–4pm; separate entrance fees). Zhengyangmen, the tallest gate in Beijing at 40 metres (130 feet), has a collection of old photographs and models upstairs showing how it looked in the past when it was joined with Jianlou. Unusually, all are captioned in English.

## Foreign Legation Quarter

In contrast to Shanghai and neighbouring Tianjin (*see page 203*), European traders never established much of a presence in Beijing. Yet after the Second Opium War, the British and the French, followed by various others, were grudgingly permitted to establish a concession in the heart of the city. At first they made use of existing palace buildings, and the quarter where they lived was integrated into the rest of the city. But during the 1900 Boxer Rebellion, which culminated in a 55-day siege on the quarter, almost the

*Jianlou, the Arrow Tower, is separated from its other half (Zhengyangmen) by busy Qianmen Jie. Getting between the two on foot is not easy, involving a circuitous route via pedestrian subways. In fact, Jianlou, surrounded by its lush lawn (no access), is cut off in all directions by roads and metal barriers. The only way in is via pedestrian subway or directly from the rail subway.*

**BELOW:** Jianlou formed the southern part of Qianmen Gate.

*The former City Bank of New York, now the Municipal Fire Department.*

entire area was destroyed. In the subsequent rebuilding, high walls were added for protection, and colonial-style edifices replaced the older Chinese buildings. Eventually evicted from the premises in 1950, the foreigners left behind these anomalies of colonial-style architecture.

Some buildings were destroyed, but others were put to use by the government and are still well maintained. They are off limits to the public and hidden behind high walls and guarded gates, but, even so, the area is well worth strolling through; the villas and mansions remain ensconced in quiet, tree-lined streets, a world away from the crowded, jostling arteries of downtown Beijing.

### A stroll around the quarter

Towards the northern end of Taijichang Dajie (formerly Rue Marco Polo), the grand red-brick towers of the former **Italian Legation** Ⓐ are now the headquarters of the Chinese

People's Friendship Association. The building was also used to accommodate "foreign friends" who supported the Chinese Revolution. Two well-known residents in the past have been the American writer Anna Louise Strong and the New Zealander Rewi Alley. Down the hutong to the east is the grey-and-white Greek-temple facade entrance to the **Austro-Hungarian Legation** Ⓑ, now housing the Institute of International Studies. Back on Taijichang is the grey-blue-walled **Peking Club** Ⓒ. Built in 1902, complete with tennis courts and a swimming pool, this is the exclusive haunt of high-ranking Chinese Communist Party officials.

Further south, on the corner of Dongjiaomin Xiang and partly hidden by a newer building, is **St Michael's Catholic Church** Ⓓ, built by the French Vincentian fathers in 1902. It was nearly destroyed during the Cultural Revolution, then renovated

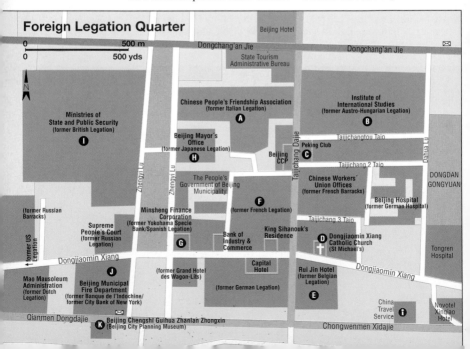

**Foreign Legation Quarter**

Beijing Hotel

0 ————— 500 m
0 ————— 500 yds

Dongchang'an Jie

Dongchang'an Jie

State Tourism Administrative Bureau

N

Ministries of
State and Public Security
(former British Legation)
Ⓘ

Chinese People's Friendship Association
(former Italian Legation)
Ⓐ

Institute of
International Studies
(former Austro-Hungarian Legation)
Ⓑ

Beijing Mayor's
Office
(former Japanese Legation)
Ⓗ

Taijichangtou Taio

Peking Club Ⓒ

Beijing
CCP

Taijichang 2 Taio

DONGDAN
GONGYUAN

Zhengyi Lu

Zhengyi Lu

Taijichang Dajie

Dahua Lu

The People's
Government of Beijing
Municipality

Chinese Workers'
Union Offices
(former French Barracks)

(former French Legation)
Ⓕ

Beijing Hospital
(former German Hospital)

(former Russian
Barracks)

Supreme
People's Court
(former Russian
Legation)

Minsheng Finance
Corporation
(former Yokohama Specie
Bank/Spanish Legation)
Ⓖ

Taijichang 3 Taio

(former US
Legation)

Bank of
Industry &
Commerce

King Sihanouk's
Residence

Dongjiaomin Xiang
Catholic Church
(St Michael's)
Ⓓ

Tongren
Hospital

Dongjiaomin Xiang

Ⓙ

(former Grand Hotel
des Wagon-Lits)

Capital
Hotel

Rui Jin Hotel
(former Belgian
Legation)
Ⓔ

Dongjiaomin Xiang

Mao Mausoleum
Administration
(former Dutch
Legation)

Beijing Municipal
Fire Department
(former Banque de l'Indochine/
former City Bank of New York)

(former German Legation)

China
Travel
Service
ⓘ

Novotel
Xinqiao
Hotel

Qianmen Dongdajie

Beijing Chengshi Guihua Zhanlan Zhongxin
Ⓚ (Beijing City Planning Museum)

Chongwenmen Xidajie

in 1989. Just past it on the left is an old post office, now functioning as a very plain restaurant. The rear entrance to the expansive grounds of the former **Belgian Legation** ❸ is across the street. The buildings, originally modelled after a villa belonging to King Leopold II (1835–1909) now function as a state guest house. Nearby is the old **French Legation** ❶, the Beijing residence of Cambodia's King Sihanouk, distinguished by an imposing grey gate with red doors and two large stone lions standing guard.

On the corner of Dongjiaomin Xiang and Zhengyi Lu is the large red-and-white-brick building of the **Yokohama Specie Bank** ❻, where Cixi supposedly took out a loan. Looking south is the site of the **Grand Hôtel des Wagon-Lits**, which was *the* fashionable place to stay, and was close to the old railway station outside the wall. The station still stands, just southeast of Tiananmen Square, but is now used as a shopping mall.

Head north on Zhengyi Lu, an attractive street with shady parkland running up the middle, and you will come to an impressive red-towered gate. This is the **Japanese Legation** ❶, and it was here that the Chinese

were forced to accept the infamous "Twenty-One Demands" on 7 May 1915, whereby the Japanese obtained special rights over Manchuria. It is now the offices of the Beijing Municipal People's Government. Almost opposite is the old **British Legation** ❶. Previously a prince's palace, this building was the city's largest foreign legation. Many sought refuge here during the siege of 1900. It is now occupied by the Ministries of State and Public Security. South on Qianmen Dongdajie are the buildings of the **Banque de l'Indochine** and the **City Bank of New York** ❶.

The **Beijing City Planning Museum** ❶ (Beijing Chengshi Guihua Zhanlan Zhongxin; open Tues–Sun 9am–4pm; entrance fee), at 20 Qianmen Dongdajie has displays that illustrate 3,000 years of the city's history. It also showcases plans for Beijing's future development, which will include the creation of 11 satellite towns intended to ease the pressure of the city's ever-expanding population. One of the museum's prize possessions is a 90-square-metre (35-sq-ft) bronze relief that depicts Beijing on the eve of liberation. The relief includes an astonishing 5,000 people, 60,000 trees and 118,000 structures. ❑

Map on page 88

*Part of the giant model of Beijing in the City Planning Museum.*

***ORIENTATION***
*The area covered in this chapter extends from Tiananmen Square to the Meridian Gate (entrance to the Forbidden City), and southeast to Chongwenmen.*

# RESTAURANTS

*Imperial Cuisine*

**Laijinyuxuan Restaurant**
Zhongshan Park. Tel: 6605-6676. Open: 11am–2pm, 5:30–9pm. $$$.
Resembling a traditional garden house, this renowned restaurant in Zhongshan Park serves up food featured in the famous Qing Dynasty novel *The Dream of the Red Chamber*.

*Peking Duck*

**Tiananmen Quanjude**
44 Dong Jiaominxiang, near

**Tiananmen Fangshan**
near SE corner of Tiananmen Square. Tel: 6523-3105. Open: 11am–2pm, 5–8pm. $$$$.
It may lack the atmosphere of its lakeside parent in Beihai Park (*see page 134*), but the imperial cuisine is on a par.

SE corner of Tiananmen Square. Tel. 6512-2265. Open: 11am–2pm, 5–8pm; fast food available all day. $$$$.
A new branch of the famous Peking Duck restaurant specialising in Shandong cuisine.

*Muslim Cuisine*

**Tiananmen Donglaishun**
SE corner of Tiananmen Square. Tel 6524-1042. Open: 11am–2pm, 5–8pm. $$$.

A branch of the well-known Muslim restaurant, specialising in mutton hot-pot.

● ● ● ● ● ● ● ● ● ● ● ●
*Prices are for a typical dinner for one (three dishes with beer in Chinese restaurants, or a three-course meal with a half bottle of house wine in Western-style restaurants).*
*$ = under 50 Rmb*
*$$ = 50–100 Rmb*
*$$$ = 100–150 Rmb*
*$$$$ = over 150 Rmb*

# THE FORBIDDEN CITY

The great palace complex at the heart of Beijing
functioned as the fulcrum of the ordered
cosmos that was imperial China

At the heart of modern Beijing, lies the most complete historical site in all of China. This remarkable complex, a full square kilometre, is simply a must-see for any visitor to the city: try to get here early in the day, and buy an all-inclusive ticket *(tao piao;* 60 Rmb), as some of the halls have exhibitions which otherwise require separate tickets. The **Forbidden City**, also known as the Imperial Palace (Gugong in *pinyin)* is open daily from 8am until 5.30pm in summer (April–September) and 4.30pm in winter, but the ticket office closes an hour before this.

The Forbidden City was the hallowed nucleus of the Chinese empire for nearly five centuries. Within its thick red ramparts a succession of emperors lived and ruled, aided and served by tens of thousands of officials, eunuchs, maids and concubines. Its importance in the political cosmology of imperial China is indicated by its other name, the Purple City. Purple was considered to be the colour of the North Star, thought to be the centre of the universe, and its parallel here on earth was the emperor, whose seat of power was thus designated by the same colour.

As the theoretical centre of the terrestrial world, the Forbidden City was a sacred ground in which ceremony and ritual dominated every aspect of life for all inhabitants, from the emperor himself to the lowliest serving girl. Its massive courtyards were regularly filled with processions of officials robed in embroidered silk gowns of many colours. Through its labyrinthine side corridors coursed a stream of young maid-servants – 9,000 of them in the Ming dynasty – and eunuchs. While the maids usually served only during their teenage years, the eunuchs were employees for life, and their mincing

Map
on page
94

**LEFT:** the Golden Water River (Jinshahe) bisects the Forbidden City's southernmost courtyard.
**BELOW:** keeping tradition alive.

*The Imperial Throne in the Palace of Heavenly Purity.*

**BELOW:** huge urns were filled with water as a precaution against fire, a constant threat to the palace's wooden buildings.

footsteps, high voices and – some said – scent of urine were a fixture of palace life. So, too, were the concubines, highly-educated young women forever cut off from their families and the world outside, fated to spend their days sewing – and, perhaps, conniving – as they awaited the emperor's pleasure.

Devoid of the people who were its lifeblood, the Forbidden City today in some ways resembles a well-touristed ghost town. Indeed, in recognition of this fact, the Chinese no longer refer to it as a "city" at all, but as a "museum", and its official appellation is now the **National Palace Museum**. But, with a little reading and imagination, it is still possible to conjure an image of life as it was once lived at the heart of imperial China.

The complex is undergoing its most significant renovations in a century, and parts of it will be shrouded in scaffolding until 2008. The main audience halls and palaces are all scheduled for refurbishment as is the Lodge of Retirement where Emperor Qianlong spent his last

years. Sadly, the process has been complicated by the dearth of workers skilled in such dying arts as *trompe l'œil* painting and paperhanging. The craftsmen involved in the restoration all have decades of training and experience – but no successors to whom they can pass on skills for which the modern world has little use.

## Sacred geometry

The Forbidden City was not meant to be a home for a mortal king but for the Son of Heaven, the divinely appointed intermediary between heaven *(yang)* and earth *(yin)*, who was responsible for peace, prosperity and the orderly life of the world. According to legend, the Ming emperor Yongle, who began the building of the palace in 1409, received the plans from the hands of a Daoist priest who had descended from heaven especially for that purpose. The complex is sometimes jokingly referred to as the "place with 9,999-and-a-half rooms", as only heaven has 10,000. (In fact it has 8,706 rooms and halls.)

Its architecture raised the court above all earthly things. Huge red walls enclosed the inner sanctum, an area forbidden to ordinary mortals. No building in the rest of Beijing was permitted to be taller than the walls of the palace or to outshine them in splendour. The exact, grid-like, geometric pattern of the palace complex reflects the strongly hier-archical structure of imperial Chinese society, with its fixed and ordered harmony as an expression of cosmic order. The buildings were aligned on north–south lines, the most important of them orientated to face south, towards the sun. Many of them have names based on Confucian philosophy – endless combinations of "harmony", "peace" and "quiet" – which were considered to have fortunate connotations.

## History of the palace

The Mongols (Yuan dynasty, 1279–1368) built their palace to the west of today's Forbidden City, before moving the capital to Nanjing in central China. In 1403, the third Ming emperor, Yongle, decided to move the capital back to Beijing. He ordered a new palace to be built, of which the basic structure has remained to the present day. Between 1406 and 1420 some 200,000 people were occupied in building the palace, which was finally occupied by the Ming rulers in 1421. The stones had to be brought on wagons from quarries in the countryside around Beijing. In winter, they were drawn on ropes over the icy ground.

The buildings of the palace were mostly wooden and were constantly being altered; the wood came from the provinces of Yunnan and Sichuan in the southwest of China. Their main enemy was fire, and often entire great halls burned down. For this reason, there were a number of large water containers in the palace, many made of gilded copper and still present today, albeit supplemented by modern fire-fighting equipment. Most of the present buildings date from the 18th century. Even as late as 1987, one of the smaller buildings fell victim to fire.

Until the overthrow of the last emperor, the general public had no

Map on page 94

*Follow Xichang'an Jie for a few hundred metres west from Tiananmen. On the right-hand side, framed by red walls, is Xinhuamen, the gate leading into Zhongnanhai, the seat of the Communist Party of China and a modern-day Forbidden City. It was here that Mao Zedong used to reside as the Great Leader; today this area is still the inner sanctum of the Party leaders.*

**BELOW:** the Court of the Imperial Palace.

# Forbidden City

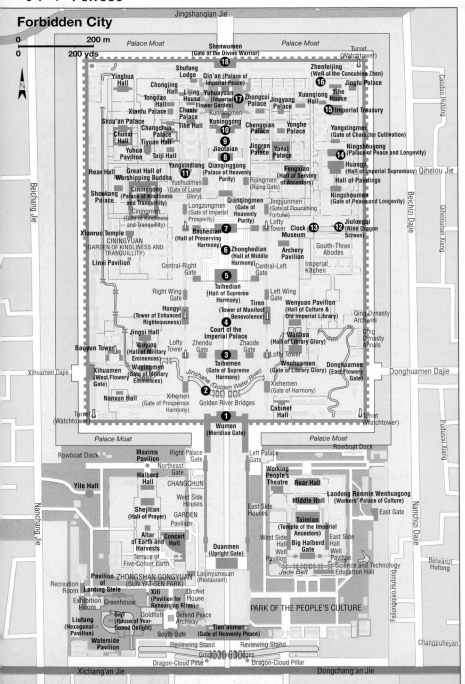

0 ___ 200 m
0 ___ 200 yds

N

Palace Moat

Palace Moat

**18** Shenwumen
(Gate of the Divine Warrior)

Turret
(Watchtower)

Shufang
Lodge

Qin'an (Palace of
Imperial Peace)

**16** Zhenfeijing
(Well of the Concubine Zhen)

Yinghua
Hall

Chongjing
Hall

Lijing
House

Yuhuayuan
(Imperial
Flower Garden)

Zhongcui
Palace

Jingyang
Palace

Xuanqiong
Hall

Jingfu Palace

Tongdao
Hall

Yihe
House

Xianfu Palace

Chuxiu
Palace

**17** Kunningmen

**15** Imperial Treasury

Shou'an Palace

Tihe Hall

Kunninggong

Chengqian
Palace

Yonghe
Palace

Yangxingmen
(Gate of Character Cultivation)

Chunxi
Hall

Changchun
Palace

**10** Jingren
Palace

Yanxi
Palace

Yuhua
Pavilion

Tiyuan Hall

**9** Jiaotaian

Ningshougong
(Palace of Peace and Longevity)

Taiji Hall

**8**

**14**

Rear Hall

Yangxindiang

Qianqinggong
(Palace of Heavenly
Purity)

Fengxian
(Hall of Serving
of Ancestors)

Huangji
(Hall of Imperial Supremacy)

Qihelou Jie

Great Hall of
Worshipping Buddha

**11**

Yuehuamen
(Gate of Lunar
Glory)

Rijingmen
(Rijing Gate)

Hall of Paintings

Shoukang
Palace

Ciningong
(Palace of Kindness
and Tranquility)

Longzongmen
(Gate of Imperial
Prosperity)

Qianqingmen
(Gate of
Heavenly
Purity)

Jingyunmen
(Gate of Flourishing
Fortune)

Ningshoumen
(Gate of Peace and Longevity)

Ciningmen
(Gate of Kindliness
and Tranquility)

Lofty
Tower

Clock
Museum

**13**

Jiulongbi
(Nine Dragon
Screen)

**12**

Xianruo Temple

CININGYUAN
(GARDEN OF KINDLINESS AND
TRANQUILLITY)

Baohedian
(Hall of Preserving
Harmony)

**7**

Zhonghedian
(Hall of Middle
Harmony)

Archery
Pavilion

South-Three
Abodes

Linxi Pavilion

**6**

Central-Left
Gate

Imperial
Kitchen

Central-Right
Gate

**5**

Right Wing
Gate

Taihedian
(Hall of Supreme
Harmony)

Left Wing
Gate

Wenyuan Pavilion
(Hall of Culture &
Old Imperial Library)

Qing Dynasty
Archives

Hongyi
(Tower of Enhanced
Righteousness)

Tiren
(Tower of Manifest
Benevolence)

Qing
Dynasty
Annals

Jingsi Hall

**4**

Court of the
Imperial Palace

Wenhua
(Hall of Library Glory)

Baoyun Tower

Wuying
(Hall of Military
Eminences)

Zhendu
Gate

Zhaode
Gate

Wuyingmen
(Gate of Military
Eminences)

Lofty
Tower

**3**

Taihemen
(Gate of Supreme
Harmony)

Lofty Tower

Wenhuamen
(Gate of Library Glory)

Donghuamen
(East-Flowery
Gate)

Donghuamen Dajie

Xihuamen Dajie

Xihuamen
(West Flowery
Gate)

Jinshahe (Golden Water River)

Xiehemen
(Gate of Harmony)

Nanxun Hall

**2**

Xihemen
(Gate of Prosperous
Harmony)

Golden River Bridges

Cabinet
Hall

Turret
(Watchtower)

Turret
(Watchtower)

Palace Moat

**1**

Wumen
(Meridian Gate)

Palace Moat

Rowboat Dock

Rowboat Dock

Maxims
Pavilion

Right Palace
Gate

Left Palace
Gate

Working
People's
Theatre

Halberd
Hall

Northeast
Gate

CHANGCHUN

Rear Hall

Yile Hall

West Side
Houses

East Side
Houses

Middle Hall

Laodong Renmin Wenhuagong
(Workers' Palace of Culture)

Shejitian
(Hall of Prayer)

GARDEN
Pavilion

Taimiao
(Temple of the Imperial
Ancestors)

East Gate

Altar
of Earth and
Harvests

Concert
Hall

West Side
Hall

Big Halberd
Gate

East Side
Hall

Terrace of
Five-Colour Earth

Well
Pavilion

Well
Pavilion

Duanmen
(Upright Gate)

Pavilion
of

Recreation
Room

ZHONGSHAN GONGYUAN
(SUN YAT-SEN PARK)

Laijinyunxuan
(Restaurant)

Jade Belt

Science and Technology
Education Hall

PARK OF THE PEOPLE'S CULTURE

Beiwanzi
Hutong

Lanting Stele

Exhibition
Room

Greenhouse

Xili
(Pavilion for
Rehearsing Rites)

Orchid
House

Liufang
(Hexagonal
Pavilion)

Siyi
(House of Year-
Bound Delight)

Goldfish

Defend Peace
Archway

Changpuheyan

Waterside
Pavilion

Tian'anmen
(Gate of Heavenly Peace)

Golden River Bridges

Reviewing Stand

Reviewing Stand

South Gate

Dragon-Cloud Pillar

Dragon-Cloud Pillar

Xichang'an Jie

Dongchang'an Jie

Beichang Jie

Nanchang Jie

Beichizi Jie

Caodou Hutong

Nanchizi Dajie

Qiqelounan Xiang

Pudusixi Xiang

Qilelou Jie

access to the Forbidden City. Although the older parts were made into a museum as early as 1914, the last emperor and his court lived in the rear parts of the palace until 1924. The first tourists were admitted in the 1920s, but after 1937 there was not much left to look at, as items were removed to Nanjing and Shanghai for safe keeping from the advancing Japanese. From there, palace treasures were in turn "removed for safe keeping" to Taiwan, during Chiang Kai-shek's retreat in 1949.

Following the founding of the People's Republic, extensive restoration work was undertaken. Zhou Enlai is credited with protecting the renovated palace from zealous Red Guards during the Cultural Revolution. Today, this complex of imperial buildings is officially designated a "palace museum", and is protected by law.

The Forbidden City covers an area of 720,000 square metres (861,000 square yards), running a distance of 961 metres (3,150 ft) from north to south and 753 metres (2,470 ft) from east to west. It is surrounded by a broad moat and protected by a rectangular wall 10 metres (35 ft) high, with mighty watchtowers standing at the four corners. It is divided into two main areas – the southern (front) section or **Outer Courtyard**, comprising three large halls, in which the Ming and Qing emperors held state ceremonies, and the residential northern (rear) section or **Inner Courtyard**, consisting of three large palaces and a few smaller ones, and the Imperial Gardens.

## The Outer Courtyard

To the north of Tiananmen Gate (*see page 84*), past the Duanmen Gate, is the massive bulk of the **Meridian Gate ❶** (Wumen), the entrance to the Forbidden City (*for opening times see page 91*). At 38 metres (125

ft) it is the tallest gate of the palace. Because of the five pavilions on its U-shaped base, this gate was also known as the Gate of the Five Phoenixes. The number five is of great symbolic importance as it represents the five Confucian cardinal virtues – humanity, justice, refinement, education and trust. The emperor could only represent the *dao* of heaven, the order that pervades the world, and bring harmony on earth if he remained faithful to these virtues.

From a throne in the middle pavilion of the gate the emperor reviewed military parades, announced new calendars and ordered rebellious officials to be punished. The only other people allowed to use this gate were the empress on her wedding day, and scholars who had passed the palace examinations.

Once inside the Meridian Gate you enter a large courtyard, bisected by the **Golden Water River ❷** (Jinshahe), crossed by five marble bridges. Across this first courtyard to the north is the **Gate of Supreme Harmony ❸** (Taihemen), rebuilt in 1890. Inside it there is a large map

Map on page 94

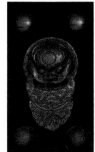

*The palace's huge wooden doors feature lions and heavyweight golden knobs – the number of which signifies the door's importance.*

**BELOW:** looking north from Tiananmen Gate to Duanmen Gate.

*The Forbidden City's own Starbucks branch is located outside the Gate of Heavenly Purity. Its opening in late 2000 caused some consternation, but, in truth, the Forbidden City is already so littered with popsicle vendors and kitschy souvenir shops that the tiny two-table coffee shop is hard even to find.*

**BELOW:** dressing up in Qing-style costume.

of the palace. Beyond this gate is the largest courtyard in the complex, the **Court of the Imperial Palace ④**, where the imperial shops selling silk and porcelain were situated.

There are three large audience and throne halls at the end of this courtyard: the Hall of Supreme Harmony, the Hall of Middle Harmony and the Hall of Preserving Harmony. They stand on a marble platform more than 8 metres (26 ft) high, which is divided into three levels. The balustrades on each level are decorated with dragon heads that spout water when it rains.

## Halls in harmony

The **Hall of Supreme Harmony ⑤** (Taihedian) is the largest of the three halls and in the time of the Ming and Qing dynasties, its 35 metres (115 ft) made it the tallest building in Beijing. Within the hall stood the **Dragon Throne**, from where the emperor ruled. Only he could enter the hall by walking up the ramp adorned with dragon motifs. On the platform in front of the hall are two symbols – a grain measure on the

left and a sundial to the right – representing imperial justice and agriculture. Also present are bronze figures of cranes and tortoises – symbols of good luck and longevity.

On state occasions, such as a coronation, the first day of the New Year or the empress's birthday, a formal court ceremony was conducted in the hall. Outside the hall, officials and the more important dignitaries lined up according to their rank, waiting to be summoned before the emperor. Incense and bells strengthened the impression of the otherworldly nature of the emperor.

The roof of the hall is supported by 72 pillars, with the inner six adorned by dragons. The hierarchy of Chinese feudal society was even reflected in roofs, which were designed to indicate the social position of the householder. The roofs of the Imperial Palace symbolised the highest degree of power through their colour, construction and material. Their breathtaking beauty makes it worth taking the time to see them again and again from different perspectives. The U-

shaped corbels typical of Chinese wooden buildings – all built without the use of nails – were reserved for great palaces and temples.

The Hall of Supreme Harmony has the most imposing roof in the palace, with a horizontal ridge, four rooftrees and double eaves. The varnished ornaments are also a sign of the building's status. Its dragons, for instance, at a weight of 4.5 tons and a height of 3 metres (11 ft), are the largest in the palace. These dragons are supposed to attract clouds and water and so protect the building from fire. Altogether, there are the figures of 10 animals on the roof, and one immortal, to serve as protection against evil spirits.

In the smallest of the three halls, the **Hall of Middle Harmony** ❻ (Zhonghedian), the emperor prepared for ceremonies before entering the main hall. There is an imperial palanquin on display here. The last of the three great halls, the **Hall of Preserving Harmony** ❼ (Baohedian), was used in the lavish New Year's banquets, as well as for examinations.

Once beyond the Hall of Preserving Harmony, stairs lead down from the platform. In the middle of the stairs, along the former Imperial Way, lies a ramp hewn from a single block of marble weighing 250 tons and decorated with dragon motifs.

### The rear courtyards

The northern section of the Imperial Palace is entered through the **Gate of Heavenly Purity** (Qianqinmen), which leads to three large palaces: the Palace of Heavenly Purity, the Hall of Union and the Palace of Earthly Tranquility. These palaces were the living and working quarters of the Ming and Qing emperors, and the scene of plots and intrigues between eunuchs and concubines in their manoeuverings for power and influence within the court.

The **Palace of Heavenly Purity** ❽ (Qianqinggong) was the bedroom of the Ming emperors, but later in the Qing dynasty it was used for audiences with officials and foreign envoys, and also for state banquets. The inscription above the throne reads "just and honourable". The

Map on page 94

*The dragon and phoenix figures perched on the palace rooftops bring protection against lightning and fire. The phoenix-riding figure at the outermost tip is the son of the Dragon King – ruler of the sea, with powers over the waters.*

**LEFT:** As a court concubine, Cixi provided Xianfeng with his sole male heir.

## Prolonging the Dynasty

At night, the Forbidden City emptied of mandarins and other royal relatives, leaving the emperor the sole mature male. During the Qing dynasty, he might have had over 120 empresses and concubines at his disposal. They were not all chosen for their beauty, but for their political ties to various Manchu noble houses. This perhaps explains why so many emperors found their way outside the walls in disguise, to the brothels not far outside the gates at Qianmen.

To prolong the dynasty, there were rules for ensuring that the primary empress was impregnated. It was thought that the male life force *yang* (i.e. semen) was limited, while the female life force, *yin* (her bodily fluids), was inexhaustible. To build up sufficient potency to father a Son of Heaven, the emperor required a great deal of *yin*. The best way for the female life force to transfer to the emperor was for him to engage in lots of sex with his concubines without achieving an orgasm. In this way he could store up lots of *yang* for his one monthly tryst with his empress. In practice, the emperors did not always restrain themselves. Most of them found one concubine that they liked, and ended up impregnating her. Cixi, for instance, got her start this way, providing the Emperor Xianfeng with his only male heir.

# The Golden Prison

It may not be obvious from a visit to the Imperial Palace that although the emperor and his court moved daily around buildings of stunning beauty, contemplated extraordinary collections of art and played in gardens beyond compare, their privileged life of luxury came at a price.

Reginald Johnston, tutor to Pu Yi, wrote: "If ever there was a palace that deserved the name of a prison, it is that palace in the Forbidden City of Peking, in which emperor Shunzhi pined for freedom, and in which the last but one of his successors, the emperor Guangxu, ended his dismal days nearly twelve years ago."

From the first, a Chinese emperor was a slave to a system built around the cult of his divine personality. His life, and the lives of his empress and concubines, were effectively not their own. From the moment they rose to the moment they went to sleep – and even while they slept – they were kept under scrutiny by attendant eunuchs, so that they never experienced any real privacy.

The emperor could not leave the confines of the palace grounds without official escort and usually not unless it was to attend an official function or to travel to another palace. Empresses and concubines led even more sheltered lives, because their sex made it impossible for them to be seen by any other males outside the immediate family circle.

Days in the palace were governed by routine. Rising early, sometimes at three or four in the morning to ready themselves for official audiences, they would be bathed by eunuchs and maidservants who carried water from the Golden Water River. When necessary, a chamber pot was brought, placed in the corner of the room, and emptied immediately.

The young sons of the emperor, and perhaps a privileged cousin or two, spent their days in lessons with the most learned of Confucian scholars, learning Chinese language, calligraphy and the Confucian classics, the philosophy on which the civil service was based and which governed official life. This prepared them for the day when one of them would be emperor and the others his officials, who would have to accept and write imperial memorials at court. Memorials, written on scrolls, were the way in which officials from all over the country sent information and subtle advice to the emperor.

Even when the emperor moved from one part of the palace to another, it was a major expedition involving a considerable amount of organisation. Pu Yi described a walk in the garden in his autobiography: "At the head marched a eunuch, a herald whose function was like that of a car horn. He walked twenty or thirty yards in front of the others, constantly hissing 'chi, chi' to shoo away any other people in the vicinity. He was followed by two of the higher eunuchs walking like crabs on both sides of the path... If I was carried in my palanquin, two of the younger eunuchs walked at my side, ready to attend to my wishes at any time. If I was walking, they held me under the arms to support me. Behind me followed a eunuch with a great silken canopy. He was accompanied by a great crowd of eunuchs carrying all kinds of paraphernalia..." ❏

**LEFT:** an audience with the emperor.

successor to the imperial throne was announced from here. Immediately to the north is the **Hall of Union** ❾ (Jiaotaian), where imperial concubines were officially approved. Within the hall are the imperial jade seals as well as a water clock dating back to 1745. The third palace, to the rear, is the **Palace of Earthly Tranquillity** ❿ (Kuninggong), the residence of the Ming empresses. The Qing rulers, following their religious traditions, also used the rear part of this hall for ritual sacrifices that entailed slaughtering pigs and cooking votive offerings. In the eastern wing is the bridal chamber of those Qing emperors who married after their accession, namely Kangxi, Tongzhi and Guangxu.

The last time the room was used for this purpose was in the winter of 1922, by the deposed last emperor Pu Yi. He later wrote: "After we had drunk the marriage cup at our wedding and eaten cakes to ensure children and children's children, we entered this dark, red chamber. I felt very uncomfortable. The bride sat on the *kang*, her head lowered. Sitting beside her, I looked about for a while and saw nothing but red: red bed curtains, red bedclothes, a red jacket, a red skirt, red flowers in her hair, a red face… everything seemed to be made of red wax. I felt most dissatisfied. I did not want to sit, but to stand was even less desirable. Yangxindiang (the Hall of Mental Cultivation) was, after all, more comfortable. I opened the door and went back to my accustomed apartments."

To the sides of the Palace of Heavenly Purity lie the **East and West Palaces**, grouped like the constellations around the pole star. Here, the emperor was the only mature adult male, surrounded by concubines, eunuchs, the empress, serving women and slaves. As late as 1900, there were still 10,000 people living in the palace.

The male palace servants were without exception eunuchs, therefore ensuring that after dark the emperor would be the only male capable of begetting a new generation. For many Chinese, especially for the poor, it was lucrative to enter the imperial service as a eunuch. Surgeons, called "knifers", stationed themselves at the gates to the Forbidden City. Here, they would perform castrations at "reasonable rates", but then sell the sexual organs back to the victims at a high price, for the organs had to be presented in a bottle for inspection at the palace.

As eunuchs were the only people who lived permanently in the Forbidden City and were allowed to leave it and return they became not only well-informed, but also skilled at intrigue. Some of them became powerful people in their own right – and a few virtually ruled the country. Corruption was a problem amongst eunuchs; the Jesuit Matteo Ricci called them "monsters of vice".

One of the most important buildings in the palace, the **Hall of Mental Cultivation** ⓫ (Yangxindiang)

Map on page 94

*There are several sundials in the Forbidden City, symbols of heaven and the* yang *element.*

**BELOW:** gateways lead through the endless network of courtyards to the rear of the complex.

*On display in the clock museum, an ornate Qing-dynasty celestial globe maps the heavens.*

**BELOW:** the Nine Dragon Screen, made of 1,773 glazed bricks.

functioned as the living quarters of Emperor Qianlong (1736–96) and, a century later, the Empress Dowager Cixi. Pu Yi also had his private apartments here. The working, living and sleeping rooms can be seen, as can the room where Cixi received audiences while hidden behind a screen. Strict Confucian protocol required that as a woman, and as an empress, she could not be seen by any Chinese of low birth or foreigners.

## Dragons and longevity

To the southeast is the **Nine Dragon Screen ⓬** (Jiulongbi), built out of brightly coloured glazed bricks. The dragon is a symbol of heaven and, therefore, of the emperor, as is the number nine, the highest unit. It is no surprise that the dragon had, according to Chinese mythology, nine sons. Each of these nine dragons had different skills. Chao Feng, for instance, loves danger and is set on roofs to protect against fire – as seen in the Hall of Supreme Harmony.

Near the gate you pass through on your way to the Nine Dragon Screen there is a fascinating **clock museum ⓭** (entrance fee payable unless you bought an all-inclusive *tao piao* ticket at the Meridian Gate; *see page 91*), filled with a spectacular array of timepieces collected by Qing emperors. As the temporal guardians of the harvest, emperors were responsible for predicting weather patterns, and were intensely interested in the scientific knowledge brought to China by the Jesuits.

Opposite the Nine Dragon Screen is the **Gate of Peace and Longevity** (Ningshoumen), which leads to the **Palace of Peace and Longevity ⓮** (Ningshougong). The 18th-century Emperor Qianlong had this complex built for his old age. The **Imperial Treasury ⓯** (entrance fee without a *tao piao* ticket), which gives some idea of the wealth and magnificence of the Qing imperial court, is now housed in the adjoining halls to the north. On display are golden cutlery and table silver, jewellery, robes, porcelain, cloisonné, hunting equipment and golden religious objects (many of the Qing emperors were followers of Tibetan Buddhism), as well as pictures made of precious

and semi-precious stones, usually depicting animals and landscapes – symbols of longevity, health and good fortune.

## The northern exit

On the way to the northeastern exit is a small well, the **Well of the Concubine Zhen** ⓰ (Zhenfeijing). Rumours were reported in the Western press, and passed down by historians who had no other record, that Cixi ordered Zhen Fei to be thrown to her death down this well before the imperial family fled to Xi'an in the wake of the Boxer Rebellion. It was said that Zhen Fei, a favourite of Guangxu, had supported the emperor in his ill-fated reforms of 1898, and that she begged Cixi to let her stay with him in Beijing to continue the fight. Cixi, the story goes, disapproved, ordered Zhen Fei to be executed, and forced Guangxu to accompany her to Xi'an. There is, however, little evidence to support these claims, and the well in question seems too small for someone to drown in. The legend may have more to do with reports from foreign

armies entering the city, who found frightened concubines hiding in wells for fear of being raped.

Follow the red palace walls to the west. Before leaving the palace it's worth taking time to see the **Imperial Flower Garden** ⓱ (Yuhuayuan). Laid out during the Ming period, it exemplifies the traditional Chinese skill at landscape gardening. The artificial rocks, pavilions, pines, cypresses, flowers and bamboo work together to produce a harmonious whole. This garden was the only chance for many of the people who lived in the palace to catch a glimpse of nature. The hill of rocks in the garden's northeast corner is one of the few places from which the world beyond the palace could be viewed. The imperial family climbed it each year on the Double Ninth Festival to pray for family members and friends who lived in far off places.

Leave the Imperial Palace by way of the **Gate of the Divine Warrior** ⓲ (Shenwumen). There is a panoramic view of the entire Forbidden City from Jingshan (Coal Hill), across the street (*see page 125*). ❑

Map on page 94

*The Forbidden City is Beijing's number-one tourist attraction.*

**BELOW:** the palace walls are 10 metres (33 ft) tall.

# BEIJING'S BICYCLES AND TRICYCLES

**Cycles have ruled the roads of Beijing for more than 50 years, but they face an uncertain future in a city that has been promoting motor vehicles**

Despite the building of multi-lane ring roads and boulevards to accommodate the growing number of cars, most Beijingers still rely on pedal power to get to work, go shopping and take the children to school. Affluent youngsters ride expensive mountain bikes, while older and poorer people make do with classic black Flying Pigeon and Forever designs. People selling pancakes and kebabs cooked on small grills the size of a bicycle rack are the most prominent of tens of thousands who do business by bicycle or tricycle.

China has some 500 million bicycles, more than half the world's total. Greater affluence has brought not only private cars, but also an unprecedented number of cycles. Today, 10 million bikes glide around the flat roads of Beijing, three times the 1980 total. Bicycles are still used for more than 50 percent of all journeys in the capital, though this figure is slowly beginning to fall.

## BICYCLE "POLLUTION"

Despite the number of bicycles, the World Bank concluded back in 1995 that modern Chinese cities, including Beijing, were "mainly dominated by motor vehicle traffic." As a showpiece capital, Beijing is image-conscious; cars are a key part of its modernisation drive. Planners' and architects' drawings have a conspicuous absence of bicycles, and some officials even discuss the problem of bicycle "pollution."

**ABOVE:** At peak times, 20,000 cyclists per hour pass through the major intersections of Beijing. To the outsider, it may look like mayhem, but cyclists face on-the-spot fines for breaking the rules.

**ABOVE:** Some farmers cycle overnight from the outlying suburbs to bring fruit and vegetables to Beijing's early morning markets, often risking arrest by police or tax officers.

**BELOW LEFT:** Tricycle rickshaws, often known as trishaws or pedicabs, ply many of Beijing's main streets, train and bus stations, and tourist areas. Most are licensed, but all prices are negotiable.

**BELOW RIGHT:** People who cycle for a living work up to 12 hours per day, in all weather. Most are self-sufficient, carrying all their own equipment and spares.

**LEFT:** Trishaws tours provide one of the best means of exploring the *hutong* of Beijing. Weaving a path between poky courtyards, visitors can peer into the life of the traditional Beijinger.

## RENTING A BIKE

Despite the increase in road traffic, many tourists still find a bicycle to be the perfect means of transport in this hugely spread-out city. Bicycle lanes are usually wide, and for those of a nervous disposition there is comfort to be had in following the mass of other cyclists. The pace tends to be sedate, particularly at peak times when two-wheeler traffic jams form at major junctions. Park in official lots, which are easy to find; the fee is usually 2 jiao, payable when you leave. As always when renting a bicycle, check that the brakes work properly, that the tyres are in reasonable condition and that the lock isn't broken. Luxury hotels charge about three times the standard rental rate. For more details, and safety tips, *see page 211.*

**ABOVE:** Armed with flags and whistles, traffic wardens, usually pensioners or unemployed youngsters, control the bicycle lanes that flank most main streets.

**BELOW:** Some families use customised three-wheelers to get around, though most now own an average of one bicycle per person.

# SOUTH OF TIANANMEN

The labyrinth of narrow *hutong* to the south of
Qianmen Gate is traditionally the liveliest part of
Beijing. Something of a den of iniquity in imperial
times, it retains an identity at odds with the rapidly
modernising city that surrounds it. The areas further
south and west contain key religious sights

The southern area of Beijing beginning south of Tiananmen Square has changed less than any other part of the city over the past twenty-five years. The buildings are lower, the pavements narrower, the drainage poorer and the life on the streets more frenetic. This comparatively timeless quality holds charm for the tourist, but is less than desirable for residents who live in sub-standard housing and share filthy public bathrooms. Acknowledging this, the Beijing government has made "speeding up the development of the southern part of the municipality" a key goal of its current five-year plan. Work is already underway to replace dilapidated residential buildings and add tracts of greenery and facilities for culture and sports. Necessary and desirable though these efforts are, they will inevitably alter the character of one of Beijing's most distinctive neighbourhoods.

## The Qianmen area

Just to the south of Tiananmen Square, beyond the Qianmen Gate, is the area referred to as **Qianmen**, which used to be one of the busier sections of town near the gates in the wall linking the Inner (Tartar) City with the Outer (Chinese) City. In earlier times, officials came from the south and had to leave their horses outside Qianmen, or when they reached the side gates of Tiananmen (demolished in 1912 in order to open up the square). They then passed through the gates into the Forbidden City (for more on the gate *see page 87*).

To the north of Qianmen Gate were the spacious estates of the imperial household, and tranquil temples set aside for ancestral and godly worship. To the south was the bustling mass of everyday life,

Map on page 106

**LEFT:** Dazhalan is one of Beijing's best shopping streets.
**BELOW:** outside the old railway station at Qianmen.

*Artists' supplies are easy to find along Liulichang.*

where the pursuit of more earthly delights was also allowed. The brothels and opium dens of Qianmen were so renowned that Manchu officials and even emperors in disguise would come to sample their pleasures. The area was also famed for its opera houses – Mei Lanfang made his start in the now-shuttered Guanghe Theatre in a little street just off Qianmen. Brothels are a thing of the past, at least in theory, and opera theatres are fast joining them. However, Qianmen was also known for its shops and restaurants, and many of these survive.

**Dazhalan** ❶ is a small *hutong* heading west from Qianmen Dajie that is famous for its old shops and businesses, which draw customers from the suburbs and the provinces, as well as overseas tourists. It was completely renovated several years ago and is now a pedestrianised zone. The name Dazhalan (sometimes referred to as "Dashilar" or

"Dashilde" in Beijing dialect) literally means "big stockades", and is an echo of Ming times when the streets were closed off at the evening curfew.

One of Dazhalan's best-known shops is the **Tongrentang Pharmacy**, which hoards secret recipes of the Qing court and is reputed to be the oldest Chinese medicine shop in the entire country, founded back in 1669. Tongrentang has not only survived, but flourished – it now has branches throughout China, around Asia, and even in such far-off places as London and Sydney. Other famous shops include the Neiliansheng Shoe Store, the Ruifuxiang Silk and Cotton Fabrics Store and various shops specialising in tea leaves and musical instruments.

Take time to head off the beaten track into the side alleys, a world of tiny workshops and dimly lit stores selling all kinds of odds and ends. This densely packed warren of

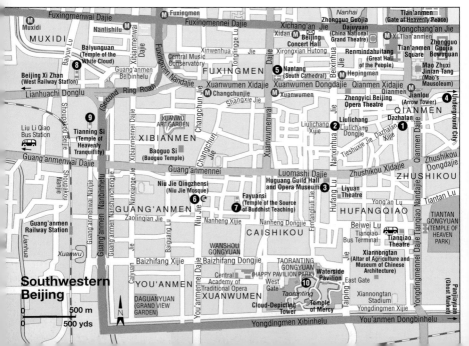

**Southwestern Beijing**

poverty is in stark contrast to the vast emptiness of Tiananmen Square just to the north, and the glitzy shopping malls beyond.

Further to the west through the maze of *hutong* is **Liulichang ❷**, literally meaning "glazed tile factory", a shopping street restored in the 1980s to its original style, which offers a wide range of Chinese arts and crafts with a generous helping of kitsch. Its name derives from the five kilns that were established nearby during the Ming dynasty to provide glazed tiles for the palaces and halls being built in the new Imperial Palace. Later, during the Qing dynasty, the area was inhabited by Chinese officials serving a Manchu government who were not permitted to live in the Tartar City to the north. A thriving economy grew up around the community, catering to the mostly male officials, young men studying for their civil service exams and the many itinerant merchants who passed through here.

There are many long-established companies on Liulichang. On the eastern stretch are most of the antique (or purported antique) shops. Here you can also find the **Cathay Bookstore** (at No. 115), with its collection of old books, while **Yidege** (No. 67) has been selling artists' and calligraphers' supplies since 1865. **Daiyuexuan** (No. 73) is the place to go for quality paintbrushes, which it has been selling since 1916. The western branch of the street has bookshops and art galleries as well as more calligraphic supplies. An interesting shop to visit is **Wen Sheng Zhai**, formerly suppliers to the palace and imperial officials of the ubiquitous red lanterns and fans. The shop's lanterns are still hung on Tiananmen Gate for Chinese New Year.

A short distance to the north is the **Zhengyici Beijing Opera Theatre**, the oldest Beijing Opera theatre constructed entirely of wood. It was built in the 18th century but was later converted into a hotel, which eventually closed in 1949. Through much effort, the theatre finally reopened in 1995, but closed again in 2003 following the SARS panic. Funding for renovation has been allocated by the

Map on page 106

**TIP**

The Huguang Guild Hall, at 3 Hufang Lu (Tel. 6351-8284) is a good alternative to the Zhengyici. It offers nightly performances of famous opera excerpts accompanied by tea and snacks.

**BELOW:** shops along Dazhalan and Liulichang sell colourful Chinese teaware.

*The Cultural Palace of the Nationalities (Minzu Wenhuagong) on Fuxingmennei Dajie is a pre-eminent center for the studies of China's non-Han peoples. The Chinese Ethnic Culture Park (see page 133) in the northern suburbs is now the focus for tourist- (and school-child-) oriented exhibits and performances.*

**BELOW:** a typical shop along Liulichang.

city government, but it remains unclear when it will reopen. When it does, it will be a beautiful setting in which to see Beijing Opera performed. In the meantime, the **Huguang Guild Hall ❸** on Hufang Lu near the western end of Liulichang is perhaps the best place to see opera in the city. There is also a small museum on site.

Alternatively, a few minutes' walk south, the **Liyuan Theatre** at the Qianmen Hotel has performances every evening.

To the east of Qianmen Dajie and south of Qianmen Dongdajie, are more scruffy hutong, home to small shops and restaurants. An unusual sight here is Beijing's **Underground City ❹** (Dixia Cheng; open daily 8.30am–5pm; entrance fee), a network of tunnels and bunkers built amid fears of Soviet attack following the 1960 bust-up between the two countries. The passageways extend all the way from Qianmen in the south to Ditan in the north and Yuetan in the west. The vast tunnel system was never needed to escape Russian bombs,

but it was subsequently used for everything from growing mushrooms to training athletes. Although parts are crumbling due to poor maintenance, some sections remain in use to this day. To reach the entrance at 62 Xidamochang Jie, turn south from Qianmen Dongdajie into Zhengyi Lu, then left at the end, first right and then left again at the T-junction.

## Christianity in China

A few hundred yards west, across Xuanwumen Dongdajie, is Beijing's oldest extant church, **South Cathedral ❺** (Nantang; open daily). The church was founded in the period around the end of the Ming dynasty and the beginning of the Qing dynasty, when Christianity began to establish itself with the arrival of Matteo Ricci (1552–1610) and Johann Adam Schall von Bell (1592–1666). Schall von Bell was responsible for the original structure which burned down in 1775. Money from Emperor Qianlong helped to rebuild it, but it was later destroyed by the xenophobic Boxers in 1900.

The spires of the missionary churches that seemed so breathtaking to Westerners were considered to be bad *feng shui* by the Chinese, and blamed for many current evils. It did not take much to encourage people to destroy the foreign building that was held responsible for the bad harvests of the previous few years. The current structure dates from 1904, but this in turn was heavily damaged during the Cultural Revolution. The building has been open to the faithful again since the early 1980s.

The cathedral also serves as the seat of the Chinese Catholic Patriotic Association, founded by the government in 1957 as a means of co-opting Catholics while at the same time attempting to give the appearance of religious freedom. The Association does not recognise the authority of the pope, and Catholics who remain true to the papacy have to practise their religion in secret.

### Beijing's Muslims

There are more than 200,000 Chinese Muslims living in Beijing today. Known as the Hui minority, they have 6 million members throughout China. Many of them are no longer orthodox Muslims, but, whether believers or not, they share one custom important to all Muslims: they don't eat pork. For this reason, there are in Beijing, as in many other Chinese cities, *Huimin Fandian*, or Hui restaurants, in which ritual-clean hands prepare snacks and meals, substituting mutton for pork.

The Hui use the Chinese language and can hardly be distinguished from Han Chinese. However, if you have the opportunity to visit a mosque in Beijing during prayers, or to take a stroll along Niu Jie, you will see many non-Han faces. The largest concentration of Hui in Beijing – an estimated 10,000 or more – is along **Niu Jie** and in its many little side streets and hutong. The street's name – which translates as "Ox Street" – is often said to indicate an association with the Hui community,, but is in fact a corruption of an earlier name, Liu Jie, which derived from the presence of a pomegranate orchard in the vicinity. Walking down Niu Jie you pass Hui butchers, Hui shops and a Hui elementary school before arriving at a mosque on the east side of the street.

The **Niu Jie Mosque** ⑥ (Niu Jie Qingzhensi; open daily, 9am–8pm; entrance fee), with its curved eaves and colourfully painted support and cross beams, looks more like a Chinese temple than a Muslim place of worship – in common with all mosques in the city, there is no dome and no minaret. Instead, it follows the Chinese palace style, with main and side buildings laid out symmetrically, and roofs of glazed tiles; roof arches and posts are often adorned with texts from the Koran or other Islamic motifs.

Map on page 106

**TIP**

The Niu Jie Mosque is open to non-Muslims (including women), but it is important to dress respectfully – no shorts or sleeveless tops. The prayer hall is closed to non-Muslims.

**BELOW:** Beijing's Hui Muslim population is mainly concentrated in the south of the city.

Also unusually for a mosque, there is a shop inside the complex, selling necklaces and teapots as well as copies of the Koran.

The mosque was built in 966 in the style of a Buddhist temple, after the Islamic faith had spread into China during the Tang dynasty (618–907). Right behind the main entrance is a hexagonal building, the **Tower for Observing the Moon** (Wangyuelou). Every year, at the beginning and at the end of the fasting month of Ramadan, the imam climbs the tower to observe the waxing and waning of the moon and to determine the exact length of the period of fasting.

Beyond the tower is the **main prayer hall**. This is where the faithful come for religious ceremonies, after ritually cleansing themselves in the washrooms. Like all mosque prayer halls, this one has no adornment or pictures inside. There is a sign requesting people not to enter the hall unless they are Muslim. Since Islamic tradition dictates that Muslims have to pray facing Mecca, the front of the hall faces

west. Beyond the prayer hall are a few smaller religious buildings and steles. In the little courtyard garden that runs east is the tombstone – with an Arabic inscription – of the founder of the mosque. During the Cultural Revolution, the faithful managed to save this by burying it next to the wall.

With state support, the mosque was restored in the 1990s (although by 2004 it was in dire need of repainting), and it is once more a meeting place for Muslims. Many Hui children also come here to study the Koran. Other regulars here include the staff of the embassies of Islamic countries, and the local Uighur community.

## Buddhist Beijing

Just to the east, on Fayuansi Qianjie (a *hutong* leading off Niu Jie), is what is thought to be the oldest temple in the inner city of Beijing, **Fayuansi** ❼ (Temple of the Source of Buddhist Teaching; open Thurs–Tues, 8.30am–4pm; entrance fee).

It was built on the orders of the Tang emperor Li Shimin, in honour of soldiers killed in battle in the unsuccessful Korean campaign, and took over 40 years to construct. It was completed in 696 and named Minzhongsi, but since 1734 it has been known as Fayuansi. Almost the entire structure has been renewed over the centuries, mostly during the Qing dynasty. The temple houses the **Buddhist Academy**, formed in 1956 by the Chinese Buddhist Society. The Academy is devoted to the teaching and study of Buddhism, and trains young monks for four to five years before they can enter other monasteries in China. The Fayuansi Temple also contains a library of more than 100,000 valuable books.

The large complex has six halls. Enter through **Shanmen**, the Mountain Gate, which is guarded by two stone lions. In the first temple court-

**BELOW:** the entrance to the main prayer hall at the Niu Jie Mosque.

yard are two bronze lions in front of the **Hall of the Celestial Kings** (Tianwangdian). The Celestial Kings rule the four points of the compass and can keep away all evil spirits and the enemies of Buddhism. Enthroned in the middle of the hall is a Milefo, a laughing, fat-bellied Buddha, who encourages the faithful to "come in, follow me on the way to release in nirvana".

Such Milefo Buddhas represent Maitreya, the Buddha of the Coming Age. They can be seen at the entrance to almost all Chinese Buddhist temples, and are always flanked by the four Celestial Kings. These five statues are Ming dynasty bronzes, a rarity in Chinese Buddhist temples.

Behind the Milefo Buddha is the Guardian of Buddhism, with his face turned to the main hall of the temple, the **Hall of Heroes** (Daxiongbaodian). This is reached by leaving the first hall and crossing a garden with a bronze cauldron and stone steles. Within the hall is a Buddha flanked by two Bodhisattvas and surrounded by 18 Luohan, or saints, the lowest rank in the Buddhist divine hierarchy.

Leaving the main hall, you will pass a small hall with stone tablets and come to the **Hall of a Thousand Buddhas**. Here, on a stone base, is a 5-metre (15-ft) high sculpture dating back to the Ming dynasty, showing the Buddhas of the five points of the compass; towering over all of them is the Dharma Buddha.

In the last hall there is a Reclining Buddha and an exhibition of Buddhist sculpture, with some pieces dating back to the Han dynasty A splendid Guanyin Bodhisattva with 1,000 arms is also on display.

## Daoist Beijing

To the northwest, in an unpromising area dominated by thundering traffic and tower blocks, is one of the few Daoist temples left in Beijing, **Baiyunguan** ❽ (Temple of the White Cloud; open daily 8.30am–4pm; entrance fee). Used as a factory during the Cultural Revolution, the temple was restored to its original purpose and today is a thriving centre for China's only indigenous

*Incense burners are a feature of Buddhist and Daoist temples.*

**LEFT:** Buddhist monk.

## Buddhist Academy

The Buddhist Academy at Fayuansi is the most prestigious in the nation and accepts only one out of every four applicants who pass tests in Buddhism, Chinese, politics, English and scripture. Once accepted, a young novice will be indoctrinated in Buddhist theory and history and required to take courses in philosophy, Chinese history, politics, writing and foreign languages. Elective courses include tea ceremony, calligraphy, music, art, computers and law. While this curriculum may sound rather worldly for a monk, the fact is that Buddhist monks do not live in isolation. Indeed, most urban monks have cellphones, email addresses and even websites. Those with high positions in their temples also have cars and drivers. "Monks do not lead secluded lives," a professor named Chi Zhen told *Beijing Weekend* in 2004. "They should have knowledge of the law so they know how to protect themselves by law. They should also pay attention to politics. A monk without any idea of current affairs is a blind man."

Upon finishing their studies, most monks either stay on for further cultivation, become abbots at local temples or pursue further studies abroad. Unfortunately, those who leave tend not to return, and school leaders complain of a Buddhist brain drain.

*Daoist priests sometimes earn extra income as fortune tellers, as here outside Baiyunguan Temple.*

**BELOW:** certain animals are linked with Daoist deities; touching the donkey at Baiyunguan brings good health.

**RIGHT:** the hexagonal pagoda at Tianning Si.

religion, popular with pilgrims and home to around 35 monks – easily identified by their white stockings and top-knotted hair.

The temple site dates from the Tang dynasty (although the building itself dates from the Ming) and is the centre of the Daoist Dragon Gate sect. Daoist temples on the grand scale were not built until the Yuan dynasty and the reign of Kublai Khan, who appointed a priest named Qiu Chuji as "National Teacher"; Qiu took up residence in the temple, and from that time on Baiyunguan has been the centre of Daoism in northern China (the other principal Daoist centre in Beijing is Dongyue Temple, in the east of the city *(see page 143)*.

The complex contains several courtyards, the overall design being similar to Buddhist temples in that it faces south and its structures lie one behind the other along a straight line. Pass through the entrance gate into the first courtyard; the main attraction here is the pair of gong-like copper coins with a bell in the centre suspended on strings. The

idea is to throw (normal-sized) coins from the bridge – hitting the bell means good luck. As Chinese currency is almost exclusively in paper form, you must buy a bag of "coins" from the nearby kiosk. Other ways to bring luck involve touching animal motifs and figures – the stone monkey at the entrance gate, or the bronze donkey in a western courtyard – or rubbing the belly on the large bronze statue of Wen Cheng, the scholar-deity in one of the western courtyards.

There are several halls spread around the large complex, each dedicated to a different deity or group of deities, concerned with everything from health to wealth. Unusually, Baiyunguan is well endowed with English signage which explain each of these.

In the centre of the furthest courtyard is the **Hall of the Four Celestial Emperors**, and on its upper floor is the **Hall of the Three Purities**. Daoist manuscripts are kept here in a compendium similar to those found in Buddhist temples. In a hall off one of the side courtyards

of the western section there are old bronze guardian figures, and in a building behind this are 60 relatively newly made figures of Daoist divinities, each one appointed to a year of the traditional 60-year Chinese calendar. Visitors can find their personal Daoist divinities according to this calendar. The Daoist priests who reside here will be pleased to help.

Daoist temples use obvious symbolic motifs more frequently in their decoration than Buddhist temples. Common designs include the Lingzhi mushroom (which is supposed to prolong life), Daoist immortals, cranes and the eight trigrams from the Book of Changes.

A short distance to the south of Baiyunguan is **Tianning Si ❾** (Temple of Heavenly Tranquillity; open daily 9am–4pm; entrance fee), thought to be the oldest building in Beijing. All that remains of the original building is the spectacular 58-metre (190-ft) hexagonal pagoda. This is one of the few tall buildings in the city at the time it was built in the 12th century, towards the end of the Liao dynasty – of which

its style is thought to be typical – it now peers out from behind a threatening overpass, tower blocks and smokestacks. The pagoda rises in 13 storeys from a richly decorated podium that symbolises the mountain of the gods, Sumeru. The first level has windows and doors but is otherwise unadorned. Major restoration work was underway in 2004.

Near the southern entrance of **Taoranting Gongyuan ❿** (Happy Pavilion Park), is the **Temple of Mercy**, dating from the Yuan dynasty. In 1695 a three-room wing west of the old temple was built, from which the park gets its name. Li Dazhao, co-founder of the Chinese Communist Party, rented one of these rooms while he was in Beijing working to further the revolution, and held many meetings here. Nearby are two *pailou* (gates of honour) which once stood on Chang'an Jie. In the past, Taoranting Park was one of the few open spaces open to common people who did not have access to the imperial parks. The boating lake and swimming pool are popular in the summer. ❑

*Throwing coins at the central bell brings good luck at Baiyunguan.*

# RESTAURANTS

*French*

**Maxim's de Paris**
2 Chongwenmen Xidajie. Tel: 6512-1992. Open: 5–9pm. $$$$.
Beijing's first joint-venture restaurant is now past its prime, but the sheer size and opulence still make it worth a visit.

*Peking Duck*

**Liqun Roast Duck**
11 Beixiangfeng. Tel: 6705-5578. Open: 11:30am–1:30pm, 4.30–10pm. $$–$$$.

Hidden away in the labyrinth of *hutong* east of Qianmen. An atmospheric place, and good value.

**Quanjude**
32 Qianmen Dajie. Tel: 6701-1379. Open: 11am–2pm, 5–9pm. 14 Qianmen Xidajie. Tel: 6302-3062. Open same hours. $$$.
The first Quanjude opened its doors in 1852. It continues to be state-owned, and now has several palatial branches around the city.

*Other Chinese*

**Duyichu**
36 Qianmen Dajie. Tel: 6702-1555. Open: 10.30am–9pm. $$.
This is one of Beijing's *laozihao*, or "old famous brand" restaurants. It specialises in Shandong cuisine and *shao mai* (*jiaozi*), for which it is renowned.

**Fengzeyuan**
83 Zhushikou Xidajie. Tel: 6318-6688. Open: 11am–2pm, 5–9pm. $$$.
Shandong cuisine is the hallmark of one of the city's most praised restaurants.

**Ye Shan Jun Wild Fungus House**
2A Qianmen Dongdajie. Tel: 6512-2708. Open: 11am–2:30pm, 4–11pm. $$$.
Hot-pot and exotic mushrooms, with dishes from Yunnan and Fujian.

• • • • • • • • • •
*Prices are for a typical dinner for one (three dishes with beer in Chinese restaurants, or a three-course meal with a half bottle of house wine in Western-style restaurants).*
*$ = under 50 Rmb*
*$$ = 50–100 Rmb*
*$$$ = 100–150 Rmb*
*$$$$ = over 150 Rmb*

# THE TEMPLE OF HEAVEN

The magnificent buildings of this peaceful complex, once used for imperial ancestor worship, are now among the city's top tourist sights; the surrounding parkland is popular with locals practising everything from tai chi to ballroom dancing

The spectacular **Temple of Heaven** (Tiantan) complex is set in the middle of one of the city's most visited parks, popular with Beijing residents, Chinese tourists and foreigners alike. The park itself is open daily 6am–8pm, the temple complex 8am–5.30pm; it's best to buy an all-inclusive ticket *(tao piao)*, although if you only wish to visit the park then a separate, cheaper ticket is available.

It is easy to get here from the city centre by bus or by taxi, and the park can be entered through several gates. The buildings are divided into two main groups: northern and southern. The northern group, built to a semicircular layout representing Heaven, gathers around one of the most impressive buildings in China, the Hall of Prayer for Good Harvests. The southern group, meanwhile, has a square layout that symbolises Earth.

The sizeable park surrounding the ancient buildings is a favourite place for locals to practice tai chi and various other forms of exercise. It is also very popular with men wielding traditional Chinese musical instruments, or playing dominoes or Go – it's all very picturesque, and not just a show for the tourists. Come early in the morning before the tour groups arrive.

## A place of ritual

Built in 1420, the Temple of Heaven served as a place of ritual for Ming and Qing emperors. Every year at the time of the winter solstice the emperor would come here in a magnificent procession lasting several days, in order to honour his ancestors and to pray for a good harvest in the season to come. In the middle of the first lunar calendar month, the emperor prayed once more in the Temple of Heaven, this time in the Hall of Prayer for Good

Map on page 116

**LEFT:** the unmissable Hall of Prayer for Good Harvests, centrepiece of the Temple of Heaven.
**BELOW:** the park is popular with musicians.

*Dragon detail from a circular roof tile at the Temple of Heaven.*

Harvests. This ceremony was last carried out in 1914 by the self-proclaimed emperor Yuan Shikai.

The observation of such ritual was more than a mere formality. The sacred nature of the emperor's rule had been established in the 3rd century BC: as the Son of Heaven, he administered heavenly authority on earth. According to the Chinese, natural catastrophes, bad farming practices, failing harvests, and increasing corruption were all signs that the emperor had lost the favour of Heaven and of his ancestors. In such circumstances, it was considered a legitimate act to overthrow him. Exact attention to the practice of the sacrificial rites in the Temple of Heaven was therefore given the appropriate importance by the ever-wary emperor.

## Ceremonies of the solstice

The procession for the winter solstice began at the Qianmen Gate at the southern edge of the Forbidden City.

When it arrived at the Temple of Heaven the emperor changed his robes in the **Hall of Heaven** ❶ (Huangqiongyu). Built in 1530 and restored in 1730, this hall has a round, pointed roof with a golden spire. The ancestor tablets of the emperors were stored inside (the spirit of the ancestor was thought to be present in the tablet during the ceremony).

A brick wall surrounding the courtyard of the Hall of Heaven has become famous as the **Echo Wall** ❷. If you stand facing the wall and speak to someone who is also standing by it, he or she will be able to hear every word at every point anywhere along the wall. Of course, it is necessary to wait until only a few people are present, which, unfortunately, is very rarely the case.

The three stone slabs in front of the stairs to the main temple are the **Echo Stones** (Sanyinshi), which produce another peculiar effect. If you stand on the first slab and clap

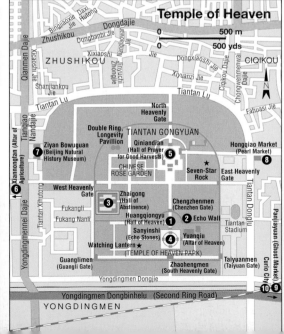

Map on page 116

your hands, you will hear a single echo. On the second step you will hear a double echo, and on the third, a triple. The secret of this ingenious phenomenon has to do with the different distances at which each stone slab is placed from the wall. Again it's practically impossible to witness the acoustics because every other visitor is trying the same thing.

Before the winter solstice ritual, the emperor would fast in the **Hall of Abstinence** (Zhaigong) ❸, which stands in the west of the temple complex. Then, by the first rays of the sun on the day of the solstice, he would offer sacrifices and prayers at the **Altar of Heaven** (Yuanqiu) ❹. This is the most spectacular of the city's imperial altars (*see following page*), consisting of a stone terrace of three levels surrounded by two walls – an inner round one and an outer square one. The lowest level symbolises the Earth, the second, the world of human beings, and the last, Heaven. The altar is built from stone slabs and its construction is based on the number nine and its multiples. In earlier times, odd numbers were

considered the attribute of Heaven or *yang*. Nine, as the highest odd unit, was the most important number of all, and therefore became associated with the emperor. The innermost circle on the top level consists of nine slabs, the second of 18, the third of 27 and so on until the final ring on the lowest level, which, as the 27th circle, contains 243 slabs.

Here another odd sound effect can be heard. If you stand in the middle of the upper level on the round stone slab and speak in a normal voice, your voice is heard more loudly than those of any other people around you. This effect is caused by the echo retained by the balustrades, and by a hollow space within the stone slab that functions as a resonating cavity. This stone in the centre was considered by the Chinese to be the most holy place in the Chinese empire, indeed the centre of the Earth.

### Prayers for the harvest

Walk along the central causeway that links the southern and northern buildings to reach the most striking building of the Temple of Heaven

**BELOW:** pillar and ceiling inside the Hall of Prayer for Good Harvests.

*Panjiayuan market is one of the best places in Beijing to look for scroll paintings, lacquerware, silk items such as cushion covers, and all kinds of interesting odds and ends.*

**BELOW:** animatronic dinosaurs at the Natural History Museum.

complex, the **Hall of Prayer for Good Harvests ❺** (Qiniandian). First constructed in 1420, the hall was struck by lightning in 1889 and burned to the ground. It was rebuilt according to the original plans.

The structure is built on a three-level marble terrace, each level surrounded by a balustrade. The pointed roof, with its three levels, its 50,000 blue-glazed tiles – blue symbolises heaven – and its golden point, was constructed without using a single nail and has no spars or beams. It is supported by 28 wooden pillars; the central four, the **Dragon Fountain Pillars**, are almost 20 metres (66 ft) tall and represent the four seasons. The first ring of pillars surrounding them represents the 12 months; the outer ring, also of 12 pillars, the 12 divisions of the day. The wood for the pillars came from the southwestern Chinese province of Yunnan. In the centre of the floor is a marble plaque with veining showing a dragon and a phoenix (symbolising the emperor and the empress).

To the east are more imperial buildings and the **Long Corridor**, a favoured spot for elderly musicians. This can be accessed with a simple "park only" ticket.

## Outside the park

Leave the Temple of Heaven via the west gate, and follow Tianqiao Nandajie. Before 1949, this was a meeting place of acrobats, fortune-tellers, sellers of miraculous elixirs, and other shady characters. Even today, the markets around here bustle with life, and the residents of this district are considered a separate breed.

A sports park on this street marks the site of the **Altar of Agriculture ❻** (Xiannongtan; open daily 9am–5pm; entrance fee), which stood symmetrically opposite the Temple of Heaven and was dedicated to the legendary emperor Shennong, the "first farmer" in China. This was one of the eight altars which, in addition to the Temple of Heaven, were central to the ritual life of Ming and Qing emperors. Parts of the site have been demolished or converted in recent times, but some old structures survive intact, notably the Hall of Jupiter, now housing the instructive **Museum of Chinese Architecture** (Gudai Jianzhu Bowuguan).

Beijing's **Natural History Museum ❼** (Ziyan Bowuguan; open daily, 8.30am–5pm; entrance fee), is in an ivy-clad building just to the west of the Temple of Heaven. The museum has an exhibition of more than 5,000 species in palaeontology, zoology and botany, but captions are in Chinese only. It has a number of dinosaurs: in the centre of the hall is the skeleton of the one-horned Qingdaosaurus. The skeleton of Mamenchisaurus, twice the size, was dug up in the village of Mamenxi in Sichuan Province. In contrast to these giants, there are the remains of a Lufengsaurus – 2 metres (6½ ft) high and 6 metres (20 ft) long – from Yunnan Province, and of a parrot-beaked dinosaur that was no

bigger than a cat. There is also an entertaining collection of animatronic dinosaurs in the poorly lit basement, which growl and bellow at passers-by, sometimes in Mandarin.

Just across the street from the Temple of Heaven's east gate and reached via a footbridge, is an ugly twin-towered building housing the ever-popular **Hongqiao Market ❽** (open daily 8.30am–7pm). Clothes, shoes, watches and fake designer goods are sold on the first and second floors; antiques, silk and – emphatically – pearls on the second and third.

At the time of writing, the upper floors were being renovated, but will eventually be the jewellery centre. The many stalls are densely packed and manned by merchants from the pearl-producing provinces who vie for customers' attention. Bargaining usually brings good results here. China now supplies 95 per cent of the world market of cultured freshwater pearls. Quality has steadily improved. Most pearl vendors come from families that produce cultured freshwater pearls, and will usually help you compare strands of pearls to

learn about lustre and shape. They will also string pearls to order. If you buy, be sure to bargain, request that knots be tied between each pearl, and purchase a good clasp.

About 4 km (2½ miles) to the east, past Longtan Park and close to the Third Ring Road, is **Panjiayuan Market ❾** (Ghost Market; Huawei Lu Dajie), also sometimes known as the Dirt Market. Formerly a small gathering of merchants selling goods of variable quality, it has expanded into a sprawling market offering a vast array of goods; scroll paintings, porcelain, silk items and Mao memorabilia are here in abundance. This is a good place to buy antiques such as old mah-jong sets, antique clocks, watches and gramophone players. Prices can be low if you bargain hard.

Just to the south, by the ring road, is **Beijing Curio City ❿** (Dongsanhuan Nan Lu, west of Huawei Bridge): four floors filled with more antiques, paintings, jewellery and furniture. It also has a duty-free shop, but remember to bring your passport, or you will not be allowed to buy anything. ❑

Map on page 116

*Hongqiao Market is the place to come for pearls.*

# RESTAURANTS

*Beijing/Chinese*

**Old Beijing Noodle**
29 Chongwenmen Dajie.
Tel: 6705-6705. Open:
11am–2:30pm, 5–9pm. $.
This restaurant has revived the lively tradition of (old-style) Beijing fast food. Waiters announce the arrival or departure of each customer at high volume.

**Tiantan Restaurant**
West gate of Tiantan Park.
Tel. 6702-0422. Open:
6am–1am. $$.
Good location near the Temple of Heaven, with

Beijing and Shandong cuisine, as well as some imperial-style dishes.

*Imperial*

**Yushan Restaurant**
87 Tiantan Lu. Tel: 6701
4263. Open: 10:30am–
1:30pm, 4:30–8pm. $$$.
A popular place, located just a few hundred yards west of the north gate of the Temple of Heaven.

*Vegetarian*

**Gongdelin**
158 Qianmen Nan Dajie. Tel:
6702-0867. Open:

10:30am–8:30pm. $$.
Specialises in amazing mock meat dishes, carefully crafted from beancurd, mushrooms and vegetables. Some are almost *too* realistic.

*Yunnanese*

**Daijiacun**
80 Tiantan Donglu. Tel:
6714-0145. Open:
9:30am–9:30pm. $$$.
The Dai people of China's southwestern Yunnan Province are related to Thais. Their slightly spicy food often uses pineapple and coconut. Among the

specialities are rice and other dishes steamed in bamboo tubes, wild mushrooms, snake, and rice wine. Dancers entertain you during your meal – and invite you to join them.

• • • • • • • • • • • •
*Prices are for a typical dinner for one (three dishes with beer in Chinese restaurants, or a three-course meal with a half bottle of house wine in Western-style restaurants).*
*$ = under 50 Rmb*
*$$ = 50–100 Rmb*
*$$$ = 100–150 Rmb*
*$$$$ = over 150 Rmb*

# THE LAKE DISTRICT AND THE NORTH

Part of the former lakeside pleasure grounds of the
imperial family, Beihai Park is now accessible to all.
To the north are the attractive back lakes, and the
famous Bell and Drum towers, while further
east is a cluster of notable temples

I n the 15th century, the large lake
in the middle of Beijing was
divided into two parts. Today, the
area around the Northern Lake,
**Beihai Park** ❶ (park open daily,
6am–9pm, closes at 6pm in winter;
buildings open daily 8am–5pm;
entrance fee *see margin note on page
123)* is one of the most beautiful and
popular places to spend a day out in
the Inner City, no matter what the
season. In winter, the lake is used for
skating. The very youngest enjoy
themselves on ice sledges – daring
contraptions consisting of a wooden
chair, or sometimes just a large plank,
fastened onto two runners. In days
gone by, the ice was smoothed with
glowing irons for imperial celebrations, but modern-day skaters must
make do with a less even surface.

During the rest of the year, the lake
is used for boating – some children
even swim in it during the summer –
and its banks attract those who enjoy
strolling and alfresco dining.

The other part of the lake, **Zhongnanhai** ❷ (literally "Central and
Southern Lake"), and its surroundings, were a pleasure garden for the
court. Right next to the Forbidden
City, this is where horse races and
hunts, birthday receptions and celebrations of the Lantern Festival took
place. After 1949, Mao, Zhou Enlai,
Liu Shaoqi and other notables lived

here, and Mao's private library is
still here today. Surrounded by its
massive wall, Zhongnanhai has been
the seat of the politbureau and the
state council since 1949. Foreigners
are not admitted into this modern-
day Forbidden City unless they are
invited to an audience.

## Islands in the lake

The location of the park – west of
Jingshan (Coal Hill) and northwest
of the Imperial Palace – marks the
centre of Kublai Khan's Mongol

Map
on page
122

**LEFT:** the White
Dagoba towers over
Beihai Park.
**BELOW:** picturesque
Yinding Bridge is
surrounded by bars
and restaurants.

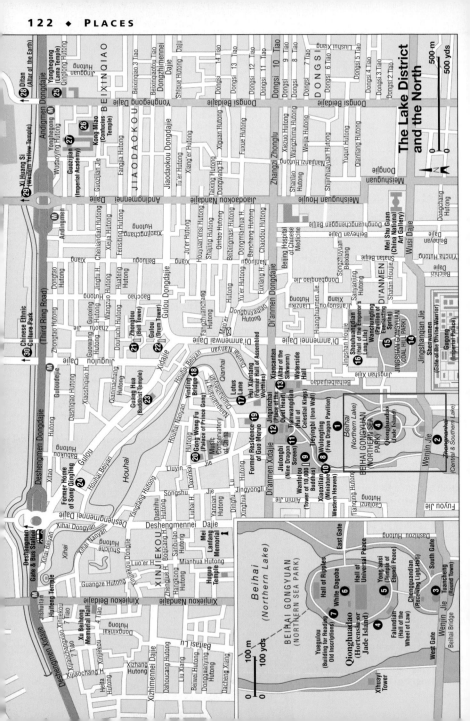

capital, Khanbaliq (known as Dadu in Chinese). In the south of the park, with a separate entrance, is the **Round Town** ❸ (Tuancheng; open Tues–Sun 8am–4.30pm; entrance fee), one of three islands in the Northern Lake. The khan had this island landscaped, along with the surrounding area, and from this spot, according to Marco Polo, he ruled in inimitable splendour. However, only the trees remain from that time, all the architecture of the Mongol Yuan dynasty having been destroyed.

An exquisite 1.5-metre (5-ft) wide nephrite container, in which Kublai Khan kept his wine, also survives; it stands next to the entrance of a pavilion with white marble pillars and a blue roof. In the 18th century, a poem by the emperor Qianlong praising the beauty of this work of art was engraved on the inside of the vessel. A second jewel in the Round Town is a 1.5-metre (5-ft) white jade statue of Buddha with inlaid jewels. It can be seen in the **Receiving Light Hall** (Chengguandian).

**Hortensia Island** ❹ (Jade Island or Qionghuadao) is the most impressive part of the park as far as scenery and history are concerned. Going from the main south gate leads to a bridge more than 600 years old, across which is the **Temple of Eternal Peace** ❺ (Yong'ansi), and beyond it, the **Hall of the Wheel of Law** (Falundian). From here, a twisting path leads up uneven steps to the 35-metre (115-ft) **White Dagoba** ❻, an onion-shaped shrine in the Tibetan style, built on the ruins of a Ming palace in honour of the fifth Dalai Lama on the occasion of his visit to Beijing in 1651. It was this onion shape that led foreigners living in Beijing during the republican era to refer to it as "the peppermint bottle". In 1679, and again in 1731, the dagoba was destroyed by earthquakes, but was rebuilt on both occasions. It suffered only cracks during

the 1976 Tangshan earthquake, and during restoration a golden reliquary containing two small bone fragments, probably of prominent lamas, was found. The view from here of the Forbidden City, Beihai and Zhongnanhai, and the numerous *hutong* of the Inner City, is only surpassed by the view from the peak of Jingshan.

On the northern side of the dagoba, the path leads through a labyrinth of stairs, corridors, pavilions and bizarre rock formations carved into grottoes intended to resemble the houses of Daoist saints, and goes steeply down to the lake shore, which is bordered by a long, semicircular covered walkway. Halfway up the northwestern slope of the island is a statue, nearly 4 metres (13 ft) tall, called the **Plate for Gathering Dew** (Cheng Lu Pan), which was placed here by Emperor Qianlong. It is thought to represent one of the Eight Immortals and records a legend from the life of the emperor Wudi, who ruled early in the first century. When Wudi heard that drinking dewdrops would make him immortal, he commanded

As with the Forbidden City and Temple of Heaven, it's worth buying an all-inclusive ticket *(tao piao)* when visiting Beihai Park. This entitles you to access all the places of interest within the park.

**BELOW:** musicians using traditional instruments perform in the Temple of Eternal Peace in Beihai Park.

*Beihai Park is a popular place for weddings.*

**BELOW:** keeping pet birds is one of Beijing's enduring hobbies.

a slave to sit outdoors overnight with a bowl to catch the dewdrops falling from Heaven, and bring them to him so that he could refresh himself and become immortal.

Directly below this statue is the **Building for Reading Old Inscriptions** ❼ (Yuegulou). A collection of 495 stone tablets is kept here, engraved with the work of famous Chinese calligraphers. Most of them date from the 18th century; some, however, go back more than 1,500 years. Rubbings were taken from the tablets – one of the earliest forms of printing.

Next door, in the Hall of Ripples, is the **Fangshan Restaurant** *(see page 134)*, established in 1925 by chefs of the imperial household who were suddenly left unemployed when Pu Yi was forced out of the Imperial Palace in 1924.

### By the lake shore

From here, a ferry takes visitors to the **Five Dragon Pavilion** ❽ (Wulongting), on the northwest lake shore. These buildings from the Ming era are built in a zigzagging

line over the water and connected by walkways. The largest pavilion, with its double-stepped, curved roof, forms the head of a curving dragon when seen from above. Emperors used to fish from this point. Beside the quay where the boats tie up is the 700-year-old, 4-metre (13-ft) wide **Iron Wall** (Tieyingbi), although it is not iron at all, but igneous rock. It was originally placed in front of a Buddhist convent which had been a bell foundry in the Ming dynasty: hence the idea that it was made of iron. It was moved to its present location in 1947.

The path leads west from the waterfront to the **Tower of 10,000 Buddhas** ❾ (Wanfolou), built by the Emperor Qianlong in the 18th century on the occasion of his mother's 80th birthday. The pure gold statuettes of Buddha that filled the niches inside the tower were stolen – like so many other treasures – by European troops in 1900.

To the south stands what is probably the biggest pavilion in China, the **Miniature Western Heaven** ❿ (Xiaoxitian), which was built in 1770

as a shrine to Guanyin, the goddess of mercy. In the Mahayana Buddhist tradition that established itself in China, the idea of the "Western Heaven" is similar to Christian concepts of paradise. Inside, Buddhist paintings are exhibited. The **Nine Dragon Screen ⓫** (Jiulongbi) originally served to ward off the god of fire from a workshop for translating and printing Lamaist scriptures that Qianlong had built in honour of his mother. When, in an ironic twist of fate, that building succumbed to fire in 1919, a gymnasium was built in its place, and the screen was moved here. A few steps to the east of the Dragon Screen is the **Hall of the Celestial Kings** (Tianwangdian), a Ming-dynasty workshop for the translation and woodblock-printing of Buddhist scriptures.

The **Place of the Quiet Heart ⓬** (Jingxinzhai), just beyond, invites walkers to rest and pause in contemplation. It is a delightful garden within a garden laid out by Qianlong, interspersed with lotus pools, halls, pavilions and living quarters. Empress Cixi often used to lunch here. At other times, Manchu princes used these peaceful surroundings to wrestle with Confucian classics. Pu Yi used this space to write his memoirs, *From Emperor to Citizen*.

On the other side of the bridge is the **Altar of the Silkworm ⓭** (Xiancantan), one of the eight altars that played a large part in the ritual life of Ming and Qing emperors. Here the empress would come to perform a ceremony honouring the goddess of silkworms – the wife of the mythical Yellow Emperor, who supposedly discovered the secret of the silkworm – and to pray for a good harvest. Turned into a tea house during the republican era, it presently serves as a nursery school for children of high-level officials.

## Imperial viewpoint

Directly behind the Forbidden City is **Jingshan ⓮** (Coal Hill; open daily 6am–9pm; entrance fee), an artificial land form which came into existence at the beginning of the 15th century, when the Ming emperor Yongle had moats dug all around the Forbidden City. Feng

**BELOW:** trishaw tours are very popular.

*Water calligraphy, as here at Jingshan Park, is thought to stimulate mind and body. The characters are usually painted with plain water so the fine brushwork quickly disappears.*

**BELOW:** there are views across the Forbidden City and much of central Beijing from the top of Jingshan.

shui – Chinese geomancy – probably played a decisive part in the choice of a suitable spot to tip the spoil. The aim of feng shui is to site buildings in harmony with the topography and, by this means, to influence them positively. Jingshan served to protect the Forbidden City from malignant influences from the north. Pragmatism must also have played a role in the choice, as any approaching enemy could be seen at a distance by a lookout placed at such a height.

Five pavilions, dating from the 16th century, crown the chain of hills and emphasise their zigzagging lines. Each pavilion once housed a bronze figure of Buddha, but four of these were plundered by European troops in 1900. The surrounding park was not opened to the public until 1928. Before this, it was a private imperial garden, and eunuchs, palace ladies and the imperial family members spent their leisure hours strolling in its picturesque scenery.

This is where Chongzhen, the last Ming emperor, committed suicide in 1644, after the rebellious peasant armies walked into Beijing through gates left open by traitorous eunuchs. Upon hearing the terrible news, the beleaguered emperor jumped on a horse and tried to flee the city, but was forced to turn back. His route took him past the Jesuit residence, and Father Johann Adam Schall von Bell saw him – for the first and last time – as he galloped by. When he got back to the palace, Chongzhen ordered his wife to hang herself and his sons to hide. He attempted to kill his 15-year-old daughter, but she defended herself, losing a hand to his sword in the process. The emperor then went out the back gate of the palace, climbed Jingshan and hanged himself from a locust tree. The tree was uprooted during the Cultural Revolution, but was replaced in 1981 and is now a favourite photo spot for Chinese tourists.

Skyscrapers have taken over from the hill as the highest point in Beijing. Yet the view from the **Pavilion of Everlasting Spring** ⑮ (Wanchungting), on the middle of the five peaks, is still superb. Looking straight along the north–south axis of the city, the sea of curved golden roofs that is the Forbidden City lies to the south, with the White Dagoba towering over Beihai Lake to the west. To the north are the massive Drum and Bell towers; and on a clear day you can see, on the horizon to the northwest, the silhouette of the Western Mountains.

In the north of the park is the **Hall of the Emperor's Long Life** ⑯ (Shouhuangdian), where the corpses of empresses were laid before being removed to tombs outside the city. It now houses a children's cultural centre.

## Shichahai and the back lakes

The **Sea of the Ten Buddhist Temples** (Shichahai) is a complex of lakes north of Beihai Park. Historically, this area has harboured many

beautiful courtyard palaces of Manchu princes and Qing-dynasty officials. Today it remains one of the most attractive parts of Beijing.

In the last few years the attractions of the so-called "back lakes" have been increasingly capitalised on by entrepreneurs, who have opened innumerable restaurants, bars and cafés here. Their business received a major boost during the SARS panic of 2003 when many stir-crazy Beijingers apparently reasoned that it was safe to go to bars and restaurants so long as they were outdoors, or partly outdoors.

The most recent – and high-end – concentration is along **Lotus Lane** ⓱, which used to be known as Lotus Flower Market. A pedestrian-only area on the southwestern shore of Qianhai Lake, the lane is lined with bars, restaurants and coffee houses. On sultry summer nights, it is packed with young people eager to enjoy the lake, the stars, the bars and each other. Another nightlife area is concentrated around dinky little **Yinding Bridge** ⓲ (Silver Ingot Bridge), where Houhai meets

Qianhai Lake. New "designer" bars are popping up all the time by the lake shores; a long strip of them runs along Houhai Nanyan on the southern shore of Houhai, and also along Qianhaibeiyan, the street between Lotus Lane and the Yinding Bridge.

Nearby on Qianhai Xijie is the former **residence of Guo Moruo** ⓳ (open Tues–Sun, 9am–4.30pm; entrance fee), an influential figure in the rise of communism in China. Guo was born in Sichuan Province in 1892, the son of a wealthy landlord. Following a spell in Japan, where he studied at Kyushu Imperial University, he returned to China in 1921 and became known as a respected author as well as a proponent of change, having been profoundly influenced by the Russian October Revolution of 1917. He soon became an early adherent of the fledgling Chinese Communist Party, meeting with Mao in 1926. Although exiled to Japan for ten years by the Guomindang government (having written an article criticising Chiang Kai-shek), he again returned to China in 1937, and later

Map on page 122

**BELOW:** relaxing at one of the many lakeside bars in the area.

*The Palace of Prince Gong is thought to have provided inspiration for the classic novel,* Dream of the Red Mansions.

**BELOW:** it is possible to climb up the 55-metre (180-ft) Drum Tower to admire the original drum inside.

held several posts in the new Communist state. Guo was one of the first people to be attacked by the Red Guards during the Cultural Revolution. The buildings are set in leafy grounds; inside, among the polished floors and old furniture, are photographs and quotations from the great man, but most are captioned in Chinese only.

Also nearby is the **Palace of Prince Gong ⑳** (Gong Wang Fu; open daily 8.30am–4.30pm; entrance fee), the world's largest extant courtyard house and a very popular destination for tour groups. Prince Gong, the brother of emperor Xian Feng, virtually ran the country during the minorities of the emperors Tongzhi and Guangxu, from 1861 to 1884. His home and its 5.7-hectare (14-acre) grounds, including lush gardens, are now occupied by the China Conservatory of Music. The historic structures in the complex include Beijing's only preserved Qing-dynasty theatre. Here, guests are served by women wearing traditional costumes of the period and treated to a sample of Beijing Opera.

## The Bell and Drum towers

On the east side of the back lakes are two towers dating from the rule of Kublai Khan. They have endured so many twists and turns of history that surviving the wars and revolutions of the twentieth century seems relatively unremarkable. Both of the towers stand at the northern end of Di'anmenwai Dajie, and once formed the northernmost point of the city. However, during the period of Mongol rule they stood at the centre of the capital city of Dadu. Under Emperor Yongle, the towers were rebuilt in 1420, somewhat to the east of their original position.

After the original wooden **Bell Tower ㉑** (Zhonglou; open daily 9am–5.30pm; entrance fee) was destroyed in a fire, the present tower, 33 metres (108 ft) high, was built in 1747. The **Drum Tower ㉒** (Gulou; open daily 9am–5.30pm; entrance fee) was last restored in 1800. In earlier years, 24 big drums were kept inside – only one has survived – which were struck 13 times every evening at 7pm to signal the start of the night hours and also the closing of the city gates. The drums were struck again every two hours, the last time being at 5am. By that hour, the officials to be present at the imperial morning audience were supposed to have taken up their kneeling positions just in front of the Hall of Supreme Harmony – failure to do so brought heavy penalties.

The day officially began at 7am with the ringing of the huge iron bell of the Bell Tower. When this proved too quiet, an even bigger bronze bell was installed in the tower, which could be heard 20 km (12 miles) away. The bronze bell has now disappeared, but the iron bell is on display behind the tower. The building is so sturdy it survived the earthquake of 1976 without major damage: only one stone ornamental figure on the roof is said to have fallen down.

Inside the recently refurbished Drum Tower is the one remaining original drum, damaged during the Opium Wars of the 19th century, now flanked by two brightly painted replicas. Climb the steep staircase of 69 steps for an unmatched view of a disappearing old-style neighbourhood. Looking down upon the grey and often grass-covered tile roofs, separated into a variety of geometric shapes by the walls of the *hutong*, you can get a sense of how each *siheyuan* courtyard is a community in itself.

Beyond the Yinding Bridge, on the east bank of Houhai, is the **Guang Hua Buddhist Temple** ㉓ (open daily 8.30am–5pm; entrance fee). Constructed during the Yuan dynasty, this active temple is now home to the Beijing Buddhist Society. While it is only medium-sized in relation to some temples, it is well preserved and stocked with the usual colourful array of Buddhist statues and artefacts.

The **former home of Song Qingling** ㉔ (open Tues–Sun 9am–5pm; entrance fee), honorary president of the People's Republic of China, and wife of Sun Yat-sen, is

nearby at 46 Beiheyan Jie, on the western bank of Houhai. The grounds were formerly part of the palace of Prince Chun, Pu Yi's father. The house where Pu Yi was born is just south of here, and occupied by the Ministry of Health.

Song Qingling moved into the house in 1963 and lived there until her death in 1981. The guest room contains an exhibition of photographs, documents, and objects from her life: her pampered Shanghai childhood as a daughter of one of China's most prominent families; her years as a student, her marriage to Sun Yat-sen, and her political activities and support for the resistance to Japanese occupation. An extract from her most famous speech, the essay, *Sun Yat-sen and his cooperation with the Communist Party*, is also on display.

## The Lama Temple

Further to the east is the **Lama Temple** ㉕ (Yonghegong; open daily 9am–4.30pm; entrance fee), one of the city's most beautiful and interesting temples. A visit here can

**BELOW:** remnants of the Cultural Revolution are hidden away in the city's remaining *hutong*.

*ORIENTATION*
*The area covered in this chapter extends north and east from Beihai Park and Jingshan to the Lama Temple. The final section covers the area north of the Second Ring Road out to the northern suburbs.*

**BELOW:**
the Lama Temple.

easily be combined with a walk in Ditan Park *(see page 133)*, on the far side of the Second Ring Road, or a tour of the Confucius Temple and the Imperial Academy, to the west.

At first glance, you might think it odd that a Tibetan Buddhist temple enjoys such prominence in the capital, given Beijing's high-profile squabbles with the Tibetan government-in-exile. But China's relationship with Tibet and its religion goes back further than the contemporary clashes. The presence of a Lamaist temple has been part of a centuries-long policy of pacifying the fractious "Land of the Snows", as well as other Lamaist states, such as Mongolia.

The name Yonghegong ("Palace of Eternal Harmony") points to the courtly and imperial origins of the temple. Built in 1694, when it formed part of the city wall, it served as a residence for Yongzheng, the fourth son of Emperor Kangxi, before he ascended to the throne in 1722. Traditionally, the home of an heir to the throne would be turned into a temple after he had become ruler, or – as in this case – after his death.

Yongzheng's son and successor, Qianlong, sent for 300 Tibetan monks and 200 Chinese pupils and installed them in his father's old palace. The palace then served as a temple-cum-monastery from 1744 to 1960, and was considered one of the most notable centres of Lamaist Buddhism outside Tibet. During the Qing dynasty, the temple was closed to the public except for the annual performance of the "devil dance", which was staged as a warning against succumbing to human weaknesses – anger, greed, wine, sex and so on. The dance can still be seen today during the Spring Festival.

During the Cultural Revolution, the monastery was closed, with parts of it converted into a shoe factory. Red Guards took over the complex, but they were forbidden to destroy or plunder it by order of Zhou Enlai. In spite of this, many monks were ill-treated and sent away to do manual labour in the countryside. In the early 1980s, the monastery was reopened and completely restored. More than 70 monks now live here in the rear part of the complex.

The Lama Temple belongs to the Yellow Hat or Gelugpa sect of Buddhism, predominant in Tibet, whose spiritual head is the Dalai Lama. While the Dalai Lama lives in exile, the second spiritual head of Tibetan Buddhism, the Panchen Lama, resides in Beijing. In contrast to the Dalai Lamas, the Panchen Lamas have recognised Chinese authority since the beginning of the 20th century. However, they have also defied the Chinese on at least one occasion.

Following the death of the 10th Panchen Lama in 1989, the Chinese government assembled a group of lamas known to be sympathetic to their wishes, and asked them to find a successor – a boy reincarnation of the previous Panchen Lama. But in 1995 it was revealed that the abbot in charge of the search committee had quietly asked for the Dalai Lama's approval of the chosen boy. When they discovered this, the Chinese authorities had the abbot arrested and put the boy and his parents under detention. They then announced that a new boy would be selected by the old method of drawing ivory lots from a golden urn. A new Panchen Lama was thus proclaimed in November 1995, but his validity is contested by Tibetans in exile.

Coming from the south, enter the temple grounds through a gate. After crossing the gardens, you pass into the inner courtyard with its Bell and Drum towers and two pavilions with steles in them. To the north is the **Hall of the Celestial Kings** (Tianwangdian), with statues of the Maitreya Buddha and two guardian divinities.

Beyond the pavilion is a stone representation of the World Mountain, Sumeru. In the **Hall of Eternal Harmony** (Yonghedian) there are three statues of Buddha surrounded by 18 Luohan. The buildings to the left and right of this inner courtyard

house a mandala and valuable *thangka* – figures representing the founder of the Yellow Hat sect, Tsongkhapa. Crossing the next courtyard, you come to the **Hall of Eternal Protection** (Yongyoudian), with statues of the Buddhas of longevity and medicine.

The halls to the left and right of the following courtyard contain, among other items, statues of Yab-Yum, a male and female divinity whose intimate sexual connection symbolises the cosmic unity of all opposites. This courtyard is bounded by the **Hall of the Wheel of Dharma** (Falundian), in the middle of which is a 6-metre (20-ft) high statue of Tsongkhapa. Behind this statue is the monastery's treasure: a miniature mountain of sandalwood, with 500 Luohan figures of gold, silver, copper, iron and tin.

The fifth inner courtyard ends at the **Pavilion of Ten Thousand Happinesses** (Wanfuge). This contains a 25-metre (80-ft) high Maitreya Buddha made from a single piece of sandalwood. The three-storey pavilion is linked by bridges to the two-storey side buildings that flank it.

*This inscription at the Lama Temple reads in Manchu, Tibetan, Chinese and Mongolian scripts.*

**BELOW:** an artist selling his calligraphy.

## The Confucius Temple

To the west, Guozijian Jie is graced by two of only a few existing *pailou* (decorative gates) left standing in Beijing. Along this street are two important landmarks.

The **Confucius Temple**  (Kong Miao; open daily 8.30am– 5pm; entrance fee) is now the centrepiece of the Capital Museum (Shoudu Bowuguan), which has a permanent display of artefacts related to the history and culture of Beijing. The temple remains one of the largest outside of Qufu, the birthplace of Confucius.

For many years after 1949, Confucianism was seen as the embodiment of the feudal ways that Communism was trying to eradicate. Most Confucian temples throughout China were thus converted to other uses, or simply abandoned. Beginning in the late 1980s, there was an effort to revive some of the basic precepts of Confucianism, such as respect for authority and the elderly. But a real comeback seems impossible in the diverse and ever-evolving society that is modern China.

*The ancient cypress tree at the Confucius Temple.*

**BELOW:** tea for sale.

Before the wide staircase leading up to the main hall, look out for a cypress tree. It is said that a branch came loose from this tree and brushed off the head of a disloyal officer as it fell to the ground. In the main hall, the **Hall of Great Achievements** (Dachengdian), there are some of the musical instruments which were so important in Confucian ceremonies.

Confucian thought is the basic underpinning of traditional Chinese society. The philosophy was especially apparent in the system of choosing mandarins for the civil service, which endured for 2,000 years. Candidates – who were locked up in cells for three days as they wrote the exam – were required to demonstrate flawless knowledge of the Confucian classics and mastery of a highly formulaic "three-legged" essay. Practical knowledge was not valued in this system.

One of the most impressive sights in the temple is the 198 stone tablets recording the names and hometowns of 51,624 candidates who successfully passed such tests held during the Yuan, Ming and Qing dynasties. The stone tablets can be seen in the pavilions around the **Gate of the First Teacher** (Xianshimen).

Tradition dictated that on the right of a temple there should be an academy. So in the year 1306, during the Yuan dynasty, the **Imperial Academy** (Guozijian: open daily 9am–4.30pm; entrance fee) was founded as a school to teach the Chinese language to Mongol boys and Mongol to Chinese boys, as well as educating all pupils in all of the martial arts. Later, the academy became a university which, in 1462, had 13,000 students. In total, the academy was responsible for producing 48,900 successful *jinshi* scholars. The building was subsequently turned into the Capital Library, and is now part of the Capital Museum.

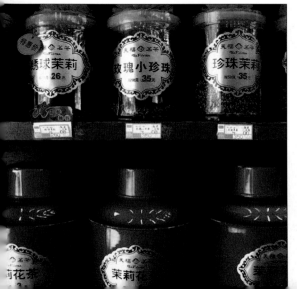

## North of the Lama Temple

North of the Lama Temple is **Ditan Park** (open daily 6am–9pm; entrance fee) which spreads around the **Altar of the Earth** (Ditan; entrance fee) **28**, one of the original eight altars, along with the Temple of Heaven, that played a great role in the ritual life of the Ming and Qing emperors.

To the northwest, near the junction of Huangsi Dajie and Andingmenwai Dajie, between the Second and Third Ring Roads, is the **Western Yellow Temple** (Xi Huang Si; no fixed opening times or fee) **29**, among the best surviving examples of Lamaist architecture in Beijing. Originally two temples, Eastern and Western, stood here, but they were destroyed in 1958 during the Great Leap Forward. The Eastern Temple was built by the Qing emperor Shunzhi in 1652 for the fifth Dalai Lama, on the occasion of his visit to the imperial court. A year later, the Western Temple was built to house his retinue. The most spectacular surviving structure is the **White Pagoda**, which Qianlong had built in 1780 to honour the sixth Panchen Lama, who died of smallpox while visiting Beijing. Subsequent Chief Lamas at the Lama Temple were required to have had smallpox and recovered (and be therefore immune) so that they could avoid similar fates.

The **Chinese Ethnic Culture Park** **30** (open daily 8.30am–6pm; entrance fee) on Minzu Lu, just west of the main Olympic complex and south of the Fourth Ring Road, is a large "cultural" theme park popular with school groups.

The park, which is divided into two halves, features a large number of fairly convincing reconstructions of buildings from all over China, as well as song and dance performances and other assorted theatrical entertainment. The Ethnic Culture Park has taken over from the Palace of the Minorities *(see page 108)* as the place to come for a (government-approved) crash course in minority culture in China. Most visitors, however, are likely to find it rather tacky. ❑

Map on page 122

*The Gateway to the Altar of the Earth (Ditan), one of the original eight altars in the city.*

**BELOW:** performance at the Chinese Ethnic Culture Park.

# RESTAURANTS & BARS

## Restaurants

### Beijing / Chinese

**Beijing Noodle King (Jingweimian Dawang)**
35 Dianmen Xidajie, Xicheng District. Tel: 6405-6666. Open: 10:30am–10:30pm. $.
A bustling, bright place with a sedan chair outside, and doormen in old-style clothing and fake braids who shout out the arrival of each guest.

**Mei Mansion**
24 Da Xiang Feng Hutong. Tel: 6612-6845. Open: 11am–2pm, 5–10pm. $$$$.
This pleasant restaurant features food created for the great Beijing Opera star, Mei Lanfang. Mei was a northerner but his chef was a southerner who created a kind of north-south fusion cuisine which the family reportedly still eats to this day.

**Shuaifu Restaurant**
19 Qianhai Beiyan. Tel: 6618-5347/48. Open: 5pm–2am. $$.
This old-style restaurant features food that Marshal Nie Rongzhen used to serve at banquets; it was originally started by the famous military leader's chef.

**Yiwanju Old Beijing Noodles**
Yayuncun (Asian Games Village) branch, Building 6, Anhuili District 4. Tel: 6491-1258. Open: 11am–11pm. $.
Popular with locals, Yiwanju is a cheaper, more understated version of the old-time Beijing noodle house. Plates still clatter, and waiters still holler in the mock-Qing setting.

**Yueming Lou**
21a Ya'er Hutong, Shichahai, Xicheng District. Tel: 6400-2069. Open: 9am–midnight. $$.
A former church that has been converted into an old Beijing-style restaurant, with beautiful views of the lakes and surrounding *hutong* from its third floor terrace.

### Hakka

**Ke Jia Cai**
Shichahai Qianhai Nan Yan. Tel: 6404-2259. Open: 11am–10:30pm. $$.
A sprawling restaurant with a lantern-hung patio that specialises in the wholesome food of the Hakka people.

### Muslim

**Kaorouji**
14 Qianhai Dongyan. Tel: 6404-2554. Open: 11am–2pm, 5–11pm. $$.
This is an old Muslim restaurant popular with Beijing's Hui residents. The caged mynah birds that greet diners in Chinese as they enter the restaurant are always a hit with children. Staff may also be able to arrange for a meal to be eaten on a boat on nearby Qianhai Lake.

### Hunanese

**Yuelu Mountain Dining Place (Wushan Luyu)**
10 Lotus Lane (He Hua Shi Chang). Tel: 6617-2696. Open: 11–2am. $$.
Splendid Hunanese food in a sleek setting that combines traditional with modern. Chinese readers will find interesting books on its wooden shelves while those seeking privacy can reserve private rooms upstairs.

### Imperial

**Fangshan Restaurant**
1 Wenjin Jie, inside Beihai Park South Gate. Tel: 6401-1889. Open: 11am–1:30pm, 5–8pm. $$$$.
Opened in 1925 by three imperial chefs in a traditional courtyard on the shore of Beihai Lake, Fangshan produces dishes once served to Qing emperors. Calligraphy and antique furniture adorn the stylish dining rooms. An extensive menu features haute cuisine from across China. Set banquets start at 150 Rmb per person for a relatively simple meal to more than 1,000 Rmb for a truly imperial feast.

**Li Family Restaurant (Lijia Cai)**
11 Yangfang Hutong, Deshengmennei. Tel: 6618-0107. Open: 6–8pm. $$$$.
This family-run place in

**LEFT AND RIGHT:** modish bars along Lotus Lane.

an old courtyard house
specialises in imperial
cuisine. It's very popular,
s book at least two days
in advance.

### Shaoxing

**Kongyiji**
Shichahai Houhai Nanan. Tel:
6618-4917. Open:
10am–2pm, 4–10:30pm. $$.
This popular themed
diner recreates the
ancient flavours of
Shaoxing, the southern

home town of famed
writer Lu Xun. Reserva-
tion advised.

### Sichuanese

**Beijing Bamboo Garden
Hotel**
24 Xiaoshiqiao Hutong
Jiugulou Dajie. Tel: 6403-
2229. Open: 7–11am,
noon–2pm and 6–9pm. $$.
Delicious Sichuan food
served in the middle of a
bamboo garden; eat on
the terrace or in the wide-
windowed dining hall.
**Sichuan Restaurant**
14 Liuyln Jie, Xicheng District. Tel: 6615-6924. Open:
11am–2pm, 5–9pm. $$.
This well known restau-
rant serves excellent
Sichuan food in the
midst of the gardens of
the Prince Gong Palace,
one of the best-pre-
served – and most elab-
orate – courtyard homes
in the city. A memorable
experience.

### Southeast Asian

**Buffalo**
6 Lotus Lane (He Hua Shi
Chang). Tel: 6617-2242.
Open: 9:30–2am. $$$.
This restaurant has artis-
tic decor and traditional-
style wooden furniture
adorned with plush silk
pillows. An excellent place
for a candlelit dinner of
southeast Asian cuisine.
**Café Sambal**
43 Doufuchi Hutong (east of
Jiugulou Dajie). Tel: 6400-
4875. Open: noon–midnight.
$$–$$$.
Flavoursome Malaysian
food in stylish surround-
ings, with an attractive
courtyard for the summer.

### Vietnamese

**Nuage**
22 Qianhai Lake East Bank.
Tel: 6401-9581. Open:
11–1am. $$.
This Vietnamese restau-
rant's languid style and
lakeside location give it

the sultry, airy atmos-
phere of a tropical
escape.

### Bars

The back lakes area,
from Lotus Lane in the
south to Houhai in the
north, is full of bars.
Lotus Lane is the most
"designer" area and
prices are relatively high
– worth it if you want to
have a seat right by the
water's edge. **The Water
of Life Bar**, **Lotus Blue**,
**Sex and Da City** and
**Wanrong's Flowers** all
vie for your attention.
There are plenty more
bars to choose from on
Qianhai Beiyan leading
up to Yinding Bridge; the
area around the bridge is
very lively, and there is
also a long line of bars
on the south shore of
Houhai Lake along
Houhai Nanyan.

# BEIJING'S PARK LIFE

**From first light, Beijingers begin to fill parks, pavements, alleys, grass verges and any space large enough to swing a leg or bat a shuttlecock. It's a fascinating spectacle**

Walk along any Beijing street early in the morning, and you will see old men shuffle out of their homes to escape the chaos of their tiny apartments. In their hands are bird cages, which they swing back and forth as they make their way to the nearest park, where they join people of all ages enjoying myriad activities.

Stroll through one of the larger parks, such as Longtan, Tiantan or Ditan, and watch the fascinating mixture of martial arts, breathing exercises, Beijing opera, calligraphy, ballroom dancing, *Yang Ge* dancing, badminton, jogging, hanging from trees, shouting exercises, meditation, kite-flying and, the newest addition, walking the dog. *Tai chi* shadow boxers draw the eye with slow, flowing movements as they practice "monkey's retreat" or "send the tiger over the mountain."

As the exercisers disperse, elderly people spread out chessboards, mah-jong tiles, dominoes or playing cards. Spectators roll jangling steel balls around their hands, a practice said to prevent rheumatism.

By the time of the rush hour, the parks have regained a little of their tranquillity – until the onslaught of lunchbreakers arrive on the scene to break the quiet once more.

**RIGHT:** Fighting fit. Sword drills are a key element of the martial art of *wushu*.

**ABOVE:** *Qigong* practitioners use slow, precise breathing exercises as a means of focusing their strength. *Qi* means "vital energy" or "life-force", which adherents believe can be positively channelled.

**ABOVE LEFT:** In order to clear the mind, some people stand for tens of minutes, even hours, apparently staring at a tree. Others balance on bricks to maintain a precise position.

**ABOVE RIGHT:** New regulations have allowed most of Beijing's estimated 1 million canines to come out from hiding. Dog registration fees have been cut from $600 to $125 a year and owners are now allowed to walk their pets in daylight. But the relaxed regulations apply only to dogs 36cm (14 inches) and under.

## MUSICIANS IN THE PARK

It's not all limb-stretching in the parks of Beijing. In Temple of Heaven Park, aficionados of folk music and traditional Han music gather with their instruments to practise their skills (and earn a few *kuai* from passing tourists).

In keeping with the Confucian ideals of moderation and harmony, musicians keep it simple, playing variations on a single melodic line. The instruments, which have changed little over the centuries, range from the *erhu* (a simple, two-stringed fiddle) and the *zheng* (zither) to the *pipa* (four-stringed lute) and *dizi* (wooden flute).

With the advent of recent Western influences on China, traditional music has taken a back seat to pop and rock music. The latter, which developed as a youthful expression of protest, was outlawed until the late 1980s, when an official ban was reluctantly lifted by the authorities. Pop anthems are today the mainstay of the music scene. Still, it isn't hard to track down the traditional strains of Chinese music – either at formal performances in the Beijing Concert Hall or at casual gatherings in Temple of Heaven Park.

**ABOVE:** After all that communal exercise, there's nothing like a solitary nap on a park bench.

**BELOW:** *Tai chi* is the world's most popular martial art. By maximising the flow of *chi*, practitioners believe they can maintain good health. The most common form of *tai chi* is a slower version of the original martial art, enabling both young and old, fit and infirm, to partake.

**BELOW:** Ballroom dancing is popular with older people, who see it mainly as a form of exercise, and with younger people who take the art form seriously.

# EASTERN BEIJING

**The Dongcheng and Chaoyang districts in the east of the city are Beijing's business and commercial hub, home to five-star hotels, Western restaurants and an ever-expanding expat community. It's a prime shopping and nightlife area, too**

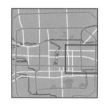

Map on page 140

Most travellers to Beijing arrive in the city's burgeoning eastern area, be it on a flight into Capital Airport or a train into Beijing Zhan, the main railway station. It is also in this part of the city that many find themselves staying, in a gleaming high-rise hotel where English is the official language and a McDonald's or Starbucks is certain to be just around the corner. For first-time visitors, it is not uncommon to feel shocked – even cheated – by the international modernity of it all, as though China should forever eschew high-rises, foreign fast-food outlets, ring roads and cars in order to preserve a more authentically "Chinese" environment for tourists.

The reality, of course, is that the West does not hold the patent on modernity. Eastern Beijing – especially Chaoyang District – may look a lot like big metropolitan cities around the world (albeit with more construction work), but it is still Chinese. This is the economic heart of the modern capital, and it is on this area that the government is focusing some of its grandest plans and greatest resources.

Eastern Beijing has long been the city's international district, home to scores of embassies and the diplomats who staff them. It is also the area in which, in the past, international journalists were required to live, and in which most still do. Beijing's first modern office building – the CITIC Building – was built here soon after Deng Xiaoping started his economic reforms,, and the area is now home to the China headquarters of hundreds of companies from around the world. A new Central Business District is being created around Chang'an and Jianguomen Avenue, in which more than 300 new high-rises are scheduled to be built. On the downside,

**LEFT:** Eastern Beijing is full of shopping opportunities.
**BELOW:** fountains outside the China World Centre.

*Upmarket shopping at Oriental Plaza.*

and somewhat paradoxically, this part of town can be somewhat insular – there are many people, both Chinese and foreign, who rarely ever venture out of its comfortable confines, or even into its side roads and back alleys where pockets of a more traditional lifestyle still carry on in the shadows of the modern capital.

## Wangfujing and around

A short distance to the east of the Imperial Palace is **Wangfujing ❶**. This street was originally called Shiwangfu, or "Ten Imperial Brothers Street". It was supposedly given this name when a Ming emperor ordered his ten brothers to take up residence here, so that he could keep an eye on them. It used to be referred to as "Morrison Street" by foreigners living in the Legation Quarter to the south, after the famous *Times* correspondent, George Morrison, who lived here at No. 98.

Always a smart address, in recent times Wangfujing has established itself as Beijing's premier shopping street. Pedestrianised as far up as Dong'anmen Dajie, it's a great place to stroll, window-shop and people-watch. Over the past few years,

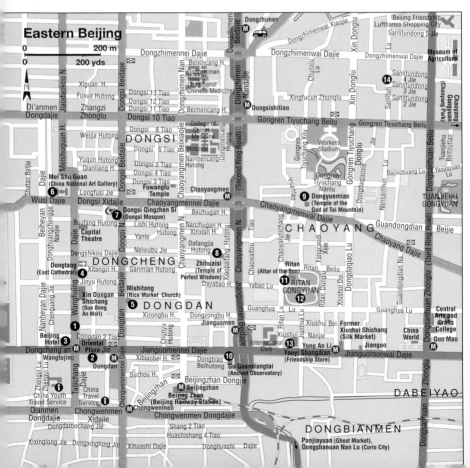

practically every building has been rebuilt, with the assistance of huge amounts of Hong Kong capital. This is the place to come to browse in upmarket Western-style shopping malls and department stores, both above and below street level.

For a time in the 1990s there was a flagship McDonald's on the southeast corner, at the junction with Chang'an Jie; it was knocked down to make way for Li Kai-shing's enormous **Oriental Plaza ❷**, a gleaming Hong-Kong-style shopping mall with a vast array of shops, food courts, and the **Sony Explora Science Centre** (open Mon–Fri 9am–5.30pm, Sat–Sun 10am–7pm; entrance fee), an interactive science museum popular with children.

The huge **Beijing Hotel ❸**, once the only place where foreigners could stay in the capital, is on the corner of Wangfujing and Dong Chang'an Jie. It was built in four stages. The earliest part of the building is the centre, dating from 1917, where ornate French-style vaulted ceilings and a sweeping staircase evoke the decadent days of the

1920s. The hotel was extended in 1954, and this section reflects the optimism of the early years of the People's Republic. The East Wing, added in 1974 towards the end of the Cultural Revolution, is, not surprisingly, somewhat bleak. The western section was added in 1989 and is a tribute to the financial freedoms of the Deng era. To the north is the **Sun Dong An Mall**, a pedestrian area renovated for the PRC's 50th anniversary.

Mixed among, and dwarfed by, the commercial high-rises are a few remnants of times past. The **East Cathedral ❹** (Dongtang; access for worship only), also known as St Joseph's, was burned to the ground in 1900, and had to be rebuilt. Prior to that the site was occupied by part of the house of Schall von Bell (see page 20), who died here in 1666. The grey-brick cathedral has an active congregation, and masses are held here on Sundays. With the redevelopment of Wangfujing, the churchyard has been converted into one of Beijing's most popular, and attractive, squares. Nearby on Dong'anmen

Map on page 140

*Beijing's East Cathedral has a large congregation. Christianity is a growth phenomenon in China, its popularity boosted by its association with the West.*

**BELOW:** Partly pedestrianised Wangfujing is Beijing's most prestigious shopping street.

# Beijing's New Architecture

**B**eijing is arguably undergoing its biggest architectural revolution since Communist planners swept through the city in the 1950s and began ordering the destruction of its ancient walls and traditional neighbourhoods. Indeed, the same government that razed a gracious imperial capital and built an ugly modern metropolis on its ruins is now hiring the world's top architects to come in and create buildings that would be considered daring in any city on earth.

Not everyone agrees with the unwritten policy to make the Chinese capital a design laboratory for the world, so it remains to be seen how many of the planned buildings will ultimately be completed, and in what manner. Even so, it is certain that by the start of the 2008 Olympics, Beijing will be architecturally a very different city than it is today.

The most prominently located of these adventurous architectural undertakings is the National Grand Theatre, located just behind the Great Hall of the People and across from the Zhongnanhai leadership compound. Designed by the French architect Paul Andreu, the theatre is a dramatic titanium and glass dome that has been dubbed "The Eggshell". Water and light play an important part in the theatre's design – the translucent shell will be illuminated by different colours, and entry is through an underwater tunnel. Complaints and controversy have dogged the design ever since it was selected, but the building is near completion so there is no turning back.

The "Eggshell's" counterpart, at least in the minds of irreverent Beijingers, is the "bird's nest", as the Beijing Olympic Stadium has been nicknamed. Designed by the firm of Herzog & De Meuron, in cooperation with the China Architecture Design Institute, the bowl-shaped, steel stadium does indeed resemble a bird's nest. Olympic swimming events will take place in the "Water Cube," as the solar-heated, cube-shaped National Swimming Centre with its extraordinary bubbled exterior is known.

Arguably the most avant-garde of all the new buildings in the works is the new headquarters for China Central Television, designed by superstar architect Rem Koolhaas and his firm. The building, which will stand just outside the eastern section of the Third Ring Road, consists of two leaning towers that bend to 90-degree angles at the top where they meet and form a tube – some call it a "Z" and some a trapezoid. A new terminal for Beijing's airport is also underway, designed by Norman Foster and billed as the world's most advanced – at a projected cost of nearly $2 billion, it is also likely to be one of the world's most expensive.

But expensive, cutting-edge architecture is not the purview of government alone. Indeed, the hip and successful Soho China real-estate firm has commissioned Pritzker Prize-winning architect Zaha Hadid to design an "independent micro-urban centre" of asymmetrical buildings. The complex is intended to be completely self-contained, so that its residents will be able to work, shop and live within its boundaries – an ultra-modern micro-city within the architecturally-evolving cosmopolis that is 21st-century Beijing. ❏

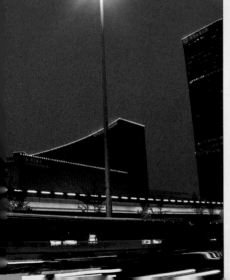

**LEFT:** the China World Centre, part of modern Chaoyang District in the east of the city.

Dajie is **Dong'anmen Night Market**, a good place to try street food. A long line of vendors sell a variety of regional specialities, including exotica such as fried locusts.

The **Rice Market Church** ❺ (Mishitang) at Dongdan Bei Jie (the next main street to the east, previously known as Rice Market Street) is an important Protestant church. The grey-brick building with its Chinese roof and double wooden eaves dates from the 1920s, when it was the seat of the Bible Society. Today it is home to the Chinese Christian Council.

At the northern end of Wangfujing is the **China National Art Gallery** ❻ (Mei Shu Guan; open Tues–Sun, 9am–4pm; entrance fee), with its 14 halls for changing exhibitions. This can be a good place to discover new as well as old trends in Chinese art. The museum employed a new director in 2004 and looks set to undertake more adventurous – even controversial – exhibitions in the future.

**Dongsi Mosque** ❼ is not open to the general public, so an appointment must be made for a visit. From the street one would hardly notice that there is a mosque at all – like Niu Jie Mosque *(see page 109)* it has no minaret or *muezzin*. The building dates from 1447, and in 1450 the Ming emperor Jiangtai gave it the title Qingzhensi (meaning "Temple of Purity and Light"), which is how all mosques are now referred to in Chinese.

## East from Wangfujing

Located to the east of Wangfujing, not far from the Second Ring Road, is the **Temple of Perfect Wisdom** ❽ (Zhihuaisi; open daily 9am–4pm; entrance fee). It was built as a family shrine by a eunuch named Wang Zhen in 1443, during the Ming dynasty, but closed six years later when Wang was executed, after which it became imperial property. Wood blocks used for printing the "Grand Collection of Buddhist Scriptures" are kept here.

On the other side of the Second Ring Road, **Dongyue Temple** ❾ (Temple of the God of Tai Mountain; open Tues–Sun 9am–4pm; entrance fee) is one of the few

*Map on page 140*

*ORIENTATION
The area covered in this chapter extends east from the Forbidden City to the Third Ring Road.*

**BELOW:** there is a wide choice of street food at Dong'anmen Night Market,

*Beijing's economic boom has made some individuals extremely wealthy, and luxury cars are now part of the scene. Mercedes-Benz, Porsche and, recently, Lamborghini have opened dealerships in the city.*

**RIGHT:** the Ancient Observatory.

Daoist temples in the city – this has less to do with a lack of Daoism in Beijing than the fact that Daoists traditionally shun urban areas.

The temple was built to honour the highest celestial ruler of the Tai mountain, one of the five Daoist holy mountains in China. Founded by Zhang Daoling during the Yuan dynasty, this was once the largest of its kind in northern China. After 1949 the temple was converted into schools and administrative offices, but reopened in 1999 after comprehensive restoration work.

Dongyue is now once more a thriving Daoist centre, and an interesting place to visit. The complex consists of three courtyards. Off the main courtyard is the **Hall of Tai Mountain** (Daizongbaodian) – in the centre of which is a statue of the god of Tai Mountain, surrounded by his high-ranking servants. Elsewhere are hundreds of other Daoist deities, dedicated to a wide variety of moral and spiritual codes – on controlling bullying and cheating, caring for animals, and upholding piety. *(For more on Daoism see pages 50 and 112.)*

At the junction of Jianguomennei and the Second Ring Road, is the **Ancient Observatory** ❿ (Gu Guanxiangtai; open Wed–Mon 9–11am and 1–4pm; entrance fee). Originally constructed in 1279 north of its present-day site, the observatory that you see today was built in the mid-15th century and sits atop a watchtower that was once a part of the city walls. It served both the Ming and Qing dynasties in making predictions based on astrology, as well as helping navigators who were about to go to sea.

Today the observatory is surrounded by ring roads and the roar of traffic, yet it remains an evocative reminder of the era in which Jesuit priests advised Chinese emperors, and reading the stars was of crucial importance to governance.

Northeast of the observatory, in the Jianguomen diplomatic quarter and not far from the Friendship Store, is **the Altar of the Sun** ⓫ (Ritan; open daily 6am–9pm; entrance fee), one of the eight altars which, along with the Temple of Heaven, played a great role in the

## Reading the Stars

In the 13th century, astronomers at the Yuan-dynasty imperial observatory fixed the length of the year at 365.2424 days – within one-thousandth of a day according to modern calculations. They achieved such precision with the aid of bronze astronomical instruments such as those on display in the Ancient Observatory. The three armillary spheres, quadrant for finding stars, celestial globe, equatorial theodolite for determining angles of elevation, altazimuth for determining the height of stars in the sky, and sextant were all used by these early Chinese scientists.

Such astonishing accuracy benefited astrology as much as astronomy. The casting of horoscopes earned the scientists the fortune and patronage they needed to develop their instruments and observatories. The *luo pan* (net tablet), a wooden or brass disc covered in hundreds of characters, was the most complicated astrological instrument. Seventeen concentric rings surround a small compass, which represents the *tai qi* (Great Origin or Ultimate Cause). The *luo pan*, backed up by the consultation of charts, was used in complex forms of divination based on calculating changes in the position of the stars and planets.

ritual life of the Ming and Qing emperors. The rebuilt altar still stands, and is sometimes used for alternative art exhibitions. **Ritan Park**  itself is a pleasant place for a stroll if you are in the neighbourhood – with rocks, ponds, meandering paths, flower beds and several good tea houses and restaurants. West of the park, **Yabao Lu** has suffered from the closure of the Russian Market, although stalls still set up along here, and cyrillic script remains almost as common as Chinese.

## Retail therapy

No trip to Beijing would be complete without some shopping. For traditional Chinese souvenirs, the **Friendship Store** is always a good source, if a little more pricey than some of the city markets. In the 1970s and 1980s this was just about the only place in town where foreigners could purchase such luxuries as wine and other Western goods. Bargaining is not countenanced here, but it remains the most reliable place to purchase Chinese goods such as silk items, porcelain and antiques.

Until it closed in January 2005, the **Silk Market**, in a cramped alleyway off Jianguomenwai, was one of the best places to hunt for bargains. Some of the vendors selling Gore-tex outdoor gear, rucksacks, suitcases, shoes and other clothing have relocated to Hongqiao Market (see page 119), while others await the opening of an adjacent (indoor) market, although high rents will dissuade many.

Further north is **Sanlitun** , a street of bars and restaurants popular with expats. In 1996 there was only one bar here, but in true Beijing style it was not long before copycat bars emerged hoping to cash in on the obvious success. Restaurants, coffee shops and even an English-language lending library have since joined the barscape.

The area is one of the city's most popular hangouts, yet despite this the spectre of the wrecking ball forever hangs over Sanlitun. Its prime location sets big real-estate developers salivating; the bars along what is known as South Sanlitun are scheduled to be torn down. ❑

Map on page 140

*The Silk Market continued to pack in the tourists right up to its controversial closure in January 2005. It is to be replaced by a new indoor market.*

**BELOW:**
nightclub in Sanlitun.

# RESTAURANTS & BARS

## Restaurants

### American

**Frank's Place**
Gongren Tiyuchang Donglu.
Tel: 6507-2617. Open:
10am–midnight. $$$.
An old favourite among
expats; the best place
for American burgers.

### Chinese (general)

**Made in China**
Grand Hyatt Hotel, Oriental
Plaza. Tel: 8518-1234.
Open: 11.30am–2.30pm,
5.30–10pm. $$$$.
Country-style cooking at
Western prices, an inter-
esting contrast of peas-
ant food in one of
Beijing's plushest hotels.

**Noodle Loft (Mianku)**
20 West Dawang Lu,
Chaoyang. Tel: 6774-9950.
Open: 11am–11pm. $$.

Food from Shanxi
Province and noodles of
every kind. Watching the
skilled chefs make noo-
dles by hand before your
eyes is almost as much
fun as eating them.

### French

**Bleu Marine**
5 Guanghua Xilu. Tel: 6500-
6704. Open:
11.30am–11.30pm. $$$$.
The chefs buy fresh
ingredients daily, and the
French menu changes
regularly. Irresistible to
homesick Europeans.
Reservations essential.

### Fusion

**The Courtyard**
95 Donghuamen Dajie. Tel:
6526-8883. Open: 6–10pm.
$$$$.
Close to the east gate of

the Forbidden City, this is
one of Beijing's top
restaurants, serving
East-West fusion dishes.
The gallery features con-
temporary Chinese art.

**The Green T House (Zi
Yun Xuan)**
6 Gongti Xilu, Chaoyang. Tel:
6552-8310. Open:
11am–midnight. $$$$.
This beautifully dec-
orated restaurant gets
its name from the tea
that is featured in many
of its dishes. Good as
the food is, the atmos-
phere and decor the
main draws.

### Hot-pot

**Mengguren**
East Chang'an Dajie. Tel:
6522-9500. Open:
11am–2pm, 5:30–10pm.
$$$.
Enjoy hot-pot, roast lamb
and other Mongolian
dishes while you listen to
live traditional songs in
this centrally located
four-storey restaurant.

### Imperial

**Red Capital Club (Xin
Hongzi Julebu)**
66 Dongsijiu Tiao,
Dongcheng. Tel: 6402-7150.
Open: 6pm– 1am. $$$$.
Located in a lovingly
restored courtyard
house, the decor here
evokes 1950s China,
and much of the furni-
ture was once used by

high-level leaders. The
menu features the
favourite dishes of such
leaders as Mao Zedong
and Deng Xiaoping.

### Indian

**Asian Star**
26 East Third Ring Road
(Dongsanhuan Beilu). Tel:
6582-5306. Open:
11am–2:30pm, 6–10.30pm.
$$$.
This large, glitzy restau-
rant features food from
China and southeast
Asia, but its best dishes
are Indian.

### Italian

**Assaggi**
1 Xingfu San Cun Bei Jie.
Tel: 8454-4508. Open:
11:30am–2:30pm,
6–11:30pm. $$$$.
Italian food served in an
elegant setting; the
glassed-in rooftop patio
is particularly pleasant.

### Peking Duck

**Beijing Roast Duck
Restaurant (Beijing
Kaoya Dian)**
Building No. 3, Tuanjiehu
Beikou. Tel: 6582-2892.
Open: 11am–2pm,
5–9:30pm. Reservations
required. $$$–$$$$.
One of the classiest of
duck restaurants, where
the meat is a little crisper
than that of most com-
petitors. Call for reserva-
tions, even on weekdays.

**LEFT:** haute cuisine at the St Regis Hotel.
**RIGHT:** the Sanlitun strip.

## Wangfujing Quanjude

9 Shuaifuyuan, off Wangfujing. Tel: 6525-3310. Open:
11am–2pm and
4:30–9:30pm. $$$.
A branch of the famous
Peking Duck restaurant.

### *Sichuanese*

## Sichuan Restaurant

37a Donganmen Jie Wang-
fujing. Tel: 6513-7591.
Open: 11am–11pm. $$.
The Wangfujing branch of
this famous restaurant
(the original is at 51
Xirongxian Hutong in
Xidan District) serves
the same combination of
Sichuan standards laced
with chillis and peppers.

## Xiheyaju

Northeast corner of Ritan
Park. Tel: 8561-7643. Open:
11am–2pm, 5–10pm. $$.
A popular Sichuan restau-
rant in attractive Ritan
Park, Xiheyaju has both
indoor and outdoor dining.

### *Thai*

## Phrik Thai

Gateway Building, 10 Yabao

Lu. Tel: 6592-5236. Open:
11:30am–2pm, 6–11pm. $$.
A good Thai restaurant in
the Russian market area.
Access via the small road
running due south from
Yabao Lu.

### *Tibetan*

## Makye Ame

A11 Xlushui Nanjie, Jian-
goumennwai. Tel: 6506-
9616. Open: 11:30–2am. $$.
An intimate restaurant
with Tibetan art and
furnishings and Tibetan-
style dishes.

### *Vegetarian*

## Tianshl

57 Dengshikou Dajie
Dongcheng. Tel: 6524-2349.
Open: 10am–10pm. $$.
Don't be fooled by the
menu, which lists a large
selection of meat and fish
dishes. This is a vegetarian restaurant and – from
the Tea-Marinated Duck to
the Sweet-and-Sour Man-
darin Fish – they are all
fake (but good)!

### *Xinjiang*

## A-fun-ti (Afanti)

A2 Houguaibang Hutong,
Chaoyangmennei Dajie.
$$$. Tel: 6527-2288 or
6525-1071. Open:
11am–11pm.
Renamed "A-fun-ti" to
reflect the fun-pub atmos-
phere, this boisterous
Xinjiang restaurant has
belly dancers and other
shows. The roast mutton,
kebabs and nans are
good. Book ahead.

### *Yunnanese & Guizhou*

## S'Silk (Chamagudao)

Soho Xiandaicheng Building
D, 3F. Tel: 6615-5515. Open:
10:30am–midnight. $$$.
Fashionable restaurant
in the Soho residential
district. The food is from
Yunnan Province – purple
rice wine is a speciality.

## Three Guizhouren
## (Sange Guizhouren)

3 Guanghuaxilu. Tel: 6507-
4761. Open: 10am–10pm.
$$$.
Features the spicy
cuisine of southwest
China's Guizhou
Province.

### Bars

The Sanlitun area is
packed with bars and
nightclubs, along the
main drag (Sanlitun Lu)

and on the smaller
streets around it. There is
another cluster of bars
around the Workers' Sta-
dium. Most are quite sim-
ilar to each other, and
cater to Western expats
and local trendies in
equal measure. Worth
looking out for is **Jazz Ya**
at 18 Sanlitun Lu, one of
the best jazz bars in
town. East of the Work-
ers' Stadium at 12 Sanli-
tun Nan Jiuba Jie, **Hidden
Tree** has a pleasant Euro-
pean atmosphere and a
nice garden. **The John
Bull**, at 44 Guanghua Lu
(west of Ritan Park), is
one of the more success-
ful attempts to recreate
an English pub. For live
music venues and
nightclubs, *see pages
219–220.*

# WESTERN BEIJING

The university, haven for revolutionaries, sets
the tone for this fascinating section of
the city, home to important temples,
churches and attractive parkland

**W**estern Beijing has long been the home of intellectuals and students. Most of the city's hundreds of universities and other institutes of higher learning are located in Haidian District, and the area has also been a base for some of the nation's best-known writers, revolutionaries and martyrs. In more recent years, its historic role as a centre of higher learning and research led the Zhongguancun area *(see page 156)* to be selected as the site for what is billed as "China's Silicon Valley". The idea to create a hotbed of future-oriented research and development in Western Beijing seemed like a silly fantasy when it was announced in 1988, but the Zhongguancun sub-district is now occupied by an increasing number of internationally funded research and development centres.

## Besieged by Boxers

Situated not far to the northwest of Beihai Park, in a side *hutong*, is the imposing Gothic-style **North Cathedral**  (Beitang, also known as Xishiku; open daily; mass on Sunday), built by Jesuits in 1889. It is best known for its role in the frenzied Boxer Rebellion of 1900; when the Boxers' frustration with foreign missionaries reached fever pitch they lay siege to the cathedral, in

which about 3,000 converted Chinese Christians had taken refuge under the protection of the French bishop Favier.

Although most of the other Boxers were rounded up, incorporated into imperial militias and marched off to face the approaching Allied troops, the Qing court allowed this one group to continue attacking the cathedral for seven weeks, resulting in the deaths of numerous Chinese converts. The siege was finally ended by the intervention of Japan-

Map on page 150

**LEFT:** *jiaozi* are a local favourite.
**BELOW:** the striking facade of the North Cathedral.

*Johann Adam Schall von Bell (1592–1666) is buried at the Jesuit Cemetery. The site is seen as an important emblem of China's long links with the West, and several scholars and officials have proposed that it be renovated and fully opened to the public.*

ese soldiers. The church survived, only to be shut down and looted during the Cultural Revolution. It was restored, and today has a sizeable congregation made up of Catholics of the Patriotic Church. Further renovation work began in 2004.

A short distance northwest, the **Earthenware and Brick Market Church 2** (Gangwashitang), in Xisi Beidajie, is one of the two most important Protestant churches in Beijing (the other is the Rice Market Church east of the Imperial Palace, *see page 143*). It was built at the beginning of the 20th century for the London Bible Society.

Another Christian monument is the old **Jesuit cemetery**, in the courtyard of the Beijing Administrative College on Maweigoulu, in the Fuchengmen District further west beyond the Second Ring Road. Sixty-three Jesuits, both Western and Chinese, are buried here. Most prominent among the tombs are

those of Matteo Ricci, Johann Adam Schall von Bell and Ferdinand Verbeist. Although the cemetery is not technically open to the public, guards at the gate will generally allow visitors to enter.

## Two temples

At the eastern end of Fuchengmennei, wedged between apartment blocks and warehouses, stands **Guangjisi 3** (Temple of Universal Rescue; open daily 7.30am–4.30pm; entrance fee), a well-used and atmospheric Buddhist temple. It is often a stop on the popular cycle-rickshaw "Hutong Tour" which starts from the north gate of Beihai Park (*see pages 47 and 232*).

Under the Ming emperor Tianshun, an existing Jin-dynasty temple on the site was renovated. This was in turn restored and extended in 1669, under Emperor Kangxi. The temple was rebuilt in 1935, following a fire, and more restoration work

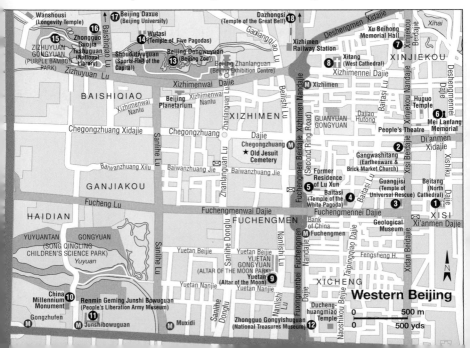

**Western Beijing**

0    500 m
0    500 yds

was completed in 1952, although it was kept closed during the Cultural Revolution. The design of the temple follows the classic Buddhist architectural plan. In the third hall, the **Hall of Guanyin**, is a thousand-armed statue of the goddess of mercy, gilded during the Qing period. A copper Guanyin figure and a Guanyin on a lotus blossom dating from the Ming period are also on view in the hall.

Stored in the library of the monastery are valuable handwritten sutras from the Tang dynasty, along with more than 30,000 old rubbings of stone inscriptions.

A 10-minute walk west from Guangjisi, towards the zoo, is another Buddhist shrine, **Baitasi ❹** (Temple of the White Pagoda; open daily 8.30am–4.30pm; entrance fee), which was built in 1096 during the rule of the Liao dynasty. Kublai Khan restored it in Tibetan style in 1271 but it was destroyed by fire soon afterwards. The monastery was rebuilt in 1457 and at the same time received its official name of Miaoy-ingsi (Temple of Divine Justice).

The temple is well known for its 51-metre (167-ft) white dagoba (a Tibetan-style shrine), which dates from 1279; it is larger and older than the similar structure in Beihai Park. Its top is adorned by an engraved copper canopy, from which little bells hang, moving in the wind in order to drive away evil spirits. In the fourth hall there are sculptures of the three Buddhas and two Buddha pupils, as well as some *thangka*, or Tibetan scroll pictures.

Baitasi and its grounds were restored in the late 1970s, when valuable objects were found in the dagoba, including Buddhist manuscripts and calligraphy by Emperor Qianlong, as well as jewellery and coins from various dynasties. A further restoration in 2000 revealed more treasures.

## Beijing of the artists

The **former residence of Lu Xun ❺** (open Tues–Sun 9am–3.30pm; entrance fee) is on a small street between Baitasi and the Second Ring Road. Lu Xun (1881–1936), one of the greatest Chinese writers

*ORIENTATION*
*The area covered in this chapter extends north and west from the Forbidden City to the Fourth Ring Road.*

**BELOW:** the museum inside Lu Xun's former residence.

of the 20th century, lived in Beijing from 1923 to 1925. The typical Chinese courtyard house – which he bought with borrowed money – is situated near **Fuchengmen**, an old imperial gate due west of Beihai Park. The eastern room in the northern part of the courtyard belonged to Lu Xun's mother; the western room to his wife. The rooms to the south served as living quarters and a library.

The small room added to the north side was the study and bedroom that Lu Xun called the "Tiger's Tail". Here he wrote the two stories, *The Tomb* and *Wild Grasses*. Photographs, unpublished manuscripts, letters and a copy of the entry he made in his diary on the day of his death are all on display.

At 9 Huguosi Jie is the **Mei Lanfang Memorial ❻** (open Tues–Sun 9am–4pm; entrance fee), dedicated to the man who was most famous for making people think he was a woman. Just as historically in Western theatre women could not perform on stage, so it was with Beijing Opera. As a consequence, certain players specialised in playing female roles exclusively. Mei Lanfang was considered to be the best such performer in the history of Beijing Opera *(see box below)*.

Further north is the **Xu Beihong Memorial Hall ❼** (open Tues–Sun 9am–5pm; entrance fee). Xu Beihong (1895–1953) was one of China's most famous modern artists, well known for his numerous paintings of horses. A Xu Beihong Memorial Hall was first established in the house he lived in.

When she died, his widow, Liao Jingwen, left this house, along with his books, calligraphy and other work, to the People's Republic, and a memorial to Xu was built in the grounds. Later, the Memorial Hall was moved here, to 53 Xinjiekou Beidajie.

Xu's studio was rebuilt in the new hall exactly as it was shortly before his death. Hanging on the walls are a copy of his painting, *Rich Harvest*, works by Ren Bonian and Qi Baishi, and a photograph of Xu taken in 1913 by Rabindranath Tagore, the Indian poet and Nobel Prize winner.

*Xu Beihong's innovation was to combine Western and Chinese techniques, to great effect.*

**BELOW:** Mei Lanfang, star of the opera.

## Hitting the High Notes

The most celebrated Beijing Opera performer, Mei Lanfang (1894–1961) was a master of the *dan* role, a central female character traditionally played by a man. Mei was born into a family of performers. He began studying opera as a child, making his stage debut at eleven. By the time he was 20, he was already a household name. In fifty years as a *dan* performer, Mei played more than 100 female roles, including concubines, generals and goddesses. He was also an innovator, designing new dances and other routines to enhance his roles. He added a sword dance to the opera *Conqueror Xiang Yu Parts with His Concubine*, and a ribbon dance, based on drawings in ancient Buddhist frescos, to *The Fairy Scattering Flowers*. Mei was an ambassador abroad for his ancient art form, visiting various European cities as well as Japan, Russia, India, Egypt and the US – which he toured in 1929 – and making many friends, including actor Charlie Chaplin and singer Paul Robeson. Berthold Brecht was among those who admired Mei's performance in Moscow in 1935.

Today, Mei's son, Mui Bo-kau (Mei Baojiu), continues the family tradition and has recently been involved in efforts to draw people back to Beijing Opera by updating it and incorporating symphonic music.

The works of art exhibited in the Memorial Hall were almost all collected by the artist himself during his lifetime. They include more than 1,200 examples from the Tang, Song, Yuan, Ming and Qing dynasties, as well as works from the time of the May Fourth Movement (1919). One of the most valuable items is a cartoon of the Tang painting, *The Scroll of the 87 Immortals*, by Wu Daozi.

Not far from Xizhimen stands another Catholic church, the **West Cathedral ❽** (Xitang). Built in the 18th century, it was destroyed during the persecution of Christians in 1811. A second church, built in 1867, was in turn a victim of the Boxer Rebellion. The present building dates from the beginning of the 20th century.

Next to the Xizhimen overpass nearby is a **Bird Market**, one of many in the city, which is particularly large and active at weekends. Birds are especially popular with older men, who wander through the city parks morning and afternoon, swinging their bird cages back and forth, so as to give the birds some air and – it is said – the sensation of flying.

## Beijing of the artists

Situated symmetrically opposite the Altar of the Sun (Ritan, *see page 144*) is another of the eight altars that played such a great role in the ritual life of the Ming and Qing emperors. The **Altar of the Moon ❾** (Yuetan; open daily 6am–8pm; entrance fee), stands in a public park – easy to find because of its large telecommunications tower.

The **China Millennium Monument ❿** is an odd, "futuristic" structure that includes a spire, bronze crossways, "Holy Fire Square" and fountains, all rife with symbolism, most of it so obscure that even the explanations offered in publicity brochures are of little help. In essence, the building seems intended as the government's answer to the Temple of Heaven – but without religious significance – and as one of Jiang Zemin's legacies to the city. It was here that the government officially rang in the year 2000 in a huge ceremony that included the running of a torch here from the site of Peking Man. It is now carving out a role for itself as a museum and gallery, and

Map on page 150

*The bird market by the Xizhimen overpass is one of the most colourful in the city.*

**BELOW:** ringing in the new century at the Millennium Monument.

*Beijing Zoo was the first in the world to breed giant pandas successfully. Each cub weighs only about 100 grams (3½ oz.) at birth – no other mammal, except marsupials, gives birth to offspring so much smaller than the adult.*

**BELOW:** artillery piece at the Army Museum.

has held several important exhibitions of items culled from collections around China. The Millennium Monument has powerful patrons and is likely to become an important fixture on Beijing's art and exhibition scene.

Boats to the Summer Palace run from Bayi Lake in Yuyuantan Park behind the monument *(see also page 161)*. Just to the south, on Fuxing Lu, is the **People's Liberation Army Museum** ⓫ (Renmin Geming Junshi Bowuguan; open daily 8.30am–5pm; entrance fee), with four floors of weapons and a motley band of tanks, planes and other military hardware lined up at the front.

On the fifth floor of the Parkson Building – a shopping mall – is the **National Treasures Museum** ⓬ (Zhongguo Gongyishuguan; open 9.30am–4.30pm; entrance fee), a good place to see examples of Chinese jade carving, porcelain and lacquerware.

### The zoo and surroundings

Further to the west, past the Second Ring Road, is **Beijing Zoo** ⓭ (Beijing Dongwuyuan; open daily,

7.30am–4.30pm; entrance fee; extra fee to enter the panda compound). Around 1900, a Manchu high official returned from a long journey abroad bringing a special gift for the Empress Dowager Cixi: a great number of animals, which he had mainly bought in Germany. To accommodate them, Cixi had a decaying park transformed into the "Park of Ten Thousand Creatures". In time this became the present-day zoo. Be warned that standards are not up to those of most Western zoos. The main attraction, of course, is the giant pandas, whose quarters are right by the entrance. Also within the zoo complex is the **Beijing Aquarium** (open same hours as zoo, separate entrance fee).

Just behind the zoo, to the north of the Shoudutiyuguan sports hall, is **Wutasi** ⓮ (Temple of Five Pagodas; open daily 8.30am–4.30pm; entrance fee). In earlier years, when en route to the Summer Palaces, it was possible to see the tops of its pagodas to the right, but the view is now blocked by apartment blocks.

The temple dates back to the 15th-century reign of the Ming emperor

Yongle. It was restored during Qianlong's reign but devastated by European troops in 1860 and again in 1900. The building, with five small pagodas standing on a massive square base, is in what is known in Buddhism as the "Diamond Throne Pagoda" style, and quite different from other temples in Beijing. Worth seeing above all else are the bas-reliefs on the outside, which depict Buddha figures, symbolic animals, lotus flowers, heavenly guardians, the wheel of Buddhist teaching, and other Buddhist symbols.

Go up two flights of stairs to the terrace where the bases of the pagodas are also adorned with reliefs. In the cloisters down below, visitors can study the various styles of pagoda architecture in China through an exhibition of photographs. An impressive collection of steles also awaits in this courtyard. The temple is a peaceful place, and does not get as crowded as most others in the city.

Across Baishiqiao to the west is the **Purple Bamboo Park** ⓯ (Zizhuyuan Gongyuan; open daily 6am–8pm; entrance fee), popular for its amusement park and playground. Around the three lakes are ten different varieties of bamboo – a rare plant in northern China. A short distance northwest of the park is the Buddhist **Wanshousi** (Longevity Temple; open Tues–Sun 9am–4.30pm; entrance fee), built in 1577 and featuring a fine collection of bronze statues, ceramics and various other ancient artefacts. The temple was a favourite of Cixi, who would break the journey to the Summer Palace here.

## Beijing University

Just north of the park is an enormous complex housing the **National Library of China** ⓰ (Zhongguo Guojia Tushuguan) open daily, 9am–5pm). Established in 1909, this is the largest library in Asia and the fifth-largest in the world, with some 21 million items. The library has an unrivalled collection of ancient Chinese texts. From here you can go north to the **People's University** (Renmindaxue), not far from the Friendship Hotel, which is home to

Maps on pages 150 & 160

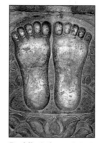
*Buddha's footprints are honoured at Wutasi.*

**BELOW:** Beijing still has enough bicycles for two-wheeler traffic jams at peak times.

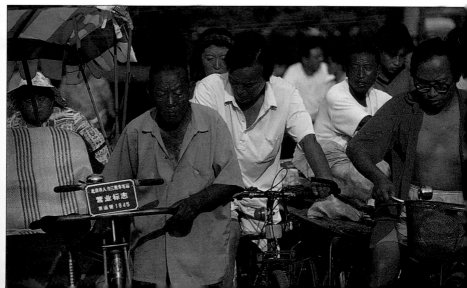

*China is nothing if not bureaucratic, and there often seem to be petty laws and restrictions on almost everything. There is an army of officialdom – from policemen to traffic controllers, security guards and park wardens.*

**BELOW:** a lecture at Beijing University.

foreign experts from all over the world. A short distance further north is **Zhongguancun**, which has been dubbed China's "Silicon Valley". Zhongguancun has nothing of the physical beauty of the other, more famous Silicon Valley in California, but it is an interesting window into the Chinese government's plans for the future. The area claims to be home to more than 400,000 of China's brightest scientists and teachers, and has become one of the nation's most important centres of science and technology research.

To facilitate its communication – virtual and actual – with the outside world, the government is developing a high-speed, broadband multimedia network for the area and building a light urban railway that will reduce travel time to Capital Airport to a swift 15 minutes. Although Zhong-guancun is still full of stores that sell pirated software products for a pittance, it is fast making the transition from copier to creator.

Still further north, out beyond the Fourth Ring Road, is the prestigious **Beijing University** ⓱ (Beijing

Daxue, or "Beida"). The university was founded in 1898, but its first campus was in the city centre, in the eastern part of the old Imperial City. The present campus, in the western district of Haidian, was previously the site of the American-founded Yanjing University, which merged with the main institution in 1953. The campus has park-like grounds with a quiet lake, and a classical Chinese pagoda with pavilions and stone figures.

Today, more than 10,000 students are studying at Beida, many of them foreigners. The students have been involved in most of the political upheavals of the 20th century; from the May Fourth Movement of 1919 to the Cultural Revolution and the 1970s and 1980s pro-democracy protests – which resulted in the demonstrations and wall newspapers of 1979 and, tragically, in the Tiananmen massacre of 1989. In recent years, the students have become known for their conservative nationalism, and some argue that the school is now dominated by the so-called "new leftists".

The remains of the old Beijing University – the so-called **Red Building** (Honglou; open daily 8.30am–5.30pm; entrance fee), at the eastern end of Shatan Jie – can still be seen. Here, Li Dazhao, one of the founders of the Chinese Communist Party, used to teach, and Mao Zedong used to work in the library. Chen Duxiu, the first General Secretary of the Chinese Communist Party, also taught at the old Beida.

The university area is well supplied with bars and cheap restaurants, with the main concentrations on Weigongcun and around Wudaokou.

### The Great Bell

Around 2 km (1½ miles) to the east of the modern Beida on the Third Ring Road, squeezed in among the new buildings and the factories, is **Dazhongsi** ⑱ (Temple of the Great Bell; open Tues–Sun 8am–5.30pm; entrance fee), dating from AD 743. This temple, like many others, was badly damaged during the Cultural Revolution, but has been restored. On display are some 160 ancient bells, from tiny 150-gram (6-oz)

specimens to the bronze giant that gives the temple its name, housed in the further part of the grounds in a 17-metre (56-ft) high tower.

The Great Bell was made in 1406 on the orders of Emperor Yongle, and measures 7 metres (23 ft) in height, has a diameter of 3 metres (10 ft) and weighs 46½ tonnes. Inscribed on the bell is the entire text of the Huayan Sutra, consisting of some 200,000 characters. At the top of this, and other every bell, is a *pulao*, a mythical creature.

The Huayan sect has had great influence over traditional Asian attitudes to nature and inspiring many artists. It was founded in AD 630 and endured until about 1000. Its teaching states that all creatures and things are imbued with a cosmic principle, that everything exists in harmony with everything else, and that every grain of dust contains all the wealth of Buddha. This teaching does not preach the need to influence the cosmic powers or to use magic, as is the case with Tantric (Tibetan) Buddhism. It relies, instead, on contemplation and observation.  ❑

*The 7-metre (23-ft) bell at Dazhongsi, the Temple of the Great Bell.*

# RESTAURANTS

### Beijing-style

**Baijia Dazhaimen**
29 Suzhou Lu, Haidian. Tel: 6265-4186. Open:11am–2pm, 5–9:30pm. $$$. Located on the grounds of a Qing-dynasty mansion. Eat in one of many pavilions or pagodas.

**Yuguotianqing**
35 Tonglingge Lu, Xicheng. Tel: 6608-9265. Open: 10:30am–10pm. $. This poetically named establishment – "the rain is over and the sky is clear" – serves good dumplings and *baozi*.

### Hot-pot

**Hongbinlou**
11 Zhanlanguan Lu, Xicheng Tel: 6899-4561. Open: 11am–8:30pm. $$$. Very good hot-pot, plus other specialities.

**Nengrenju**
5 Taipingqiao Dajie, Xicheng. Tel: 6601-2560. Open: 11am–2pm, 5–9pm. $$. Good Mongolian restaurant close to Baitasi.

### Other Chinese

**Goldpeacock Dai Nationality Restaurant**
2 Minzu Daxue Bei Lu, Haid-

lan. Tel: 6893-2030. Open: 11am–10pm. $$. Popular place featuring the sweet, spicy food of Yunnan.

**Tongheju Restaurant**
72 Sanlihe Nanjie, Yuetan, Xicheng. Tel: 6852-2917. Open: 10am–10pm. $$. A venerable establishment, with food from Shandong Province..

**Tongxinyu Mao Jia Cai**
Minzu Daxue Lu, Haidian. Tel: 6843-9049. Open: 9:30am–11pm. $$. Specialises in serving up Mao's favourite dishes from his native Hunan.

### Russian

**Moscow Restaurant**
135 Xizhimenwai Dajie. Tel: 6835-4454. Open: 11am–2pm, 5–9pm. $$$. A cavernous restaurant in the old Soviet-built exhibition centre.

• • • • • • • • •

*Prices are for a typical dinner for one (three dishes with beer in Chinese restaurants, or a three-course meal with a half bottle of house wine in Western-style restaurants).*
*$ = under 50 Rmb*
*$$ = 50–100 Rmb*
*$$$ = 100–150 Rmb*
*$$$$ = over 150 Rmb*

# THE SUMMER PALACES

The great landscaped gardens and lavish palaces built outside Beijing for the pleasure of the emperor and his court are now open to anyone who wants to escape the bustle of the city

There are two "summer palaces" in the northwestern suburbs of Beijing. Between them, they were used by the Qing emperors for more than 150 years. During this time dozens of palaces, pavilions and temples were built in contrived idyllic landscapes of artificial hills, lakes and canals. The older complex, Yuanmingyuan, was largely destroyed by foreign troops in 1860 at the end of the Second Opium War.

The "New" Summer Palace, Yiheyuan, built as a replacement by the Empress Dowager Cixi at the end of the 19th century, was also plundered by foreign troops, in 1900 during the Boxer Rebellion. This time, however, most of the buildings survived or were restored, and Yiheyuan is today one of Beijing's major sights, attracting large numbers of visitors, particularly on summer weekends. Its popularity so outweighs that of its predecessor that it is generally referred to simply as "the Summer Palace".

## The Old Summer Palace

Little remains of the original Summer Palace, **Yuanmingyuan** ❶ (open daily, summer 7am–7pm, winter 8am–5.30pm; entrance fee), although its large grounds are now a park providing a quiet retreat from the city, and are a popular place for weekend picnics. The main entrance is at the southern end of the complex. Inside, a web of paths make their way through the park. There is a fair amount of tourist tat for sale, as well as snack vendors, children's playgrounds and boating lakes. The rebuilt maze *(see page 160)* is fun. Past a wide depression in the terrain is a broad field of ruins, where the remains of ornate pillars and frescos are more reminiscent of European baroque buildings than the architecture of imperial China.

Map on page 160

**LEFT:** the Long Corridor at the New Summer Palace.
**BELOW:** ruins at the Old Summer Palace.

*Emperor Qianlong created the once-magnificent palace and gardens at Yuanmingyuan.*

The magnificent complex of park and palace that once stood here was the creation of Emperor Qianlong (1736–95). He called it Yuanmingyuan: the Garden of Perfect Purity. Qianlong was an enthusiastic admirer of southern Chinese landscape gardening, having appreciated the quiet beauty of the West Lake in Hangzhou, and the gardens and canals of Suzhou, sketches of which were used to transform the surroundings of Yuanmingyuan into a gigantic masterpiece of landscape gardening. Here, natural and artificial landscapes were merged into a perfect whole.

Similarly inspired by pictures of princely French and Italian palaces, Qianlong gave orders for buildings in the European style to be constructed in the northeastern part of the park. The architect was a Jesuit missionary and artist, Giuseppe Castiglione, from Genoa, later to be the emperor's confidante and teacher.

Between 1747 and 1759, Castiglione created a complex of buildings unique in China. There were little rococo palaces with horseshoe-shaped staircases, marble halls, fountains and even a maze (now reconstructed in stone) – a piece of Versailles in the Middle Kingdom, the counterpoint to the chinoiserie of European princes. The rooms were equipped with European furniture, and there were even European toys for the children. Qianlong and his court listened to Western music and ate Western food, making him feel like the "Emperor in Rome". During the Mid-Autumn Festival, he sat in a raised pavilion in the centre of his maze. His court ladies, with torches in their hands, had to find their way to him, the first to do so being rewarded with a present.

Qianlong was particularly fond of European fountains, simple or elaborate. The remains of some of these can still be seen just south of the

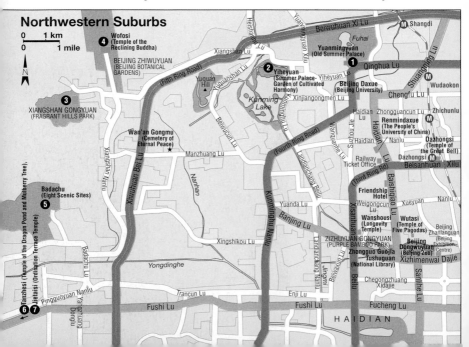

present palace **museum** (open daily 9am–5pm; entrance fee). The fountains were composed of several levels of water-spouting figures; water sprayed from stone lions' heads, dogs' mouths and stags' antlers. In the museum itself are old photographs, prints, and a large map of the site.

An interesting symbiosis of Chinese thought and European architecture was the water clock, designed by the French Jesuit, Benoît. Close to the Palace of the Quiet Sea, the ruins can be seen between the museum and the restored maze. Traditionally, the Chinese divided the 24-hour day into 12 segments, with every segment attributed to an animal. Benoît designed a construction with 12 stone animals with bronze heads, each of them spouting water for two hours.

In Qianlong's time, the French court contributed to the decoration of the buildings "in the Western style" and sent rare gifts. One hundred years later, it would be French troops, together with the British, who destroyed these very palaces.

## Destruction of the palace

During the Second Opium War (1858–60), when China vastly overestimated its strength and tried to expel permanently the unscrupulous foreign merchants, the Europeans took brutal revenge. The imperial house was considered personally responsible for the xenophobic policies, and Lord Elgin, the commander-in-chief of the British forces, ordered the destruction of Yuanmingyuan. It was said that he wanted to spare the common people and only punish the court. Before the troops attacked in October 1860, the emperor Xianfeng, together with his womenfolk (among them the concubine Cixi), managed to escape to the safety of Chengde.

The allied soldiers plundered the palace, taking away anything they could carry – some items have ended up in museums and auctions in the West. Then they set fire to the buildings, and for three days the Summer Palace blazed. The traditional wooden buildings were almost completely destroyed, and only a few of the Western-style structures survived. Attempts at restoration failed because of a chronic lack of finance, and the palace's demise was complete when, following the Boxer Rebellion, peasants from the surrounding countryside took away valuable ceramic tiles and marble to build houses.

## Yuanmingyuan today

For modern Beijingers, what was once the exclusive haunt of emperors is now a place for a day out. They come especially to enjoy **Fu Hai Lake**. In the summer, hundreds of paddle and rowing boats bob in the water and, in the winter, skaters glide over the ice. Also popular is the eastern section, the **Eternal Spring Garden** (Changchunyuan), with the European fountain ruins – one of the more intact structures in the complex.

TIP

To get to Yuanmingyuan, take the subway to Wudaokou and then a taxi, or bus 331 or 375. The latter also goes to the New Summer Palace. Bus 322 runs from the zoo to both palaces. There are now regular boats to the New Summer Palace departing from behind the Exhibition Centre next to the zoo, and from Bayi Lake in Yuyuantan Park; journey time is 1 hour.

**BELOW:** the ruins at Yuanmingyuan make a backdrop for patriotic productions.

**TIP**

For entry to the New
Summer Palace, as
with the Forbidden City
and Temple of Heaven,
it's best to purchase an
all-inclusive ticket *(tao
piao)*, unless you only
want to visit the park
and not the buildings.

**BELOW:** Foxiangge,
the Pagoda of Buddhist
Virtue, towers over the
northern shore of
Kunming Lake.

The ruins of Yuanmingyuan
remain a powerful symbol of China's
humiliation at the hands of the West.
The memory of its destruction is
regularly evoked as a reminder of the
dangers of both Western imperialism
and domestic political and military
weakness. Indeed, the large sign just
outside the eastern gate of the ruins
greets visitors with the words, "Do
not forget the national shame, rebuild
the Chinese nation."

Yuanmingyuan's potency as a
symbol has led to a lively debate
over its future. Some believe that it
should be restored to its original
glory as proof of China's triumph
over weakness and imperialism.
Others argue that to rebuild the
ruins would be tantamount to sacri-
lege. The debate is largely academic, since to restore the ruins
properly would cost astronomical
sums. However, so sensitive is the
topic that even minor repairs to
crumbling walls are controversial.
The issue is further complicated by
the fact that over the years parts of
the grounds have been occupied by
businesses and families.

## The New Summer Palace

A short distance southwest of
Yuanmingyuan is the site of the
"New" Summer Palace, **Yiheyuan**
**②** (Garden of Cultivated Harmony;
park open daily 6.30am–7pm, buildings 8am–4.30pm; closes one hour
earlier in winter; entrance fee –
unless you just want to visit the park,
buy an all-inclusive *tao piao* ticket).

The area had been used as an
imperial pleasure garden for centuries, predating the gardens of Yuan-
mingyan, the "Old" Summer Palace.
However, it wasn't until the 1880s,
when the Empress Dowager Cixi set
about expanding the original park,
and rebuilding and adding to the
existing buildings, that the new Summer Palace was created to replace the
old. The resulting mosaic of imperial
pleasure gardens and grand buildings, harmoniously arranged on hills
around a beautiful lake, was partially
destroyed in 1900 but quickly rebuilt
– and has since survived civil war
and the Cultural Revolution to
become one of Beijing's top tourist
attractions, visited by hundreds of
thousands every year.

Cixi loved her new creation. She
and her entourage effectively abandoned the Forbidden City and ruled
China from here for 20 years until
her death in 1908.

As in every Chinese garden, rocks
and water feature prominently, while
blossoming shrubs and a colourful ar-
rangement of flowering plants in tubs
have been preferred to European-
style flower beds. There is also a con-
scious use of walls and buildings to
screen sections of the gardens, so that
small pieces of the landscape appear
like framed pictures through windows in chequered, rhomboid, fan,
vase and peach shapes. Sometimes a
sudden and dramatic change of scene
is possible within only a few yards.
A walk through the Summer Palace
can be likened to the slow unrolling
of a Chinese scroll painting.

Beautiful **Kunming Lake**  covers about two-thirds of the area of the Yiheyuan complex, adding a sense of serenity and silence. In summer, the lake is covered with a carpet of huge, round, green lotus leaves, while pale pink lotus flowers rise between them. The three islands in the lake recall a 2,000-year-old Daoist myth of three islands in the Eastern Sea supposedly inhabited by immortals.

The great artificial hill, about 60 metres (200 ft) in height, which rises behind the palace was named **Longevity Hill** **B** (Wanshoushan) by Qianlong, in honour of his mother on her 60th birthday. Like a giant screen, it divides the grounds of the Summer Palace into two completely different landscapes. The southern section, with the broad lake in the foreground, is reminiscent of the idyll of the West Lake in Hangzhou; the northern section, with its romantic groves and canals, creates an atmosphere akin to that of Suzhou.

The main path into the grounds leads through a mighty wooden *pailou*, a kind of Chinese triumphal arch, past the ghost wall that is supposed to ward off all evil influences, directly to the **Eastern Gate** (Donggongmen). Visible beyond this is the **Hall of Benevolence and Longevity** **C** (Renshoudian), with its opulent furnishings and decorative objets d'art. This is where young Emperor Guangxu dealt with state business when the imperial court resided in Yiheyuan; here, grand audiences were held for imperial ministers, advisers, mandarins, and later for foreign diplomats as well.

It was in the nearby **Hall of Jade Ripples** **D** (Yulantang) that Cixi supposedly kept Guangxu under house arrest for his folly at attempting to reform a crumbling dynasty by opening China to foreign ideas in 1898. It has been argued, however, that it was pressure from a powerful faction at court which convinced her that Guangxu was endangering the regime, and told her that if she did not resume her position as regent, the dynasty would collapse.

Not far from the Hall of Jade Ripples, on the southeastern slopes of Longevity Hill, were Cixi's private

*Pleasure boats of various shapes and sizes cruise the waters of Kunming Lake. Most depart from the jetty next to the Marble Boat.*

**BELOW:** view across Kunming Lake.

Maps
Area 160
Site 165

*Cixi was an enthusiastic fan of Beijing Opera, and had an open-air stage built at the Summer Palace.*

living and sleeping apartments, the **Hall of Happiness and Longevity** **E** (Leshoutang ). Served by a staff of 48, she did not want for much except privacy.

Cixi was passionate about Beijing Opera. There was an excellent ensemble at court, composed of 384 eunuchs. Cixi herself was supposed to have appeared in some operas as Guanyin, the goddess of mercy. She had an impressive open-air stage built in the **Garden of Virtue and Harmony** **F** (Deheyuan). Its three stages, one above the other, were connected by trap doors, so that supernatural beings, saints and immortals could swoop down into the operatic scene and evil spirits could rise from the depths of the underworld. There was even an underground water reservoir for "wet" scenes.

Today, the Deheyuan has been turned into a **theatre museum**. Costumes can be seen in glass cases, and the female museum attendants wear the clothes and hairstyles of the Qing dynasty. Under their Manchu shoes are high platforms, which gave

women a swaying walk. Unlike the Han Chinese, the Manchu women – the palace elite of the Qing dynasty – did not have their feet bound. Apart from the theatre collection, there are also some of Cixi's private possessions on display. Some of her jewellery and cosmetic implements can be seen, as can the first car imported into China, a Mercedes-Benz which was a gift from Yuan Shikai. Here, one can also see the famous portrait in oils painted by the American artist Hubert Vos when the Empress Dowager was aged 70, but rendered to make her look as she would have appeared when she was 25.

A highlight in the further eastern part of the palace gardens is the **Garden of Harmonious Interest** **G** (Xiequyuan), a complete, perfect and beautiful replica of a lotus pool from the Wuxi area in central China.

## The Long Corridor

Covered walkways and galleries are established features of Chinese landscape gardening. These light, elegant, wooden structures link

## Who was the real Cixi?

The founder of the New Summer Palace, the apparently omnipotent Empress Dowager Cixi, began life as a concubine of the third rank. Her rise to prominence began when she was appointed as one of the two regents who ruled during her son Tongzhi's minority, following the death of Emperor Xianfeng in 1861. The accepted wisdom is that she was ruthlessly ambitious, removing anyone who stood in her way, and that it was she, rather than Guangxu, who effectively ruled China in the late 19th century.

There is, however, an alternative view which maintains that Cixi was merely a puppet, installed on the throne by officials who actually made policy, so that they could hide behind her and act as they pleased. As a woman she had little personal power, and was further handicapped by her inability to read or write. Her defenders point out that Cixi was unable ever to know what was really going on because the only people she had contact with were inside the court – as a woman of imperial rank she was not allowed to venture beyond the confines of the imperial palaces. The only weapon she had was her son, the royal heir, and her ambition for him was merely a form of self-defence.

Map below

scattered individual buildings to make a composite whole. The **Long Corridor Ⓗ** (Changlang) is a magnificent example; 728 metres (796 yds) in length, it runs along the foot of the hill parallel to the shore of Kunming Lake.

The ceilings and rafters of the walkway are decorated with countless bird-and-flower motifs. If humans or human-like creatures appear in the pictures, they are either in scenes from famous legends, episodes of Chinese history, or scenes from classical novels such as *The Dream of the Red Chamber*, *The Bandits of Liangshan Moor* or *The Journey to the West*, with its hero the Monkey King, Sun Wukong.

In the middle of the walkway, where the east–west axis of the palace park meets the north–south axis, the **Gate of Dispelling Clouds ❶** (Paiyunmen) – a great triumphal arch, or *pailou* – marks the start of the climb up Longevity Hill. Next to

12 massive, bizarre-shaped stones symbolising the signs of the Chinese zodiac, is an elegant pair of lions cast in bronze – perhaps the most beautiful in all of Beijing – guarding an imposing Buddhist temple complex, which is surrounded by a red wall. Go through two gates and over a bridge to reach the **Hall of Dispelling Clouds ❶** (Paiyundian).

A temple once stood on this site during the Ming dynasty. Qianlong had it rebuilt and, on his mother's 60th birthday, renamed it the **Temple of Gratitude for a Long Life**. It was destroyed in 1860, and the present form dates from Cixi's time in 1892. This was where she celebrated her birthdays with extravagant and elaborate ceremonies. Many of the presents given on these occasions are on exhibition in the rooms here, often with yellow paper labels attached, marked with words of adulation such as "Given in honour and respect by your true and loyal subject..."

*Paintings adorn each of the 8,000 ceiling beams in the Long Corridor. To prevent them from fading until they are unrecognisable, the colours are renewed – not always very sensitively – every 12 years.*

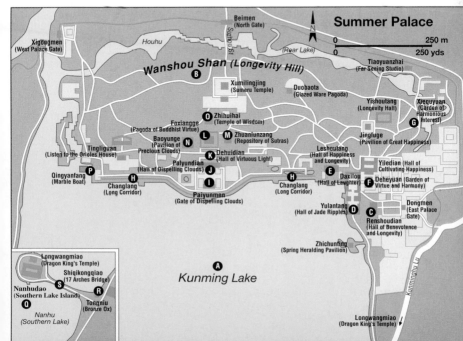

Summer Palace

*The Summer Palace is very popular with Beijingers as well as Chinese and foreign tourists.*

**BELOW:** the Marble Boat, two storeys of spectacular excess.

Go past the Hall of Dispelling Clouds, through the **Hall of Virtuous Light** 🄺 (Dehuidian), and up a steep stone staircase to reach the massive, 38-metre (125-ft) tall, octagonal **Pagoda of Buddhist Virtue** 🄻 (Foxiangge). This is the highest point of the palace, and from here is a wonderful panoramic view.

To the east is a group of buildings, the **Repository of Sutras** 🄼 (Zhuanlunzang), once used as the archives for copies of Confucian classics and Buddhist scrolls. To the west is a rare and quite extraordinary masterpiece of Chinese architecture – the **Pavilion of Precious Clouds** 🄽 (Baoyunge), framed on all four sides by smaller pavilions and walkways. In Cixi's day, Lamaist monks gathered here to pray on the 1st and 15th day of every lunar month. Its stepped roof, and its beams, columns and struts, make it look like a wooden building, yet they were all cast from bronze in 1750 with the help of wax moulds. This is why it is usually called the Bronze Pavilion (Tongting). It is one of the few buildings

of the Summer Palace to have survived the destruction of 1860 and 1900 relatively undamaged.

Behind the pagoda on Longevity Hill, a narrow path leads to the **Temple of Wisdom** 🄾 (Zhihuihai). There are countless small statues of Buddha in the niches of its greenish-yellow ceramic facade.

### Sights around the lake

A little further to the west, at the end of the Long Corridor lies the famous **Marble Boat** 🄿 (Qingyanfang) with its two stone wheels on either side. Cixi is generally thought to have squandered a fortune on this spectacular folly, money that should have gone to the Chinese navy – with the direct result a humiliating naval defeat by the Japanese in 1895. The counter-argument is that she in fact had no knowledge of where the money came from in the first place. Prince Chun, Guangxu's father, was in the habit of flattering Cixi as a way of encouraging her to support his policies, and squeezed funds from wealthy gentry and rich officials in order to pay for it. It

should also be pointed out that Qianlong had already built the base of the boat, which, like so much in the palace, was damaged in 1860.

From the Marble Boat, it is possible to cross the lake by ferry, landing either on **Nanhudao**  (Southern Lake Island), or on the neighbouring mainland. Close to the bridge leading to Nanhudao crouches the **Bronze Ox** ❶ (Tongniu). Its task, as the characters engraved on its back make clear, is to pacify the water spirit and to protect the surrounding land from floods. The script also relates how Qianlong decided to enlarge the lake; in recording this on the statue, he was identifying with the legendary Emperor Yuan, a mythological hero who is described as having commanded the damming of a flood from the back of an ox.

**Seventeen Arches Bridge** ❸ (Shiqikongqiao) crosses the water in a supremely graceful curve, linking Nanhudao with the mainland. Stone lions and other exotic creatures keep watch on the balustrades. On the small island itself is the **Longwangmiao** (Dragon King's Temple).

## The demise of the palace

The 1900 Boxer Rebellion grew out of economic hardship combined with a rise in Chinese nationalism, promoted by the government. The desire was to preserve Chinese traditions at all costs and to expel all things foreign. However, it didn't work out that way, and the foreigners ended up plundering the capital city, making off with untold cultural riches.

As the European powers plundered and partially destroyed the Summer Palace, Cixi fled to Xi'an. She is said to have become apoplectic with rage when she heard that her throne had been flung into Kunming Lake, her robes stolen, and the walls of her bedchamber scrawled with obscene words and drawings. When at last she returned to Beijing, she set about restoring the palace to its former glory with typical energy. Some buildings were not restored – the Lama Temple, for instance, on the far side of Longevity Hill, has only been partially rebuilt in the last few years. Following her death in 1908, imperial China itself was to survive only three more years. ❏

Maps
Area 160
Site 165

*Yellow roof tiles were reserved for imperial palaces.*

**LEFT:** *pailou* gateway at the main entrance to the Summer Palace.

# RESTAURANTS

*Imperial*

**Tingliguan Restaurant**
inside Summer Palace (Yiheyuan). Tel: 6288-1955. Open: 11am–2pm, 5–7pm. $$.
Serves more than 300 dishes that were popular at court in Ming and Qing times. Fish caught from Kunming Lake is a house speciality.

*Other Chinese*

**Chengdu Caotang Restaurant**
21 Yiheyuan Lu. Tel: 6287-0902. Open: 9.30am–10pm. $$.
The name comes from the grass-roofed cabin in which the poet Du Fu once lived; the food is the spicy cuisine of the poet's native Sichuan Province.

**Kejiacai**
Wanliuyuan, Kunminghu Lu, Tel: 6287-8726. Open: 10am-2pm, 4:30–10pm. $$
This branch of the popular restaurant serves up Hakka food in a comfortable setting.

• • • • • • • • • • • • • •
*Prices are for a typical dinner for one (three dishes with beer in Chinese restaurants, or a three-course meal with a half bottle of house wine in Western-style restaurants).*
*$ = under 50 Rmb*
*$$ = 50–100 Rmb*
*$$$ = 100–150 Rmb*
*$$$$ = over 150 Rmb*

# THE WESTERN FRINGES

**In the hills and valleys to the immediate west of the city are a number of tranquil temples and other sites of historical – and prehistorical – significance. Further north are the impressive imperial tombs of the Ming emperors**

I f you're staying in Beijing for more than a few days, you may want to break up your sightseeing with a trip to the hills and valleys of the pleasant rural areas to the west of the city. Not only will you get to see a China vastly different from that experienced in the urban sprawl, but you will also gain an insight into some important moments from the country's past.

## The Fragrant Hills

Whether you're escaping the heat of a Beijing summer, or just the madding crowds, a trip to the **Xiangshan ❸** (Fragrant Hills Park; open daily 6am–9pm, last ticket for entry 7pm; closes 6pm in winter; entrance fee), only an hour's drive to the northwest (beyond the Summer Palace), is a convenient way to get away from the metropolis for a day. When the sky is clear, you will be rewarded by an excellent view of the city you have left behind.

In the Liao dynasty (907–1125), noble and wealthy merchant families built elegant villas on the cool slopes of these hills, to which they could flee when temperatures in the city soared. Those that could not afford to buy or build their own property rented guest quarters in temples. The journey was undertaken on mule at an easy pace, trav-

elling through the woodlands, enjoying the feeling of communion with nature, and staying overnight in Daoist or Buddhist shrines.

Later, the Ming emperors turned the area into an imperial game preserve. As recently as 300 years ago, the Qing emperor Kangxi is supposed to have killed a tiger here. Qianlong turned it into a landscaped park, a complex of 28 scenic zones, named the Park of Tranquillity and Pleasure. As with both of the Summer Palaces, however, it was badly

Maps on pages 160 & 173

**LEFT:** figure at the Ming Tombs.
**BELOW:** Buddhist ceremony at Tanzhesi.

*The Glazed Tile Pagoda (Liulita) is a prominent landmark in Xiangshan Park.*

**BELOW:** the hills are famous for their autumnal colour.

damaged by foreign troops in 1860, and again in 1900. Few of the buildings have survived.

The Fragrant Hills were opened to the public in 1957, and quickly became one of the most popular excursions for city dwellers. Bear in mind that on summer and autumn weekends the crowds are so large it can sometimes feel as if you are still in the city. The hills are particularly popular in late autumn because of the blazing reds and yellows of the sycamore leaves.

Turn right inside the main eastern gate to the park and you come to the Tibetan-style **Temple of Clarity A** (Zhaomiao), built in 1780 for the Panchen Lama. In its grounds is the octagonal **Glazed Tile Pagoda B** (Liulita), which has little bells hanging from the corners of its eaves, the lightest breeze making them chime delicately. The **Chamber of Introspection C** (Jianxinhai), to the east of the pagoda, has a courtyard in the

southern Chinese style with a semi-circular pond, as well as the usual walkways and pavilions. Only a few steps ahead lie two lakes separated by a jetty, and known, because of their shape, as the **Spectacles Lake D** (Yanjinghu).

Beyond this is the northern gate, from which a chairlift will take you to the 550-metre (1,830-ft) summit of the "Fragrant Hill". From here you can gaze over steep, thickly wooded slopes and deep ravines to Biyunsi Temple (in a side valley on the northeast side of the park). Further away is the Jade Spring Hill, with its ancient pagoda, with the Summer Palace and Kunming Lake beyond. In the far distance are the skyscrapers of Haidian District – on a clear day, you can get a good impression of the immensity of Beijing. If you're feeling fit you can climb the hill on foot instead of taking the chair lift, but you will need good shoes and at least a couple of

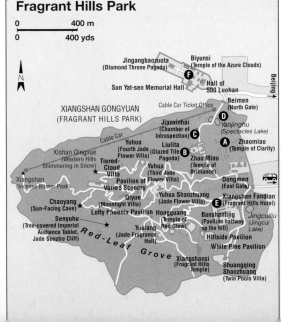

## Fragrant Hills Park

0      400 m
0      400 yds

N

Jingangbaozuota (Diamond Throne Pagoda)
Biyunsi (Temple of the Azure Clouds) **F**
Sun Yat-sen Memorial Hall
Hall of 500 Luohan
Beijing

Cable Car Ticket Office

XIANGSHAN GONGYUAN (FRAGRANT HILLS PARK)

Beimen (North Gate)

Jianxinhai (Chamber of Introspection) **C**
Yanjinghu (Spectacles Lake) **D**

Cable Car

Yuhua (Fourth Jade Flower Villa)
Liulita (Glazed Tile Pagoda) **B**
Zhaomiao (Temple of Clarity) **A**

Xishan Qingxue (Western Hills Shimmering in Snow)
Tiered-Cloud Villa
Yuhua (Third Jade Flower Villa)
Zhao Miao (Temple of Brilliance)

Xiangshan (Incense Burner Peak)
Pavilion of Varied Scenery
Dongmen (East Gate)

Chaoyang (Sun-Facing Cave)
Qiyue (Moonlight Villa)
Yuhua Shanzhuang (Jade Flower Villa)
Xiangshan Fandian (Fragrant Hills Hotel) **E**

Lofty Phoenix Pavilion
Hongguang (Temple of Red Glow)
Banshanting (Pavilion halfway up the hill)
Jingcuiliu (Jingcui Lake)

Senyuhu (Tree-covered Imperial Audience Tablet, Jade Sceptre Cliff)
Yuxiang (Jade Fragrance Hall)
Hillside Pavilion
White Pine Pavilion

Red-Leaf Grove

Xiangshansi (Fragrant Hills Temple)
Shuangqing Shanzhuang (Twin Pools Villa)

hours to spare. The steepest part of the hill bears the name Guijianchou, which means "Even the devil is afraid of it!"

Near the eastern gate stands the I.M. Pei-designed **Xiangshan Hotel** **E**, probably the most beautifully situated hotel in the region. The southern part of the park beyond the hotel is excellent for picnics. Yet only a few visitors ever seem to find their way here. Past the remains of the once massive **Xiangshan Temple** (destroyed in 1860) that rose over six levels, you will reach the remote **Twin Peaks Villa** (Shuang Qing Shanzhuang) and the **Pavilion Halfway up the Hill** (Banshanting). Here, a small tower has been restored, and from it you get a good view of the park.

## Temple of the Azure Clouds

Just to the north of Xiangshan Park is the spectacular, 600-year-old **Biyunsi** **F** (Temple of the Azure Clouds; open daily 8am–5pm; entrance fee). The structure is made up of four great halls, the innermost being the memorial hall for Sun Yat-sen. Here lies an empty coffin, a gift from the Soviet Union, which could not be used because it did not arrive until two weeks after the funeral.

To the left of the main entrance of the hall, letters and manuscripts left by Sun Yat-sen are on display. On the wall is an inscription in marble: a letter from Sun Yat-sen addressed to the Soviet Union. There are exhibition rooms on both sides of the memorial hall showing photographs from Sun's life.

Beyond the memorial hall is the pagoda courtyard. The marble **Diamond Throne Pagoda** (Jingang-baozuota) was built in 1748 under the rule of Emperor Qianlong, and is modelled on Wutasi (the Temple of the Five Pagodas) in northwest Beijing (*see page 154*). In March 1925, Sun Yat-sen's coffin lay in state in the pagoda, before being moved in 1929 to Zhongshanling, the Sun Yat-sen mausoleum in Nanjing. His clothing and personal belongings, however, remained here. The pagoda itself is 35 metres (114 ft) high, and its base is adorned with numerous statues of Buddha.

Maps
Area 160
Site 170

**TIP**

To get to Xiangshan Park on public transport, take a taxi or bus 318 from Pingguoyuan (at the western end of subway line 1), bus 333 from outside the main entrance to the Old Summer Palace, or bus 360 from Beijing Zoo. All buses will drop you at the car park, from where it is a 10-minute walk to the park entrance.

**BELOW:** Biyunsi, high in the hills.

*There are over 2,000 species of trees and plants at the impressive Botanical Gardens, some in hothouses, others in formal gardens outside.*

**BELOW:** the Temple of the Reclining Buddha.

There are other places nearby worth seeking out. The **Xiangshan Zhiwuyuan** (Fragrant Hills Botanical Gardens; open daily 8am–6pm; entrance fee), to the east of the main park, contains a large conservatory and pleasant grounds. To the north is **Wofosi ❹** (Temple of the Reclining Buddha; open daily 8am–5pm; entrance fee), dating from the Tang dynasty. The 54-ton, 5-metre (18-ft) Buddha is made of lacquered and painted bronze, and is of indeterminate age, although experts have expressed doubts that it is the original statue. Surrounding the Buddha are transcendental Bodhisattvas. Beyond the temple is the **Cherry Ravine** (Yingtaogou), a romantic spot.

### Eight Scenic Sites

On a hillside 8 km (5 miles) to the south of Xiangshan is a group of former temples and monasteries that can be visited together, the **Eight Scenic Sites ❺** (Badachu; buildings open daily 8am–5pm; park open 6am–7.30pm in summer, 6am–6pm in winter; entrance fee). In the pagoda of the second temple

you come to, **Lingguangsi** (Temple of the Sacred Light), there is a holy relic reputed to be a tooth of the Buddha. **Dabeisi** (Temple of Great Compassion) is renowned for its 18 Luohan statues. The temple below the peak, the **Cave of Precious Pearls**, is built around a cave in which a hermit is supposed to have lived for 40 years during the Qing dynasty.

### Western temples

Beijing's oldest Buddhist temple is not to be found the city centre but in the Mentougou District on Tanzheshan Hill, about an hour away by taxi. It is easy to combine a visit to **Tanzhesi ❻** (Temple of the Dragon Pond and the Mulberry Tree; open daily 8am–5pm; entrance fee) with a side trip to Jietaisi. Both are delightful because of their rural setting and the sense of peaceful isolation which you can experience, particularly on weekdays.

Tanzhesi was built between AD 265 and 316 on terraces carved in dense woods – both Buddhists and Daoists traditionally withdraw to such beautiful places where they can

meditate undisturbed. The temple is made up of three parts set along a north–south line across the hill slope. Enter following the central axis from the south, through the **Gate of Honour,** and the adjoining **Mountain Gate.** The path is lined by picturesquely gnarled old pine trees. Beyond the Mountain Gate, one behind the other, are the **Hall of the Celestial Kings** (Tianwangdian), the **Daxiongbaodian Hall** (the main hall), the **Zhaitang Hall,** and the **Piluge Pavilion,** dedicated to the Buddha Vairocana. Above the main hall are legendary beasts, sons of the Dragon King, who are supposed to have captured a monk and chained him to the roof. There is a great view of Tanzhesi and its surroundings from here, the highest point in the grounds. Beyond Daxiongbaodian Hall are two **gingko trees,** called the Emperor's Tree and the Emperor's Companion's Tree, thought to date from the Liao dynasty (916–1125).

Take the western path from here and look into the **Temple of Guanyin,** where you can see the Paving Stone of Beizhuan, on which the nun Miaoyan, a daughter of the Mongol emperor Kublai Khan (1260–94), is supposed to have prayed to Buddha daily in penance for her father's misdeeds. The path continues to the **Temple of the Dragon King** and the **Temple of the Founding Father.**

In the eastern part of the grounds are a white dagoba dating from 1427, two groups of 12th-century pagodas, a bamboo grove and the **Pavilion of the Moving Cup** (Liubeige), where Qianlong stayed during his visits to the temple.

Eight km (five miles) to the southeast, at the foot of Ma'anshan Hill, is **Jietaisi ❼** (Ordination Terrace Temple; open daily 8am–5pm; entrance fee). This imposing temple dates from 622 and owes its name to the three-level stone terraces

Maps
on pages
160 & 173

**TIP**

To get to Badachu on public transport, take the subway to Ping-guoyuan at the western end of subway line 1, then a taxi or bus 965.

Tanzhesi and Jietalsi can both be reached by bus 931 from Ping-guoyuan, or by tourist bus 7 from Qianmen in central Beijing (April to October; departures from 6.30–8.30am only). The easy option is to hire a taxi for the day.

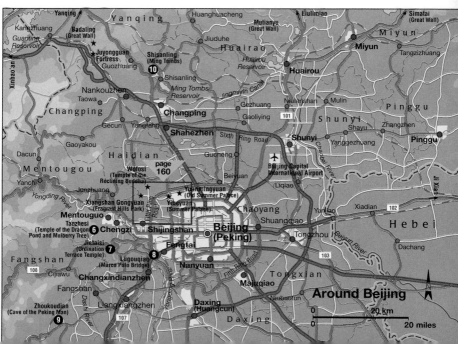

### TIP

The Marco Polo Bridge can be reached by public bus 339 from the junction of Nanxinhua Jie and Zhushikou Xidajie (across the intersection from the Huguang Opera Museum), but it's a long ride. Alternatively, hire a taxi for the day.

*ORIENTATION*
*The area covered in this chapter extends northwest to the Ming Tombs and southwest to the Peking Man site.*

**BELOW:** an offering at Tanzhesi.

which were surrounded by statues and upon which the dedication ceremony of monks took place. The main hall is the **Daxiongbaodian**, and beyond it is the **Thousand Buddhas Pavilion**. Steles with Buddhist inscriptions dating from the Liao and Yuan dynasties can be seen in front of the **Mingwang Hall**. There is no longer much to be seen inside the halls, but it is worthwhile taking a walk to enjoy the temple grounds with their old pine trees.

In Haidian District out past the New Summer Palace (take a taxi, or bus 346 from the main gate) is **Dajuesi** (Temple of Enlightenment; open daily 8am–5pm; entrance fee), at the foot of Yangtai Hill. It was founded in 1068, but the present buildings date from 1428, when the temple was rebuilt. It is known for its "six wonders", which include a 1,000-year-old stele, a millennial gingko tree and the beautifully clear **Dragon Pool** fed by a nearby spring.

To the south, in the district of Shijingshan, is the **Fahaisi Temple** (open 9am–4.30pm; entrance fee, built by the eunuch Li Tong in 1439

and today visited chiefly for its murals dating from the Ming dynasty.

## Marco Polo Bridge

The **Marco Polo Bridge** ❽ (Lugouqiao; open daily 8am–5pm; entrance fee), is 15 km (9 miles) southwest of central Beijing. The Italian merchant Marco Polo, who stayed at the court of the Mongol emperor Kublai Khan in the 13th century, admired this bridge: "Ten miles past Cumbalac (Khanbaliq)…a magnificent stone bridge crosses the river, and it has no equal anywhere in the world…The twenty-four arches and the twenty-four pillars are of grey, finely dressed and well-placed marble blocks. Marble slabs and pillars form a balustrade on both sides…It is wonderful to see how the row of pillars and the slabs are so cleverly joined together."

Lugou means "Black Ditch", and is an earlier name for the **Yongding River**, which flows under the bridge. The first crossing was built here in 1189, improved in 1444 and rebuilt following a flood in 1698. On the balustrade on either side are 140 stone posts crowned with lions, some only a few centimetres tall, others comparative giants; no two are exactly alike. At each end is a 5-metre (15-ft) stele; one records the rebuilding of the bridge in the 17th century; the other is inscribed: "The moon at daybreak over the Lugou Bridge", one of the eight wonders of old Beijing.

As the river is prone to flooding, the 11 arches of the bridge have been fastened with iron clamps to strengthen it, and it has been closed to road traffic. Upriver, a dam has created an artificial lake, so that the river bed is usually dry in summer, which has taken away some of its appeal. The river was navigable here until the early 20th century, and there was a landing place from which travellers embarked on journeys to the south.

The bridge gained notoriety in the 1930s because of the incident which is seen as the start of the Japanese invasion of Asia during World War II. On 7 July 1937, Japanese troops of the Tianjin garrison attacked the bridge, provoking the Chinese guards to fire at them. This retaliation provided a pretext for further aggression by the Japanese. By August, China and Japan were at war. A **memorial museum** (same hours as bridge, separate entrance fee) at the bridge explains the full background to these events.

## Ancestral cave

The site of the discovery of Peking Man, *Sinanthropus pekinensis*, lies close to the small town of Zhoukoudian, about 50 km (30 miles) southwest of Beijing. The **Cave of Peking Man ❾** (Beijing Yuanren Yizhi; open daily 8.30am–4.30pm; entrance fee) is on the northern slopes of Longushan (Dragon Bone Mountain).

About 450 million years ago, the site was underneath an ocean. As the waters receded, limestone caves gradually developed. Over 500,000 years ago, early hominids settled in these caves; they were to inhabit them for the next 300,000 years. When this hominid race disappeared, the caves became naturally filled in, and the tools, food scraps and bones in them remained covered by deposits until modern times.

As early as the Ming dynasty, workers digging for lime found many animal fossils, which were believed to be the bones of dragons. By the beginning of the 20th century, peasants were finding human teeth at this site. In 1921, the Swede John Gunnar Andersson found a rich source of fossils that attracted many other scientists.

More discoveries were made in the following years, until, in 1927, systematic excavations began. Two years later the complete upper skull of Peking Man was found. Java Man and Heidelberg Man were known at that time, yet the discovery of Peking Man surprised scientists and caused a great sensation.

Up until the beginning of the Japanese invasion in 1937, fossil

Map on page 173

*The Marco Polo Bridge is lined with hundreds of stone lions, no two of which are alike. A local myth says that trying to count them will drive you mad.*

**BELOW:** visiting the rural hinterland of Beijing offers a different perspective.

*An artist's impression of Peking Man.*

**BELOW:**
the entrance to the
Peking Man Cave.

remains of more than 40 individuals of both sexes had been found. The men were some 1.5 metres (5 ft) tall, the women slightly smaller. They had skulls about a third smaller than people of today, but could walk upright, use stone tools, and understood the use of fire. In the Upper Cave, the remains of *Homo sapiens,* who settled here some 18,000 years ago, were also discovered.

The actual work that led to the discovery of Peking Man seems to have been a model of international cooperation, with Chinese and Western researchers working amicably and productively side by side. In subsequent years, however, there has been a great deal of undignified squabbling over who should get the credit for finding the bones and who should take the blame for losing them. In Europe, it is common to credit the find to the Jesuit Teilhard de Chardin, who is said to have discovered the first skull. It is more likely, however, that it was discovered by the Chinese site worker Pei Wenzhong, as the Chinese have long attested.

The question as to who lost the bones of Peking man is even more vexing. Work at the site was interrupted by the Japanese occupation of China in 1937, and by 1941 it had practically come to a halt. The decision was made to get the bones out of China. Packed in specially built wooden crates, they were delivered to the office of Trevor Bowen, the American administrator of Peking Union. Mr Bowen brought the crates to the US embassy and from there they were transferred to the United States Marine Corps.

The plan was to put them aboard the SS President Harrison, for shipment to the US. However, whether the skulls actually made it onto the ship is unclear – all that is known for sure is that they have never been seen since.

There is a small, recently restored **museum** (same hours as main site, entrance fee included) on the site, close to the Peking Man Cave and the Upper Cave. The exhibits are divided into three sections and provide information on evolution in general, of Peking Man in particu-

## Political Science

The scientific importance of the Peking Man bones has diminished over the years as older hominid bones have been found elsewhere, but its symbolic importance in China has correspondingly increased. Every few years there are patriotic calls to find the missing bones, including a 1998 plea from leading palaeoanthropologists and a 2000 manifesto that opened with the words, "We call on everybody to come together and search for the lost 'Peking Man'!"... A 2003 discovery at the site of human cultural artefacts that pre-date Peking Man caused renewed interest, and led the government to channel much-needed funding into preservation of the site.

lar, and on the development of Chinese palaeontology. There are also displays of other fossils found in the area – ancient bears, tigers, elephants and rhinoceros. A sort of eternal flame at the museum symbolises the importance of Peking Man's early use of fire.

## The Ming Tombs

Although Beijing was the capital of the Middle Kingdom for five dynasties, the tombs of the Ming emperors are the only ones in relatively close proximity to the city. The tombs of the Qing emperors, both the western and eastern sites, are further out, although still within reach (*see pages 200 and 201*). The burial site of the Liao (916–1125) are in distant northeast China; those of the Jin (1125–1234) were destroyed at the end of the Ming era. The rulers of the Yuan dynasty (1279–1368) had no special burial rites and left no mausoleums behind them.

A visit to the **Ming Tombs**  (Shisanling; site open daily 8am–5.30pm; entrance fee – extra fees apply for some tombs) is often combined with a trip to the Wall at Badaling. Thirteen of the 16 Ming emperors are buried here, in a valley to the south of the Tianshou Mountains, 50 km (30 miles) northwest of Beijing. The foothills of the Yanshan Mountains form a natural entrance to the 40-sq.-km (15-sq.-mile) basin, "defended" on both sides by the Dragon and Tiger Mountains, which are said to keep harmful winds away from the holy ground.

The completion of the eight-lane Badaling Expressway has made the site more readily accessible. A visit here is usually part of an organised tour to the Great Wall, although tourist buses 1, 2, 3 and 4 all call in regularly en route to Badaling (*see page 187*), and bus 845 operates from Xizhimen to Changping, from where you can take bus 345.

Maps Area 173 Site 177

*Ming-dynasty relics on display in the Shisanling Museum.*

**BELOW:** Emperor Wanli's crown.

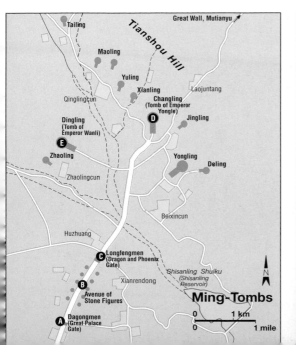

*Imperial suit of armour excavated at the Ming Tombs.*

**BELOW:** the magnificent 7-km (4-mile) Avenue of Stone Figures.

Behind the **Great Palace Gate** (Dagongmen) at the entrance to the Ming necropolis is a square stele pavilion, on which can be seen a great tortoise bearing another stele on its back. The gate marks the beginning of the **Avenue of Stone Figures** , also known as the Avenue of Ghosts. This 7-km (4-mile) road leading to the tomb of Emperor Yongle is flanked by pairs of stone lions, elephants, camels, horses and mythological creatures, followed by 12 military and civil dignitaries representing the imperial court.

Beyond these figures is the **Dragon and Phoenix Gate** (Longfengmen) with its three entrances which in earlier years were sealed off behind heavy doors.

The **Tomb of Emperor Yongle** (Changling; same hours as site; entrance fee) is the biggest and best preserved of the 13 surviving tombs. Built on a south-facing slope, its three courtyards are surrounded by a wall. The first courtyard stretches from the massive three-arched entrance gate to the **Gate of Eminent Favours** (Ling'enmen). In the

east of this courtyard is a pavilion with a stone tablet, a stone camel and a stone dragon. The **Hall of Eminent Favours** (Ling'endian) is in the second courtyard. The central section of the stone steps leading up to the hall is adorned with sea monsters and dragons. In the east and the west parts of the hall there are "fire basins", in which balls of silk and inscriptions were burned as offerings to the imperial ancestors. Four mighty wooden pillars, each one made out of a single trunk of a nanmu tree, along with 28 smaller posts, support the construction.

In the third and last courtyard, a stele tower can be found, with an incense basin and other ritual objects in front of it – the so-called "nine stone utensils". On the stele is the inscription "Tomb of the Emperor Chengzu of the great Ming dynasty" (Chengzu was the temple name of Emperor Yongle). A wall with a circumference of about 1 km (½ mile) was built to enclose the burial mound which is 31 metres (102 ft) long and 38 metres (125 ft) broad. To the east and west are the

tombs of the 16 imperial concubines, who were buried alive to serve their emperor in the underworld.

The **Tomb of Emperor Wanli ⒺE** (Dingling; same hours as site; entrance fee) lies to the southwest of Changling. Wanli (1573–1619) was buried here in 1620, together with his two wives, Xiaoduan and Xiaojing. About 30,000 workers took a total of six years (1584–90) to complete the tomb, which cost 8 million taels of silver (equivalent to the total land tax for two years).

A tunnel leads down to a depth of 7 metres (23 ft), to the first massive gate of a subterranean palace, with five rooms, mighty marble vaulting and a floor of 50,000 highly polished stones. The marble thrones of the emperor and his wives stand in the **central hall**. An "eternal lamp" (an oil lamp with a floating wick that was believed to burn for ever) and five sacrificial offerings (an incense bowl, two candelabra and two vases of yellow-glazed earthenware) can be seen in the room. Next door are two side chambers that contain pedestals for coffins. These platforms, which are covered with the "golden stones" and filled with yellow earth, are known as the Golden Fountains. No coffins were found in this chamber.

The **rear hall** is the largest and the most imposing in the subterranean palace. It is 9.5 metres (30 ft) high, 30 metres (100 ft) long and 9 metres (30 ft) wide. On pedestals in the middle of the hall are the coffins of Wanli and his empresses, surrounded by 26 lacquered chests filled with crowns, gold and jade pitchers, cups, bowls, earrings and wine containers. There are also sacred objects of jade and items of blue-and-white Ming porcelain. An extraordinarily fine filigree crown of gold adorned with two dragons playing with a pearl *(pictured on page 177)* can be viewed in the two exhibition halls within the complex, together with a valuable embroidery showing 100 playing children, and other exhibits.

Other Ming emperors' tombs are not open to the public at present, but you can wander around the grounds for several miles, discovering the ruins of other tomb structures and escaping from the crowds. ❑

*Lion pillars guard the main entrance to the Ming Tombs complex.*

# RESTAURANTS & BARS

## Restaurants

### Shandong

**Songlin Restaurant**
Xiangshan Villa, east gate of Fragrant Hills Park. Tel: 6259-1296. Open: 10am–4pm. $$
This is a massive restaurant specialising in home-style cooking from Shandong Province. There is the option of "fast food" service or full restaurant facilities.

### Shaoxing

**Huangye Cun**
Xiangshan Botanical Gardens. Tel: 8259-9121. Open: 10:30am–9:30pm. $$$
On the grounds of the Botanical Gardens, the Huangye Cun specialises in Shaoxing cuisine from southern China.

### Chinese (general)

**Fragrant Hills Hotel Restaurants**
Fragrant Hills Park, Haidian. Tel: 6259-1166. Open: noon–2pm, 6–8:30pm. $$$

There are three restaurants in here, with food from Sichuan and Shandong provinces, and specialities from Shanghai.

### Hot-pot

**Wofosi Restaurant**
Wofosi, Xiangshan Botanical Gardens. Tel: 6259-3635. Open: 10am–3pm. $$
Serves family-style cooking and hot-pot, with lamb and beef as its specialities.

## Bars

**Sculpting in Time (Diaoke Shiguang)**

50 Maimaijie, Xiangshan Tel: 8259-0040. Open: 8am–1pm. $
Popular coffee house and bar situated south of the main entrance to Xiangshan Park, with a beautiful terrace.

• • • • • • • • • • •

*Prices are for a typical dinner for one (three dishes with beer in Chinese restaurants, or a three-course meal with a half bottle of house wine in Western-style restaurants).*
*$ = under 50 Rmb*
*$$ = 50–100 Rmb*
*$$$ = 100–150 Rmb*
*$$$$ = over 150 Rmb*

# THE GREAT WALL

**The greatest fortification in human history was built to prevent invasion by nomadic tribes from the steppes to the north. Today it is one of the most famous sights on earth.**

The Great Wall is the single greatest tourist attraction in China, and one of the greatest in all the world. It has excited fascination and wonder among Westerners ever since tales of its immensity and scale began trickling back to Europe in the 17th and 18th centuries. Its popularity as a tourist attraction among Chinese is more of a 20th-century phenomenon, one given a considerable boost by Chairman Mao's comment to the effect, "If you haven't been to the Great Wall, you're not a real Chinese." An unattributed, but similar, aphorism directed at Westerners says, "If you haven't been to the Great Wall, you haven't been to China".

Thanks to the widespread expression of such sentiments, the Great Wall receives upwards of 5 million visitors a year. The part of the Wall that nearly all foreigners, and many Chinese, choose to visit is easily reached as a day trip from Beijing.

It is possible to visit the Wall in all seasons. It looks as spectacular flanked by summer greenery as by winter snow, or by autumn yellows, oranges and browns. Spring and autumn are best for hiking, however, as summer heat and dense vegetation make an excursion more of an ordeal, and in mid-winter snow and ice make the steep slopes danger-

ous. In any season, solid and comfortable footwear is advised.

### The rise and fall of the Wall

The "Ten Thousand Li Great Wall" (Wan Li Chang Cheng) represents the pinnacle of 2,000 years of wall building in northern China. The construction visible today dates mostly from the 15th century and stretches for some 4,000 km (2,500 miles). It is a structure of overwhelming physical presence; a vast wall of earth, brick and stone topped

Map on page 184

**LEFT:** an empty stretch of Wall at Juyongguan Pass. **BELOW:** crowds at Badaling.

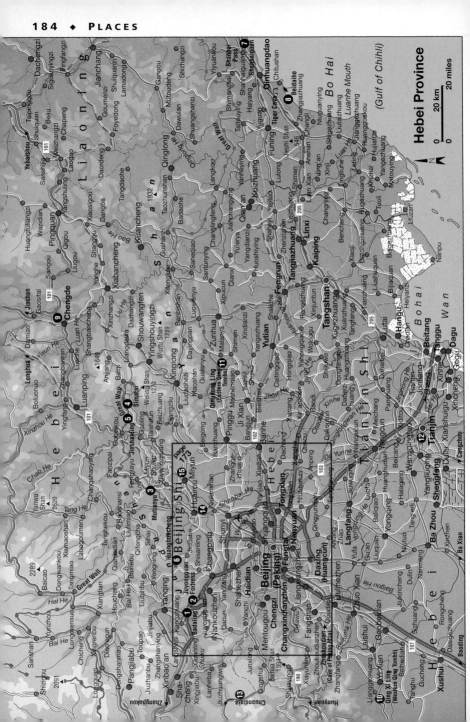

**Hebei Province**

0    20 km
0    20 miles

N

*Bo Hai*

*(Gulf of Chihli)*

*Bo Hai Wan*

by an endless procession of stout towers, rolling over craggy peaks and across deep ravines and barren deserts. But the Great Wall is more than a remnant of history. It is massively symbolic of the tyranny of imperial rule, the application of mass labour, the ingenuity of engineers commissioned to work on the grandest scale, and the human desire to build for immortality.

It is, however, misleading to speak of one wall. Archaeologists have identified many walls, some of which date back to the 5th century BC. These fortifications came into being because the flourishing agricultural settlements on the fertile plains along the Yellow River and its tributaries had to protect themselves against constant plundering by nomadic tribes. Each settlement built its own "great wall" of rammed earth, the earliest probably being in the state of Qi, in modern Shandong Province. The length of all such walls so far discovered totals some 50,000 km (30,000 miles).

It was Qin Shi Huangdi, considered to be the first Chinese emperor (221–210 BC), who conceived the idea of a single, protective Great Wall. He forced all the states of China to submit to his rule. After removing internal threats in this way, he linked the northern walls into a single defensive bulwark against the nomads. Under the leadership of General Meng Tian, an army of 300,000 forced labourers is said to have constructed the Great Wall. In those days, the Wall began in the west of Lintao (to the south of Lanzhou) and ran east through Inner Mongolia, Shaanxi and Hebei provinces. It ended in the east of what is now Liaoning Province.

The Great Wall did not always fulfil its purpose of keeping enemies out. It was breached regularly even before the Tang dynasty (618–907) extended the borders of its empire

well beyond it. Sometimes it simply had no purpose at all. The Mongol conquerors who ruled northern China from 936 to 1368 had no need of the Wall, since it lay in the middle of their territory, and served as neither a boundary nor a defence.

However, the overthrow of the Mongols by the first Ming emperor, Zhu Yuanzhang (1368–98), changed the situation. The maintenance of the Great Wall became a matter of life or death for the new Ming dynasty, which had to defend itself against attacks from the Mongols. For more than 200 years, work went on to strengthen the Wall. New sections were built, fortified towers were extended, and the logistics of defending and administering it were overhauled and improved.

The Wall was mostly left to decay after the middle of the 18th century. The Manchu rulers of the Qing dynasty were invaders from beyond the Wall, and were intent on expanding rather than consolidating their empire. Wind and weather gradually eroded away some sections of the redundant walls. Peasants recycled

*Cable cars ensure swift access to the higher sections of the Wall at Badaling and Mutanyu.*

**BELOW:** security guard on the Wall at Badaling.

*Hiring a taxi for the day makes a trip out to the Great Wall a more relaxed experience.*

**BELOW:** the Wall at Badaling is illuminated during the summer, and on special occasions at other times of the year.
**RIGHT:** dressing up as a Mongol warrior.

bricks and stones to build farmhouses and stables. This process of deconstruction continued into modern times. During the Cultural Revolution, army units built whole barracks out of bricks taken from the Great Wall.

The Wall has since been given a new lease of life as one of the most familiar images of China at home and abroad. As a patriotic symbol, it now adorns the badges of China's public-security officers. On the screen it has formed the background for Japanese children's choirs, American fashion shows, religious services, sporting events and mobile-phone advertisements. It is used as a brand name for everything from computers to wine. Plays have been staged in its towers, motorcyclists have jumped over it and parachutists have landed on it. Illusionist David Copperfield once walked through it.

## Preserving the Wall

Since Deng Xiaoping launched a campaign in 1984 to "Love China, Restore the Great Wall", many sections have been rebuilt and opened to tourists. The intentions of the campaign were good and have generally led to much greater respect for and interest in the Wall. However, over the years this increased interest has produced certain negative side effects.

The chief source of the problems is tourism itself. As more people visit the Great Wall, the popular restored areas become increasingly crowded, causing those interested in a more genuine – or at least private – Wall experience to seek out less crowded parts of the 675 km (420 miles) of Wall in the Beijing area. However, it is hard to keep anything secret in China, and as more hikers show up on a particular unrestored section of the Wall – commonly referred to as "Wild Wall" – local people begin appearing to sell mineral water.

Such small-scale entrepreneurial activity gradually grows until, in the blink of an eye, an entire village erects a bridge or a barricade on the Wall so they can charge tourists to cross it. Local officials get involved and build guesthouses or cable cars.

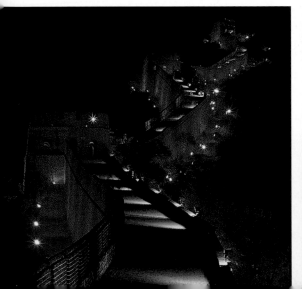

Sometimes they even undertake hastily to repair the Wall with limestone and paint. More tourists come, bringing with them their litter, noise and graffiti, and causing the more adventurous to seek undiscovered sections of Wild Wall – and thus the entire cycle begins again.

If tourism is a problem, it is not only tourists who are to blame. Ultimately, the government is responsible for protecting the Wall. However, more often than not, it is local governments who are part of the problem. Even at the central level, the lack of will and the failure to commit sufficient funding led the World Monument Fund to place the Great Wall Cultural Landscape in the area of Beijing on its list of the world's most endangered monuments in 2002. This helped bring more attention to the problem, and in 2003 the Beijing government promulgated stricter regulations banning the construction of buildings on or near the Wall, and forbade hikers from walking on the most fragile sections. The battle to protect the Wall will be forever ongoing, but the tide seems, perhaps, to have turned in its favour.

## Badaling

The most accessible section of the Wall – and consequently the most crowded – is at **Badaling ❶** (open daily 8am–4.30pm; entrance fee; cable car extra), 60 km (38 miles) northwest of Beijing. It is easily reached by the fast road from Beijing *(see margin for details)*. Despite the hordes of sightseers, avoidable in the early mornings and in the colder months, Badaling has great scenery, restored forts and exhibitions to see.

The Wall here was strategically important and heavily fortified by the Ming emperors. The gate facing west bears the inscription "The Bolt of the Northern Gate", while the one facing east states, "The First Line before Juyongguan". The towers are solidly built, with high arrow slits. The way up on both sides of the valley leads to high beacon towers, from which you can see the northern plain and the Wall snaking across faraway hills. The western side is a steeper climb.

Maps on pages 173 & 184

**TIP**

Badaling is the number-one destination for tour groups, but it is easy to get here independently, too. Tourist buses operate from April through October; no.1 departs regularly (6am–noon) from Qianmen; no.2 from Beijing Railway Station. It takes 90 minutes, and buses call in at the Ming Tombs on the way back. There is also an air-conditioned bus (919) from Deshengmen bus station just north of the Second Ring Road.

**BELOW:** souvenir stall.

*A steep climb to the strategically important Juyong Pass.*

**RIGHT:** an unrestored section of Wall.

The only drawback of Badaling is that it can seem unbearably crowded and commercialised. Vendors of tacky souvenirs and T-shirts compete for sales, not only as you approach but also on the Wall itself. In the evening, karaoke sessions and laser shows are sometimes held. Only by a brisk walk of an hour or so can you escape from the tour groups.

The majority of tourists visit Badaling as part of a tour, often taking in the Ming Tombs *(see page 177)* en route and sometimes also stopping at **Juyongguan Fortress** ❷, built to guard the narrow, 20-km (13-mile) long valley, and Beijing, against invading armies from the north. In the middle of the valley is a stone platform of white marble, the **Cloud Terrace** (Yuntai). Built in 1345, it once served as the foundation for a great gate with three stone pagodas. An arched gateway still survives. In the vaulted passage of the gate there are splendid reliefs, mostly Buddhist motifs, among them the four Tianwang (Celestial Kings), and inscriptions of Buddhist sutras in six different languages: Sanskrit, Tibetan, Tangut, Uighur, Mongol and Chinese.

The Wall climbs steeply on both sides from the fortress; this was an important stretch of Wall, and is one of the oldest. It has been renovated in recent years but is usually quite empty, and the scenery is dramatic.

## Mutianyu

The Wall at **Mutianyu** ❸ (open daily, 8am–5pm; entrance fee; cable car extra) is equally spectacular but less crowded than Badaling. A long section of restored Wall follows a high ridge, giving views over wooded ravines 90 km (55 miles) northeast of Beijing. The nearest point on the Wall is a steep one-hour climb from the car park, though a cable car offers a breathtaking alternative. Mutianyu was not part of the main Wall but a barrier wall shielding passes to the north towards Zhangjiakou. High parapets, crenellated on both sides, are part of the major Ming-dynasty renovations completed in 1569. As at Badaling, large blocks of granite were used in

## Rambling on the Ramparts

To truly experience the splendour of the Wall, you need to hike on it. Of old, parts of the wall were used as routes for porters and itinerant traders. In this age of leisure-walking many enthusiasts hope it will become the world's ultimate long-distance footpath.

Since so much of the Wall is unrestored, seeing wilder sections need not be an endurance test. Walking is mostly on the Wall itself, so it's difficult to get lost, but the going is often slow. Take great care on steep, crumbling sections. In some places, you may have no alternative but to leave and rejoin the Wall; in others, rickety piles of fallen bricks may be your only climbing aid.

Jinshanling, Huanghuacheng and Simatai are three of the more popular stretches, the last being the most popular place – and the most challenging, if you traverse the whole ridge. You can combine a trip to Simatai and Jinshanling, to the immediate west, perhaps camping overnight in one of the many towers along the Wall. Camping is not officially allowed but, while numbers remain small, it seems to be tolerated. The views from your beacon tower at dusk and dawn more than compensate for a night on the bricks. Do not light fires, and, of course, take all your litter with you.

the foundations because of the strategic importance of the area, which became known as the North Gate of the Capital.

## Simatai

Well established as a favoured section of Wall for hikers, **Simatai ❹** (open daily 8am–5pm; entrance fee; cable car extra) shows the unrestored Great Wall at its most majestic, crowning a narrow ridge and sharp pinnacles. The site is quite remote, 115 km (70 miles) northeast of Beijing, and many visitors find it best to take a tour.

You can either take the cable car to a point 20 to 30 minutes' walk below the Wall, or make a longer excursion on foot. If you opt for the latter, from the car park you will see a small reservoir between two steep sections of Wall. Go through the entrance gate and take the path to the right (east) leading to the higher section of Wall. This is the most spectacular stretch. Alternatively, turn left (west) for a quieter, easier walk towards Jinshanling.

The scramble to Viewing the Capital Tower (Wangjing Lou) via the ridge demands a good head for heights, but rewards you with some of the best views and most exciting walking anywhere on the Wall. In places, you walk on sections just two bricks (40 cm) wide, which locals call the *tianti,* or "stairway to heaven." Yet even on the most inaccessible parts you may find someone waiting to sell you a soft drink. On the lower reaches, inscriptions on bricks give details like "made by the infantry camp of suppressing enemy troops in the sixth year of the Wanli reign".

## Jinshanling and Gubeikou

First built by the Northern Qi dynasty in AD 555, **Jinshanling ❺** (open daily 7am–sunset; entrance fee), like neighbouring Simatai 10 km (6 miles) to the east, was part of a 3,000 *li* wall from Shanhaiguan to northern Shaanxi Province. Nearby **Gubeikou** was considered a weak point in the defence of the capital. It occupies a broad valley among low mountains cut by streams and rivers, allowing many possible routes to Beijing. Tribes of Mongol and other

Maps
on pages
173 & 184

**TIP**

To reach the farther-flung Great Wall sites independently, tourist buses (no.6 for Mutianyu, no.12 for Simatai) depart between 6.30 and 8am from the north-east corner of the intersection by Xuanwumen subway station (April to October). There are also minibuses to both destinations from Xizhimen and Dongzhimen stations.

**BELOW:** Simatai is one of the least developed sections.

*There are several trains daily from Beijing to Shanhaiguan and Beidaihe. Journey time on the faster trains is three or four hours. You should book tickets two days in advance of travel. There are also buses from Xizhimen and Majuan bus stations in Beijing. Frequent buses and trains operate between Shanhaiguan and Beidaihe.*

**BELOW:** one of many fortresses on the Wall.

nomads repeatedly forced their way through here. In 1554, the same group raided Beijing three times via Gubeikou. Heavy fortification followed in the late 16th century, including "arrow walls", small walls built across steep sections of the main Wall, giving protection to archers.

In the late 17th century, when Emperor Kangxi built his summer resort in Chengde, the pass which lies on the route there was heavily guarded. The 158 fortified towers are particularly remarkable for their variety of shapes: rectangular, round, oval and polygonal. Most of the towers on the section east of Gubeikou have been restored, but this is usually the quietest of all the tourist stretches. It makes a good choice for an easier walk with views east towards the more dramatic Simatai.

### Huanghuacheng

Once one of the main garrison areas guarding the capital, **Huanghua-cheng** ❻ (open daily 8am–6pm; entrance fee), or Yellow Flower Wall, lies 60 km (38 miles) north of Beijing, the closest the Wall gets to the city. At present the only viable transport here involves taking a tour, although tourist buses are expected to start operating soon. It once had few tourist facilities, but in recent years has become an unfortunate example of rapid overdevelopment. Climb up on either side from a small reservoir to the east of the road.

The more spectacular section begins across the reservoir – and across the narrow dam. If you are scared of heights, you will have to take a detour to cross the stream below the dam, leaving a steeper climb up to the Wall. Several large towers along the ridge offer great views on both sides. A stone tablet lies on the floor of the largest tower. Further on, the Wall resembles a saw blade as it drops steeply into the valley to your right (south).

To complete a circular route, descend to the valley on a path leading down from the large tower, which is the lowest point on the ridge. Once at the bottom, head west through orchards of apples, walnuts and apricots, until you reach the road back to the reservoir.

## The Hebei coast

Ancient walls still enclose about half of the small market town and former garrison of **Shanhaiguan** ❼, in Hebei Province, the place where the Wall meets the Sea. The East Gate, rebuilt in 1639, is known as the First Pass Under Heaven. Manchu troops rode through here to Beijing to replace the deposed Ming emperors in 1644.

As the Great Wall (open daily 7.30am– 5pm; entrance fee ) rises steeply inland, two sheer drops have to be climbed by ladder. From the top, you get a fantastic view of the Wall dropping below you and then bounding over the plain towards the sea. In the opposite direction is the Old Dragon's Head, where bricks and earth crumble into golden sand at the edge of the Bohai Sea. In late 2003 it was announced that half of Shanhaiguan's 20,000 residents were to be relocated as part of local efforts to protect the Wall and ancient constructions in its vicinity. Illegally built houses are scheduled to be demolished and repairs will be made to the city

wall, the drum tower and the three towers that mark the city gates.

Shanhaiguan is a favourite photo spot for the hordes of day-trippers who arrive from nearby **Beidaihe** ❽, a beach resort long favoured for company conferences and official junkets – although it was the small foreign community in Beijing and Tianjin who made the place popular in the early 20th century.

China's top leaders still meet here annually to discuss important policy issues and to enjoy a welcome respite from Beijing's polluted air, hidden away at a private beach to the south of town. Their conferences usually start in late July or early August, which is also the peak time for groups of lesser officials and army officers.

An abundance of cheap seafood restaurants line a small boardwalk area on the sandy 10-km (6-mile) main beach. On the rolling, rather Mediterranean-looking hills behind the town, old brick villas overlook the sea. Party officials and organisations have access to many of the 700 villas built around Beidaihe before 1949. ❑

Map on page 184

*A sandy stretch of beach, good transport links and warm shallow waters have made Beidaihe one of the main seaside resorts in China.*

### ORIENTATION

*This chapter covers the Great Wall from Badaling in the west to Shanhaiguan and Beidaihe in the east.*

# RESTAURANTS

### *Beidaihe*

**Kiesslings**
Dongjing Lu. Tel: 0335-404-4284. Open: 7:30am–10:30pm. $$$
The Beidaihe branch of the famous Austrian restaurant serves both Western and Chinese food. In the distant past, diners could expect to be served Viennese chocolate and caviar on sparkling crystal while White Russian musicians serenaded them at table. These days,

you can still get a good, nostalgia-laced meal.
**Hai Tian Xiang**
Dongjing Lu.
Tel: 0335-404-7159. Open: 8:30am–midnight. $$
Home-style cooking – and a menu in English – with seafood as a specialty; the restaurant is a quick five minute walk from the CITS office.

### *Simatai Great Wall*

**Simatai Restaurant**
Simatai Great Wall, 98 Jingqu Lu. Tel: 6903-5311

Open: 8am–9pm. $
Homestyle food prepared by a Sichuanese chef with long-time experience working in Beijing.
**Great Wall Villa**
Simatai Great Wall, Jingqu Lu. Tel: 6903-5159. Open: 7am–9pm. $
A small restaurant in this inexpensive hotel serves basic home-style food to hungry hikers.

### *Badaling Great Wall*

**Badaling Restaurant**
Badaling Great Wall. Tel: 6912-1486. Open: 11am–8pm. $$$
This is the main, state-

owned restaurant at Badaling, the only one tourism officials will promote to groups – it can hold up to 1,000 people, serves Sichuan and Jiangsu food, in clean and surroundings.

• • • • • • • • • • •
*Prices are for a typical dinner for one (three dishes with beer in Chinese restaurants, or a three-course meal with a half bottle of house wine in Western-style restaurants).*
*$ = under 50 Rmb*
*$$ = 50–100 Rmb*
*$$$ = 100–150 Rmb*
*$$$$ = over 150 Rmb*

# HOW THEY BUILT THE GREATEST WALL IN HISTORY

**The astonishing project, conceived as the ultimate defence, took nearly 20 centuries to complete and involved millions of conscripted labourers**

The Ming dynasty Ten Thousand Li Great Wall averages 8 metres (26 ft) high and 7 metres (21 ft) wide. Some sections are broad enough to allow five or six soldiers to ride side by side. Surveyors planned the route so that, where possible, the outer (generally north-facing) wall was higher. Countless parallel walls, fortified towers, beacon towers, moats, fortifications and garrisons completed a complex system. Local military units supervised construction. In a simple contract, officers and engineers detailed the time, materials and work required.

## HIDDEN SENTRIES

Many sections of the wall around Beijing were built on granite blocks, with some foundation stones weighing more than one ton.

Elaborate wooden scaffolding, hoists and pulleys, and occasionally iron girders aided the builders. To speed up the construction process, prefabricated stone parts were used for beacon towers, including lintels, gate blocks and gullies.

**ABOVE:** Construction of the Great Wall varied according to the terrain and the perceived level of threat. With the aim of maximising its defensive capabilities, surveyors often chose unlikely routes across near-vertical hillsides. Engineers coped with the topography by using stretches of "single" wall, bridges, viaducts, and incorporating natural features.

**BELOW:** The 7-metre- (23-ft-) thick wall was constructed of an outer layer of brick and stone enclosing an inner core of earth, rubble and, legends say, the bones of conscript labourers.

**ABOVE:** Stone tablets, like this one set into the wall at Huanghuacheng, serve as invaluable artefacts by which to measure the progress of construction down the centuries. The tablets record what was built when and by whom, as well as listing command structures.

**BELOW:** Ming-dynasty bricks were extremely heavy; pulleys, shoulder poles, handcarts, mules, and goats were used to move them into place.

**LEFT:** Towers in remote areas were built close enough together to enable the beacon system devised in the Tang dynasty to function. When trouble was spotted, guards used wolves' dung to create smoke signals, which could be interpreted by neighbouring guard posts.

## LIFE ON THE EDGE: A GUARD'S STORY

From their small rooftop sentry boxes, Great Wall guards, though they kept their weapons and torches primed, saw no enemies for months on end. If an assault came, the guards' main function was not to defend the wall but to alert the nearest garrison using a complex system of torch signals.

Most guards lived in remote watchtowers shared with five to ten others. During the day, those not on lookout tilled small patches of farmland on the hillside, collected firewood and dried cattle or wolf dung, and sometimes hunted. They ground wheat flour in stone mortars and carried out minor repairs to the wall and tower. To supplement food supplies brought by road, migration of farmers was encouraged or enforced, and guards helped them construct irrigation canals and farmhouses.

The guards' crowded living quarters also served as storage for grain and weapons. Doors and windows had heavy wooden shutters to keep out the winter cold, and often guards shared a *kang*, a heated brick bed.

**BELOW:** To minimise transportation costs, brick kilns were constructed as close to the wall as possible. Brick makers often recorded their names and the date of production on the bricks as a guarantee of quality. So far, some 50 brick kilns have been excavated. Archaeologists believe dozens – if not hundreds – more remain buried along the length of the wall.

# FURTHER AFIELD

Beyond the Great Wall, the imperial resort at Chengde offers perfect respite from the heat and noise of the city. Within easy reach south of Beijing, the port city of Tianjin offers fascinating architecture and interesting shopping

The region extending from the immediate surroundings of Beijing, largely encompassed by Hebei Province, has a great deal to offer anyone who wishes to see a different side of China, away from the frenetic energy of the capital city. Within reach are resorts of both imperial and seaside variety – mountains, lakes and grasslands, imperial tombs, and the enyoyable city of Tianjin. In the countryside, enter another world, where the air is clean, trees and grass are abundant, and life is lived at a slower pace.

## Chengde, Imperial Resort

Chengde , 250 km (150 miles) to the northeast of Beijing, is a city of more than 200,000 people that feels a lot smaller than it actually is. It is several degrees cooler than Beijing, and even though there are tall buildings and busy roads, it has kept the feel of the summer resort it once was.

Around the end of the 17th century, the Qing emperors began to look around for somewhere cool and green to retreat to when the summer heat of Beijing became oppressive. They found what they were looking for beyond the Great Wall, in the hilly countryside around the Wulie River. Here they created a summer residence, exploiting mountains, woods and other exist-

ing natural features, to which they added contrived landscapes to make settings for innumerable pavilions, palaces and temples.

The resort was first established when Emperor Kangxi (1661–1722) ordered the building of a summer palace here in 1703, and construction continued through most of the reign of Qianlong (1736–95). The result is the largest imperial residence in China that has survived in its original condition – the buildings and gardens cover an area of 560

Map on page 184

**LEFT:** overview of the Chengde palaces, with Putuozongsheng in the background.
**BELOW:** fur hats help to protect against the freezing winter cold.

TIP

There are several trains daily from Beijing Zhan to Chengde, generally taking around 4½ hours – although some take considerably longer. Buses and minibuses go from Deshengmen, Xizhimen and Dongzhimen bus stations.

**BELOW:**
Emperor Kangxi.

hectares (1,400 acres), and are surrounded by a wall 10 km (6 miles) long. Outside the palace walls, to the north and west, a total of 11 temples – mostly in the Tibetan style – were built. Seven of these can still be visited.

For over 100 years, the emperors and their retinues passed the summer months here, spending their time on hunting excursions, equestrian games and other diversions, as well as on state business. Yet after 1820, when a bolt of lightning killed Emperor Jiaqing, who was in residence at Chengde, the resort was abandoned. Fearing that fate might deal them a second blow, the court stayed away, and the buildings and gardens fell into ruin.

Xianfeng was the only emperor ever to stay here again, and he only did so when forced to flee Beijing during the Second Opium War in 1860. It was at the Imperial Resort that he was obliged to sign the

Treaty of Peking, which granted far-reaching concessions to foreigners. He died the following year.

## Around the resort

Bordering the northern edge of the town are the beautiful landscapes of the **Imperial Resort** (park open dail, 5.30am–6pm, buildings open 8am–5pm; entrance fee includes buildings in the park). The closest section to Chengde itself is **Bishu Shanzhuang** (The Mountain Resort for Escaping the Heat; open daily 8am–5pm; entrance fee), consisting of three great complexes reached by passing through the **Lizhengmen Gate Ⓐ**, which has a tablet bearing inscriptions in Chinese, Mongol, Manchu, Tibetan and Uighur. The **Inner Gate** (Neiwumen) bears an inscription in Emperor Kangxi's calligraphy, naming the resort.

As in the Forbidden City in Beijing, the first halls entered are those in which state business was

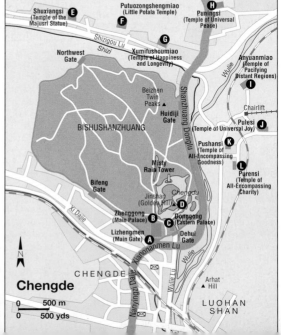

conducted and ceremonies were held, with the private imperial apartments occupying the rear of the palace. The main hall of the **Main Palace ❸** (Zhenggong) is built of precious nanmu hardwood from southwest China. This was the hall in which, in 1860, Xianfeng reluctantly signed the treaty dictated by the British and the French.

The **Hall of Pines and Cranes** (Songhezhai), to the east of the Main Palace, was the private residence of the emperor's mother. Beyond this is the **Hall of Ten Thousand Pine Valleys in the Wind** (Wanhesongfeng), from which you get a view of the northern grounds. Here, the 12-year-old Qianlong was instructed by his grandfather, Kangxi, in the proper form of answering petitions, and in classical literature. In memory of Kangxi, he later named the hall the **Hall for Remembering Kindness** (Ji'entang).

In the southeast corner of the resort are the remains of the **Eastern Palace ❸** (Donggong). In 1948 the last part standing, a three-storey theatre, completely burned down.

The **park** adjoining the palaces to the north can be divided into three areas. Directly bordering the palaces to the north is the lake area; to the northwest is a plain; and to the west is a forested, hilly landscape with ravines and valleys.

The **Lake of Pure Water** (Chengdu Lake) is divided by a number of dams into eight smaller lakes. Everywhere are little pavilions, tea houses and resting places, reminiscent of the southern Chinese lakes, such as the area around the West Lake near Hangzhou. The lake is fed from the **Warm Spring** (Requan), so it does not freeze even in the frigid north Chinese winter. Smaller lakes and pools have clever features. One, for instance, offers a daytime reflection of the crescent moon – an effect created by rocks carefully placed above the water.

The artificial **Golden Hill ❹** (Jinshan) is topped by the Jinshan Pavilion where the emperors made offerings to Daoist gods. Further north lies a broad plain, which Qianlong named the **Park of Ten Thousand Trees** (Wanshuyuan).

Maps
Area 184
Site 196

*Steam locomotives are still in use in parts of northeast China, and can sometimes be seen on the line at Chengde.*

**LEFT:** pavilion at the Lake of Pure Water.

## A Right Royal Rebuff

When Lord George Macartney visited China in 1793 in an attempt to open up normal trade relations between Britain and China, Emperor Qianlong received him at Chengde. Their meeting took place in the royal audience tent where Macartney and his delegation were treated to a banquet so splendid that Lord Macartney compared it to the "celebration of a religious mystery". However, although the audience seemed to have gone well, it was followed by Qianlong's famous letter to King George in which he praised the British king for inclining himself "towards civilisation", but informed him that... "we have never valued ingenious articles, nor do we have the slightest need of your country's manufactures. Therefore, O King, as regards your request to send someone to remain at the capital, while it is not in harmony with the regulations of the Celestial Empire we also feel very much that it is of no advantage to your country. Hence we have issued these detailed instructions and have commanded your tribute envoys to return safely home. You, O King, should simply act in conformity with our wishes by strengthening your loyalty and swearing perpetual obedience so as to ensure that your country may share the blessings of peace."

*Rare animals wandered through the grounds of the Imperial Resort, among them Père David's deer, a curiosity to the Chinese, who called it the 'four dissimilarities' – it displayed features of horse, donkey, reindeer and cow.*

**BELOW:** Tibetan architectural styles at Puningsi.

Pines, acacias, willows and old cypresses grow in abundance here, and Qianlong delighted in the many birds and deer. The court met in Mongol yurts, feasting and watching wrestling bouts, or enjoying displays of horse-riding or folk arts. To the west of the gardens was a great riding arena where the emperors chose their horses and had them broken in and trained for equestrian performances.

## The Eight Outer Temples

Many of the temples at Chengde were built in Tibetan style, a sign of the favour shown to the Lamaist religion by the Qing emperors. Eleven such temples were built on the hills northwest of the Imperial Resort during the reigns of Kangxi and Qianlong.

Divided into eight groups, they became known as the **Eight Outer Temples** (open daily 8am–5pm; individual entrance fees). The main gates of these buildings pointed towards the palace, symbolising the unity of China's various ethnic groups under central imperial rule.

Seven temples remain, with halls modelled on famous Tibetan Buddhist buildings. In a kind of giant ancient Buddhist theme park, the 18th-century replicas of the Potala Palace in Lhasa, the Tashilhunpo and Samye monasteries elsewhere in Tibet and other religious buildings from all over China, make an impressive sight. Today, several temples again have small communities of monks living in them, allowed back in the 1980s after the religious repression of the Cultural Revolution had ceased. All are open daily from 8am to 5pm.

In the extreme northwest is the **Temple of the Majusri Statue** Ⓔ (Shuxiangsi), dating from 1774. A replica of the Shuxiang Temple in the Wutaishan Mountains of Shanxi Province, it holds a Manchu translation of the Buddhist scriptures, the *Kanjur*. Further east, due north of the Imperial Resort, is the large and spectacular **Putuozongsheng Temple** Ⓕ, which bears the name of Putuoshan, a sacred Buddhist mountain on an island in the East China Sea. It is modelled, however, on the

Potala Palace, the residence of the Dalai Lama in Tibet until 1959. Building began in 1767, and the temple was completed four years later. It served as a residence for high Tibetan dignitaries when they stayed at the Chinese imperial court.

From the outside this palace appears to have seven floors, but actually it only has three. Above the Red Palace is a hall, **Wanfaguiyidian**. This contains many Bodhisattva figures. It is possible to access the roof for panoramic views across the entire complex.

The **Temple of Happiness and Longevity Ⓖ** (Xumifushoumiao) was built in 1780 for Qianlong's 70th birthday. The sixth Panchen Lama had announced his intention to travel from Tibet to attend the festivities, and, as a special honour, Qianlong recreated the Panchen Lama's residence (Tashilhunpo Monastery in Xigaze) here. The roof of the main hall is covered with scale-like, gilded copper plates, with eight gilded dragons adorning the roof beams. The bodies of the mythical animals are bent and their tails raised, so that they look as if they are about to launch themselves into the air. The main part of this temple is another Red Palace. A building to the east of it houses a throne in which Emperor Qianlong listened to sermons preached by the Panchen Lama.

A little out of the way to the northeast stands the **Temple of Universal Peace Ⓗ** (Puningsi), built in 1755. The impressive 37-metre (120-ft) high **Mahayana Hall** is China's tallest wooden pavilion, and symbolises Meru Mountain (Kang Rinpoche, or Mount Kailash, in Tibet), the cosmic centre of the Buddhist world. It is flanked by a Moon Hall and a Sun Hall, and surrounded by Tibetan stupas. Inside is a carved wooden statue of the Bodhisattva Avalokiteshvara, 22 metres (73 ft) tall, measuring 15 metres (49 ft)

across, and weighing more than 120 tons. It is said to be the tallest wooden statue in the world. Known as the Thousand Arm, Thousand Eye Guanyin Buddha, it is an incarnation of the Goddess of Mercy. Her 42 arms, each with an eye on the palm, symbolise her inexhaustible power of salvation. A statue of the Buddha Amitabha sits on the head of the goddess. The World Monument Fund has placed it and its two side statues on its endangered list; two-and-a-half centuries of visitors, dust, exposure and neglect have left the statues in "desperate need of conservation".

To the south of the Temple of Universal Peace is the **Temple of Pacifying Distant Regions Ⓘ** (Anyuanmiao), built in 1764 as a replica of the Gu'erzha temple at Ili, in Xinjiang. Only the Pududian (Hall of Universal Conversion) survives, with its statue of the Bodhisattva Ksitigarbha, the King of Hell, whom the Chinese know as Ludumu.

Further south lies the **Temple of Universal Joy Ⓙ** (Pulesi), built in 1766 in honour of Kazhak, Kirghiz

*Putuozongsheng Temple is modelled on the Potala Palace in Lhasa.*

***ORIENTATION***
*This chapter covers Hebei Province and Tianjin Shi.*

**BELOW:** martial arts outside Puningsi.

*Wall detail at the Western Qing Tombs. Both the yellow colouring and the dragon represent the emperor.*

**BELOW:** the tomb of Emperor Guangxu.

and other nobles from northwest China. The building is similar in style to the main hall of Beijing's Temple of Heaven. Beyond the entrance gate, bell and drum towers stand on either side. The main building, Pavilion of Morning Light (Xuguangge), or Round Pavilion, rests on a square terrace, the combination symbolising Heaven and Earth according to ancient Chinese cosmology. The Temple of Universal Joy also contains bronze images of Tibetan deities conquering their enemies and in erotic embrace – fine examples of the simultaneously gorgeous and terrifying imagery of Tibetan Buddhism. Behind the temple you can hike or take a cable car to the eroded rock of **Club Peak**.

Adjoining the grounds of the Temple of Universal Joy to the south is the **Temple of All-Encompassing Goodness ⓚ** (Pushansi), which has fallen into ruin. Next to this is the **Temple of All-Encompassing Charity ⓛ** (Purensi). The southernmost of the Eight Outer Temples, it was built in 1713 to celebrate Emperor Kangxi's 60th birthday.

## The Western Qing Tombs

The **Western Qing Tombs ❿** (Qingxiling; open daily 8am–5pm; entrance fee; buy an all-inclusive *tao piao* ticket to access all tombs) lie in a hilly district on the southern slopes of the Yongning Mountains, 125 km (80 miles) southwest of Beijing, near the town of Yixian. The Qing emperors Yongzheng, Jiaqing, Daoguang and Guangxu, along with three empresses, seven princes and many imperial concubines, are buried here. The site is very spread out.

The largest tomb, roughly at the centre of the site, is the **Tomb of Emperor Yongzheng** (Tailing). Yongzheng (1723–35) was extremely suspicious, and developed a network of spies who were supposed to observe the activities of his ministers. He rarely left his palace for any length of time, and only six years after ascending the throne, began to seek a suitable site for his tomb. Because he had gained the throne in an illegal manner, it is said that Yongzheng was afraid of being buried close to his father, Kangxi, in the Eastern Qing Tombs.

The **Gate of Eminent Favours** (Longenmen) is the entrance to the main part of the Tailing complex. Within the gate there are furnaces for burning offerings, and the former storehouses which now serve as exhibition halls. Offerings were made in the **Hall of Eminent Favours** (Longendian), which contains the thrones of the emperor and the empress, together with an altar for offerings and gifts. Beyond the hall are two gates, stone receptacles for offerings and a stele tower, below which lies the underground palace of the emperor.

Not far away to the west of Yongzheng's tomb is the **Tomb of Emperor Jiaqing** (Changling), completed in 1803 but not occupied until 1821. The number of buildings and their style are almost identical.

Five km (3 miles) further west is the **Mausoleum of Emperor Daoguang** (Muling), built between 1832 and 1836. After he had ascended the throne, Daoguang immediately began to have a mausoleum built in the Eastern Qing Tombs. One year after its completion, it was discovered that the subterranean palace was full of water. A new site was found at the Western tombs.

Meanwhile, new homes had to be found for dragons that had been displaced from their homes when the abortive Eastern Tomb had flooded. Hence, the unique work of art of the **Hall of Eminent Favours** (Longendian): on its coffered ceiling of *nanmu* wood, every panel bears a writing dragon, and the unpainted beams are carved in dragon forms.

The **Tomb of Emperor Guangxu** (Chongling) lies 5 km (3 miles) to the east of the Tailing. It was built in 1909, and is the last of the imperial tombs, although Guangxu was not to be the last emperor of the Qing dynasty. That dubious honour is held by Pu Yi, China's last

emperor, who died in 1967 as an ordinary mortal who could not therefore be buried beside his imperial ancestors. To the east of Guangxu's mausoleum is a mausoleum for his concubines, including Zhen Fei and her sister, Jinfei.

## The Eastern Qing Tombs

Among the largest and most beautiful tombs in China are the **Eastern Qing Tombs**  (Qingdongling; open daily 8.30am–5pm; entrance fee; buy an all-inclusive *tao piao* ticket to access all tombs), near the town of Zunhua, 125 km (80 miles) east of Beijing – a three- or four-hour drive. There is agreeable countryside to look at on the way and, once you arrive, the cobbled courtyards, stone bridges, streams and pathways make the stroll around the wooded tomb complex much more pleasant than the trudge around many tourist sites.

The Jingxing mountain range, which resembles an upturned bell, borders the area to the south.

Five Qing emperors are buried in the area: Shunzi (1644–61) chose this

Maps
Area 184
Site 196

**TIP**

The Western Qing Tombs are best reached by taxi, but it's a long drive (up to three hours) so this is expensive. There are buses from Liu Li Qiao and Li Ze Qiao bus stations in the southwest of the city. Most rail departures are from Beijing Xi Zhan (West Station); take a train to Gaobeidian, and then a taxi or minibus from there. Trains returning to Beijing are few, so it's best to take the bus or go by taxi.

**BELOW:** portrait of Guangxu.

**TIP**

To reach the Eastern Qing Tombs hire a taxi for the day, or take a bus from the Majuan bus station in the southeast of the city. Journey time is three to four hours, so you will need to make a very early start if you are planning a day trip. The bus will drop you at Zunhua, from where it's best to take a taxi the short distance to the tombs.

**BELOW:** marble bridges span the moat in front of Emperor Kangxi's tomb.

broad valley for the site of his tomb while on a hunting expedition. Kangxi (1661–1722), Qianlong (1736–96), Xiangfeng (1851–61) and Tongzhi (1862–75) followed him, as well as the Empress Dowager Cixi (who died in 1908), and a total of 14 other empresses, 136 imperial concubines and princesses.

The main entrance to the tombs is a great white **marble gate**, its rectangular surfaces covered with inscriptions and geometric designs. Pairs of lions and dragons form the base of the pillars. Beyond this is the **Great Palace Gate** (Dagongmen), which served as the official entrance to the mausoleum complex. It has a tower in which a carved *bixi* (a tortoise-like animal) bears a tall stone tablet on its shell. Engraved on the tablet are the "sacred virtues and worthiness" of the Emperor Shunzi.

Passing a small hill to the north, you come to a *shenlu* (spirit way) with 18 pairs of stone figures, similar to the one at the Ming Tombs, but a little smaller. This road leads through the **Dragon and Phoenix Gate** (Longfengmen) and crosses a marble

bridge with seven arches. This is the longest and most beautiful of nearly 100 bridges in the complex, and is known as the **Five Notes Bridge**. If you step on one of the 110 stone slabs, you will, it is said, hear the five notes of the pentatonic scale.

At the other end of the bridge is the **Gate of Eminent Favours** (Longenmen), the entrance to the **Tomb of Emperor Shunzi** (Xiaoling). Beyond the Gate of Eminent Favours is the **Hall of Eminent Favours** (Longendian), where the ancestor tablets and the offerings to the ancestors were kept. A stele tower rises behind the hall. The stele within is covered with red lacquer and bears the following inscription in Chinese, Manchu and Mongol: "Tomb of the emperor Shunzi". The underground tomb has yet to be excavated.

The **Tomb of Emperor Qianlong** (Yuling) dates from 1743. Qianlong reigned for 60 years, longer than any of the other nine Qing emperors. The three vaulted chambers of his subterranean palace covers an area of 327 sq. metres (126 sq. ft). A relief of the goddess of mercy, Guanyin, adorns the eight wings of the four double doors. Behind the doors are fine sculptures of the Tianwang, the Four Celestial Kings. Other reliefs cover the vaulting and the walls of the tomb, including the Buddhas of the five points of the compass, and Buddhist inscriptions in Sanskrit and Tibetan.

The **Tomb of the Empress Dowager Cixi** (Dingdongling) can also be visited. The tomb lies about 1 km (½ mile) to the west of Yuling. Here, the two wives of Xianfeng lie buried: the eastern Empress Dowager Ci'an, and the infamous western Empress Dowager Cixi. The two tombs were originally symmetrical and built in the same style. But Cixi was not satisfied, and had Longendian, the Hall of Eminent Favours, pulled down in 1895. The tomb that

she then had built for 4,590 taels of gold is the most splendid and extravagant of all.

As Cixi died before the work on her tomb was completed, the underground part is relatively plain, and is outshone by the fine craftsmanship of the stonework between the steps in front of the tomb and the balustrades in front of the hall. These show some exquisite carvings of dragons in the waves and phoenixes in the clouds – traditional symbols of the emperor and empress. The Hall of Eminent Favours has an exhibition of Cixi's clothes, articles for daily use and a number of other tomb offerings. Also on display is the Dharani, a robe of sacred verses, woven in pure silk and embroidered with more than 25,000 Chinese characters in gold thread.

The concubines of Emperor Qianlong occupy tombs under 38 burial mounds. Other small tombs worth seeing in the complex are the **Tomb of the Wife of Emperor Shunzi** (Xiaodongling), the **Changxiling** and the **Mudongling**. These tombs, recently excavated, had already been plundered.

The **Zhaoxiling** stands alone outside the Great Palace Gate. Although Zhaoxi, who was buried here in 1687, was a simple concubine, she was given the title of Empress Dowager because she had given birth to the future emperor Shunzi.

## Tianjin

Only an hour and ten minutes by train from Beijing (regular departures from Beijing Zhan), **Tianjin** ⑫ lives in the shadow cast by its big neighbour to the north. The city grew up as a trading post. It is the closest port to Beijing, and in imperial times it also thrived on the vast amounts of tribute rice that wended its way north along the Grand Canal. The city became a pawn in the 19th-century trading disputes and wars between the imperial authorities and those European states – particularly the British – who wanted to "open up" China. Attempting to keep the foreigners at bay, while permitting limited and regulated trade, the Chinese allowed Tianjin to become part of the "Canton System" – a scattering of cities in which foreigners could live and trade. Later, it became an outright "concession", similar to the International Settlement and French Concession in Shanghai. A number of Western buildings still dot the cityscape.

During its time as a treaty port, as the coastal cities of the Canton System were known, Tianjin was far more cosmopolitan than Beijing. Some wealthy Chinese built themselves Western-style villas in and around the city. Pu Yi, the last emperor, lived in the Japanese Concession from 1925 to 1931, fleeing the republican government who had thrown him out of the Forbidden City. **Zhang Garden**, the villa he lived in with his empress, Wan Rong, and his concubine, Wen Xiu,

Map on page 184

*At 415 metres (1,362 ft), the Tianjin Tower is one of the tallest structures in Asia.*

**BELOW:** Tianjin is one of China's largest ports.

*Wanghailou Cathedral dates from 1869, when Tianjin was part of the so-called Canton System, and had a sizeable foreign population.*

**BELOW:** Zhongxin Park is flanked by colonial-style buildings.

still stands. The house was named after the first owner, Zhang Biao, who built it in 1916.

Pu Yi was known to frequent another Tianjin landmark, the late 19th-century **Astor Hotel Ⓐ** (Lishunde Fandian), where he enjoyed many pleasant evenings in the ballroom. Due to unfortunate renovations in 1984, the hotel does not retain much of its old world charm, but it has an interesting array of historical photographs, including one of the future president of the US, Herbert Hoover, and his wife. The couple were married here in 1899, when Hoover was working as an engineer in the city.

Down Tai'an Dao, and then to the south on Zhejiang Lu, is another Tianjin institution, **Kiessling's Bakery Ⓑ**, set up by an Austrian in 1911 to supply bread to foreigners living in the concession. This is in the same building as the Qishilin hotel. There is another Kiessling's in Beidaihe (*see page 191*).

Following Qufu Dao into Nanjing Lu toward the Friendship Hotel, there is the **Monument to the Tang-shan Earthquake Ⓒ**, which struck on 28 July 1976, just a few weeks before Mao's death. The epicentre was at Tangshan, 80 km (50 miles) to the east, but surrounding areas, including Tianjin and Beijing, felt the effects and suffered many collapsed buildings. One of the worst natural disasters of recent times, an estimated 242,000 people died – although this figure went unreported by the government.

Further west along on Nanjing Lu, close to the junction with the large shopping street of Binjiang Dao, is another relic of Concession days, the **Xikai Cathedral Ⓓ**, which was built by French Catholics in 1916.

Another area evocative of the Concession period is **Zhongxin Park** (Zhongxin Gongyuan) Ⓔ, near the intersection of Heping Lu and Chifeng Dao. Within this attractive circular park, surrounded as it is by old colonial-style buildings, it is easy to feel as if you are in Europe rather than China.

From the park it is just a short walk to the northwest to Shenyang Dao. On the section of this street

Map below

closest to the river there is a well-known **Antiques Market** **F** (Guwan Shichang). If local lore is to be believed, the true antiques for sale here were confiscated from wealthy families during the Cultural Revolution, and stored in Tianjin. The government is now selling off these treasures to local merchants, who in turn sell them to tourists. Stickers occasionally appear on the merchandise, supposedly indicating from whom the piece was taken, as well as the time and place of the appropriation. The market is also a good place to buy old books and stamps as well as Cultural Revolution memorabilia. Opening hours are approximately 8am to 5pm.

Further north, where Zhangzizhong Lu meets Dongmennei Dajie, is the **Ancient Culture Street** (Guwenhua Jie). Built to look like an old Chinese city, it is now filled with merchants hawking familiar Chinese souvenirs. On

some public holidays, Chinese opera performances take place here. In the middle of the street is the **Mazu Temple** **G** (Tianhou; open daily 8am–4pm; entrance fee), dedicated to the goddess of the sea. It was originally built in 1326 during the Yuan dynasty, and is supposedly the oldest extant building complex in Tianjin.

Worshipped by seafaring people throughout China, the goddess is known as Matsu in Taiwan and Tin Hau in Hong Kong. Mazu's main temple is located on the Taiwanese island of Meizhou, where temple fairs are held every year. Tianjin, as the largest port city in northern China, had the largest Mazu temple in the area, and would hold an annual temple fair in her honour. Emperor Qianlong once visited this fair, celebrated on Mazu's birthday, the 23rd day of the 3rd lunar month. The tradition lapsed for a time, but has been revived in recent years.

*Like most coastal cities, Tianjin has visibly prospered in China's economic boom. Prices here, however, are noticeably lower than in Beijing.*

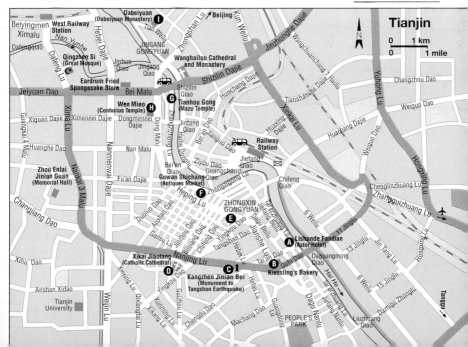

*Handcrafted chops for sale in Tianjin's large antiques market.*

## Other sights

At the corner of Dongmennei and Dong Malu is the **Confucian Temple** (Wen Miao; open daily 8.30am–5pm; entrance fee), dating from 1463. Located in what is known as the Old Chinese Quarter, the temple is now surrounded by high rise shopping malls and apartment buildings. Yet despite this and the strains of pop music that can filter in from the nearby shops, it is mostly quiet and peaceful. Stop in the *cha guan* (tea room) and sip tea while listening to Beijing opera on Sunday afternoons.

Further north, across the river on Shizilin Dajie is **Wanghailou Cathedral**, a Gothic-style Catholic church and monastery built in 1869. Still further north is the **Dabeiyuan Monastery** (open daily 9am–4pm; entrance fee), originally built in 1669 during the reign of Emperor Shunzhi. It managed to survive the Cultural Revolution intact, and was renovated in 1980.

The Hai River runs right through the middle of Tianjin, and in the city centre there is a strip of parkland on both sides of it. It is possible to take a cruise on the river from the pier close to the Astor Hotel. The irresistibly named **Eardrum Fried Sponge Cake Store** is a short distance to the southwest, on the north side of Bei Malu. It takes its odd name from a nearby *hutong* and not its speciality, which is innocuous cakes of rice powder, sugar and bean paste fried in sesame oil.

## Chuandixia

A beautifully preserved village in the hills of rural Mentougou District, some 90 km (55 miles) west of Beijing, **Chuandixia** is a growing tourist destination. Much of the tiny town's architecture dates to the late-Ming and early-Qing dynasties.

Once a prosperous farming enclave, Chuandixia had been all but abandoned by the mid-1990s. Its young people had all gone to the city to find work, and the only residents were a handful of elderly folk who depended on remittances from their children and on the sales of the honey from the bees they raised in the courtyards of abandoned homes.

However, its beauty was "discovered", and it has quickly become a booming tourist site, with dozens of rooms in which visitors can lodge and eat with local residents. Young people have moved back to manage the inns and restaurants. To avoid the crowds, try to visit on a weekday; bring your walking shoes, as the village is encircled by a trail that provides views of the homes and the surrounding landscape. There is an entrance fee payable when you first arrive.

## Huairou and Miyun

Huairou ⓮ is perhaps best known as the location of the Mutianyu Great Wall, *(see page 188)* and as the site to which the International Women's Conference was moved in 1995 after the Chinese government became anxious at the prospect of having Beijing overrun with outspoken feminists from around the world. Yet a generous supply of scenic lakes and mountains has made the area something of a weekend getaway for Beijingers seeking some fresh air, and the locals are

increasingly turning from farming to tourism. According to one source, some 2,500 local families now operate family inns and restaurants that host 2½ million tourists a year.

As such numbers indicate, this is not exactly a bucolic retreat, but it is an interesting place to see Chinese tourism in action. It is also still possible to get away from it all if you hike far enough into the Yunmeng Mountains, which are criss-crossed by trails.

Miyun ⓯ is another rural area that has become popular in recent years. It is home to the Jinshanling and Simatai sections of the Great Wall, as well as a large reservoir. Miyun contains several "folklore villages" that are supposed to show traditional rural life and also the Nanshan Ski Village, open in winter. Although those parts of Miyun close to Beijing are overrun with tourists at weekends, the county does have beautiful hills and good hiking. It is also an excellent place to spend the night in a village if you choose one that is not on the beaten tourist track. ❑

Maps on pages 184 & 205

**TIP**

Chuandlxla is accessible on bus 929 from Pingguoyuan, the western terminus of Beijing subway Line 1. There are buses from Dongzhimen bus station to various points in Huairou and Miyun counties.

**BELOW:** Mlyun reservoir, a weekend retreat for Beijingers.

# TRANSPORT

# GETTING THERE AND GETTING AROUND

## GETTING THERE

### By Air

All visitors need a Chinese visa before embarking on a flight. Many more airlines fly direct to Beijing from Europe and the US than was the case just a few years ago. From London Heathrow flight time is around 10 hours (direct). Economy return fares are typically around £500.

Cheaper fares are possible if you are prepared to change planes (Austrian Airlines via Vienna, Finnair via Helsinki and KLM via Amsterdam are often competitively priced). Direct China Air flights can also be well priced.

From North America, flights from the West Coast take around 13 hours, from the East Coast 18 to 20 hours. China Air is often the cheapest option.

**Beijing Airport**: Now fully modernised, Beijing Capital Airport, (Tel: 962580 – toll number for flight information), is about 30 km (18 miles) from the city centre. The journey takes about 30 to 40 minutes by taxi, but allow one hour or more at peak hours. Depending on the destination and category of taxi, the fare will be between 60 and 120 Rmb. Beware of drivers who approach you before you reach the taxi rank; ensure the driver uses a meter, or make sure you agree on a price before setting off. If your hotel is near the airport, drivers

## AIRLINE OFFICES IN BEIJING

**Air China**, 15 Chang'an Xidajie, Xicheng. Tel: 6601-6667.
**Air France**, Rm 512-515, Full Link Plaza, 18 Chaoayangmenwai Dajie. Tel: 4008.808.808.
**Austrian Airlines**, Rm C215, Lufthansa Centre, 50 Liangmaqiao Lu. Tel: 6462-2161.
**British Airways**, Rm 210, Scitech Tower, 22 Jianguomenwai Dajie. Tel: 8511-5599.
**Canadian Airlines**, Rm C201, Lufthansa Centre, 50 Liangmaqiao Lu. Tel: 6468-2001.
**Cathay Pacific**, Rm 1701, Capital Mansion, 6 Xinyuan Nan Dajie. Tel: 8486-8532.
**China Eastern Airlines**, 67 Wangfujing Dajie. Tel: 6468-1166.

**Dragonair**, Rm 1710, Henderson Centre, 18 Jianguomennei Dajie. Tel: 6518-2533.
**Finnair**, Rm 204, Scitech Tower, 22 Jianguomenwai Dajie. Tel: 6515 0797.
**Japan Airlines**, Hotel New Otani Changfugong, 26 Jianguomenwai Dajie. Tel: 6513-0888.
**KLM**, 5th Floor, China World Trade Centre, 1 Jianguomenwai Dajie. Tel: 6505-4898.
**Korean Air**, Rm C401, China World Trade Centre, 1 Jianguomenwai Dajie. Tel: 6505-0088
**Lufthansa**, Rm S101, Lufthansa Centre, 50 Liangmaqiao Lu. Tel: 6465-4488.
**Northwest Airlines**, Rm 501, China World Trade Centre, 1

Jianguomenwai Dajie. Tel: 6505-3505.
**Qantas**, Rm S120, Lufthansa Centre, 50 Liangmaqiao Lu. Tel: 6467-4794.
**Singapore Airlines**, 8th Floor, China World Tower 2, 1 Jianguomenwai Dajie. Tel: 6505-6891.
**Swiss International Airlines**, Rm 612, Scitech Tower, 22 Jianguomenwai Dajie. Tel: 6512-3555.
**Thai Airways**, Rm S102, Lufthansa Centre, 50 Liangmaqiao Lu. Tel: 6460-8899.
**United Airlines**, Lufthansa Centre, 50 Liangmaqiao Lu. Tel: 6463-1111.

may be unwilling to take you unless you pay extra – this is illegal, but agreeing to pay will save you much arguing and changing of taxis.

Air China offers coach services from the airport to several stops in the city centre. Destinations include the main Air China booking office on Chang'an Xidajie, close to Xidan; the Lufthansa Centre; and the Beijing International Hotel, north of Beijing Zhan station. Taxis are available at all stops. Most of the major hotels offer limousine pick-ups and free bus transfers.

**Flight connections**: Capital Airport has connections to more than 50 other cities in China. Most international flights use the newer Terminal 2, while domestic flights normally use Terminal 1. Hotels usually have flight-booking services, and most major airlines have offices in Beijing. You must check in at least 30 minutes before departure for domestic flights, although delays are common on many domestic routes, and at least an hour before departure for an international flight.

### By Rail

An exciting way to travel between Beijing and Europe, at least for those with plenty of time, is to take the Trans-Siberian railway. Trains leave from Beijing Zhan, the start of a five-day (via Mongolia) or six-day (via northeast China) journey to Moscow. The Beijing International Hotel, a short distance north of Beijing Zhan, has an international-ticket-booking office. Allow at least a week to obtain Russian and, if necessary, Mongolian visas in Beijing. Bring plenty of passport photos; otherwise there is a photo booth inside the main entrance to the Friendship Store on Jianguomenwai, or at virtually any photo developing shop.

There are also rail routes from Beijing to Moscow via Xinjiang and Central Asia, and two trains weekly from Vietnam (Hanoi) to Beijing.

### By Sea

Several ferry services connect China with Japan and South Korea. Boats from South Korea leave the port of Incheon for Shanghai, Weihai, Tianjin, Qing-dao, Dalian, Dandong and Yantai. The schedules for these trips can be found on www. seoulsearching.com/transportation/boat Ferries also ply the waters between Japan and China, connecting Osaka, Kobe and Shimonoseki with such cities as Shanghai, Qingdao and Tianjin. The schedules for these can be found at www.seejapan.co.uk/transport/sea/international

## GETTING AROUND

### Orientation

Beijing has five main ring roads (the Second, Third, Fourth, Fifth and Sixth – the latter two are still being built). Most of the other main roads run north–south or east–west, making it relatively easy to navigate through the city. Main streets are commonly divided in terms of *bei* (north), *nan* (south), *xi* (west) and *dong* (east); and in terms of *nei* (inside) and *wai* (outside the Second Ring Road). On the other hand, many housing estates are full of indis-tinguishable (unless you can read Chinese) high-rise buildings, mak-ing it easy to get lost, especially at night. The words *jie*, *dajie*, *lu* and *men*, which you'll find on all maps, mean street, avenue, road and gate respectively.

**City Maps**: *see page 230.*

### Public Transport

#### Subway

Beijing's subway system, which first opened in 1971, is still fairly limited in extent, but is fast, cheap and efficient. Most journeys cost 3 Rmb and there are trains every few minutes from 5.30am until 11pm. It is easy to find your way around, especially as signs and announcements are bilingual. Buy your ticket from the ticket office window (there are currently no ticket machines).

Line 1 (red) runs east–west underneath Chang'an Avenue through the heart of the city and out to the eastern and western suburbs, where the terminus at Pingguoyuan is a jumping-off point for reaching attractions west of the city. Line 2 (blue) is a circuit running parallel to the Second Ring Road, more or less following the demolished city wall around the north of the city. A new north–south line (Line 5) is under construction, for comple-tion before the 2008 Olympics.

In additon to the underground system, a new suburban light-railway ("Line 13") runs from Xizhimen in the northwest and loops around to Dongzhimen in the northeast.

A fast rail service is also being built from Dongzhimen to Capital Airport. In total, 148.5 km (92 miles) of new subway and rail line will be added by the start of the Olympics, quadrupling the current distance.

### Buses

The network of red, yellow and blue buses is comprehensive and operates from 5am to 11pm. Most rides only cost around 1 Rmb. A few routes have been improved, with air-conditioned double-decker buses, but jour-neys are generally slow and crowded and the gaps between stops are sometimes long. Buses are extremely crowded during the rush hours, and you will need to use your elbows, pushing and shoving like the locals do, just to get on board.

Remember to secure money and other valuables before you board.

Conductors usually sit at tall metal desks close to the doors. Give the conductor a few jiao bills and rely on her help or on that of your fellow passengers, to whom you can perhaps show your destination on a map or name card. You will find people who just struggled violently to get on the bus in front of you will now be only too happy to help if you need assistance. Fare dodgers take advantage of the chaos to get a free ride. When the conductor confronts a fare-dodger, you get an idea of the explosive powers of the Beijing dialect.

### Minibuses

Minibuses ply some of the same routes as the buses but offer a faster, more comfortable service at several times the bus fare, though they are still cheap by Western standards (1 to 10 Rmb, depending on distance). They generally seat 16 people. Tourists use the services that run between the Summer Palace and the zoo, between the zoo and Qianmen Gate (behind it is a main stop for minibuses), from the zoo to the Beijing railway station, from Qianmen to the station, and from the Summer Palace to Xiangshan Park (and of course return the same way). Minibuses have official stops but, if they have space, will usually stop wherever they are flagged down.

### Boats

A boat service operates from two points in Western Beijing to the New Summer Palace, along the Long River. Departures are hourly through the summer months, and journey time is one hour.

### Private Transport

### Taxis

Several types of taxi ply the streets of Beijing, from the cramped *xiali* (usually coloured red) which cost 1.2 Rmb per km after the initial 3 km, to Wuhan-built Citroëns (1.6 Rmb), and Audis and other large saloons (3 Rmb) – still cheap by Western standards. The rate is indicated on a red sticker displayed in the rear window. The flagfall is 10 Rmb for all taxis, so for short journeys (less than 3 km) they all cost the same. Between 11pm and 5am, the basic fare and the cost per km are higher.

All taxis are metered, and drivers are generally reliable at using them. Sometimes a driver may try to quote a flat rate to your destination. Do not accept this if you are just taking a simple one-way journey, as it will never be cheaper than the meter charge.

Drivers occasionally refuse to take passengers – foreigners and locals – to destinations they consider inconvenient. However, they can be fined for such refusals and simply showing them the number of the Taxi Complaint Hotline – 6835-1150 – is usually enough to convince them that they had better take you where you want to go.

Most taxi drivers speak little or no English, and carrying a Chinese name cards for hotels, restaurants, shops or other destinations can be useful for showing where you want to go. If you are travelling with other people, make sure the driver doesn't try to charge the meter price for each passenger. Always carry enough change, since taxi drivers are often unable, or unwilling, to change a 100 Rmb note.

Taxis can also be hired for longer trips, such as whole-day tours or visits to the Great Wall or Ming Tombs. If you plan to do this, obviously you will need to agree the total fare and itinerary in advance. Plan to spend 300–500 Rmb for a full day, depending on distance. Do not pay the full amount in advance. Here are some of the city's major taxi firms: For short distances:
**Beijing Dispatch Service**,
1 Binhe Lu. Tel: 6837-3399.

**Dial-a-Cab**, hotline tel: 96103.
For daily hire:
**Beijing Taxi Corporation**,
26 Fuchengmenwai Dajie.
Tel: 6852-4088 (24 hours).

### Tourist Buses

If travelling in a group, you will rarely need taxis, public transport or bicycles. Most tour groups travel in comfortable, air-conditioned buses. There are bus companies in several places, for instance outside Beijing Zhan (railway station) and opposite the Chongwenmen Hotel, which organise regular excursions to the most important sights.

From mid-April to mid-October, there are several special tourist bus routes suitable for independent travellers. These are more comfortable and faster than public buses, and cheaper than hiring a taxi. On most routes, several buses leave each morning, starting from about 7am, and return the same afternoon; the ticket allows passengers to get off and on at any designated stop, giving you some flexibility. Routes include Qianmen to Badaling, the Ming Tombs, the Eastern Qing Tombs, and Xuanwumen to Simatai. For a list of schedules and prices see www.bjbus.com/english/tour/lines_2.htm

### CAR RENTAL

Foreigners are now allowed to drive in China, but a local licence is required, which makes this a difficult option for short-term visitors. More practical is to hire a car with a driver. This can be done through most travel agencies and hotels, or from taxi companies. Alternatively, try negotiating a whole-day or half-day price direct with a driver. If you ask at the front desk of your hotel, most will arrange a car for the day for you, giving the driver clear instructions where you want to go and what time you want to return. Do not pay in advance.

## Bicycles

The bicycle is still the vehicle most used by Beijingers, although the number of cyclists has begun declining in correlation with the growing popularity – and affordability – of private cars. Cycling was once the most enjoyable way to see Beijing (which is mostly pancake-flat), but as cars have spilled over into bicycle lanes and air pollution has worsened, the joys of cycling have diminished and its dangers increased. Nonetheless, if you have steady nerves, strong legs and a high tolerance for pushy, aggressive car drivers, cycling is a great way to get around and will give you a completely different view of life in the city. Perhaps the best option is to rent a bike in a neighbourhood that is relatively quiet – Sanlitun, the Ritan Park neighbourhood, and the Houhai area are good bets – until you are more familiar with the rules of the road.

Bicycles must be parked in the special guarded lots (for which you normally have to pay 2 jiao to the attendant). You can have repairs done almost anywhere in the city, as there are repair people on every street corner and in every alleyway.

If you do hire a bicycle, check the brakes first, and make sure the lock is working. Many hotels and hostels have bicycles for hire, usually for around 20 Rmb per day, although prices are much higher (up to 100 Rmb) if you hire from an upmarket hotel.

If you want to experience travelling through Beijing at a cyclist's pace but don't feel up to cycling yourself, pedicabs (or trishaws) can be hired near many tourist sites.

## On Foot

Beijing is too large and too spread out to be seen primarily on foot. This said, most of its major sites demand a lot of walking and some areas of the city do lend themselves to idle strolling. The best parts of the city for wandering about on foot are the back lakes area with its willow-lined paths and meandering *hutong*; the Qianmen shopping district, which is so crowded that it can truly be experienced only on foot; the Wangfujing shopping district, which is largely a pedestrian mall; the old Foreign Legation Quarter, and the Ritan Park embassy district, although some streets are now blocked off because of terrorism fears.

Note when crossing the street: a green pedestrian light does not necessarily mean cars and bikes will stop – they are permitted to turn right on a red light signal. Take care at all times.

### Domestic Travel in China

## By Air

Beijing has flights to all other parts of China. Tourist offices and travel agencies, including many hotel travel desks, can give you the current flight schedule of the various state airlines – the number of which has mushroomed over the past few years. Accompanying this growth in the aviation business have been improvements in service. But tight budgets, especially for the smaller airlines, and the rapid growth of the industry, have led to overused airports and frequent flight delays. This was one of the reasons behind the extension of Beijing's Capital Airport.

You can buy tickets from travel agencies or airline booking offices. Travel agencies may be better; although they charge more, they are more likely to have English speaking staff. Try **Fesco Air Services**, 1st Floor, China World Trade Centre. Tel: 6505-3330. Alternatively, try CITS near the Gloria Plaza Hotel, or China Youth Travel Service (CYTS), around the corner from the CITIC building to the east of the Friendship Store. Since some flights are fully booked, it is advisable to buy your tickets as far as possible in advance.

## By Rail

Beijing has two main railway stations: Beijing Zhan (Beijing Station) and Beijing Xi Zhan (Beijing West Station). The former is centrally located and connected to the subway system, the latter is out in the southwestern suburbs and less easily accessible. A few trains to other parts of China run from the city's three smaller stations.

It is possible to buy rail tickets through a travel agency, but it's cheaper to use the foreigners' booking office inside Beijing Zhan, where you can also buy tickets for trains leaving from Beijing Xi Zhan (which has its own foreigners' booking office on the first floor). If you want a sleeper berth, especially in summer, it is essential to buy your ticket as soon as they go on sale, usually four days in advance. Return tickets can be purchased for most routes.

There are generally four different classes on Chinese trains: soft sleeper (*ruanwo*; four beds in one compartment), hard sleeper (*yingwo*; six beds in an open compartment), soft seat (*ruanzuo*) and hard seat (*yingzuo*). All are comfortable for both long and short journeys, except for the hard seats, which live up to their name and are not recommended for anything other than short trips. Some trains running between Beijing, Shanghai, and Guangzhou/Hong Kong have one and two person private compartments with bath, while the new "Z" trains that connect Shanghai and Beijing are soft-sleeper only.

There are good services between Beijing and most other Chinese cities. Trains to Shanghai take 11–14 hours, and most people prefer the overnight services which depart around 7pm. Trains to Xi'an take 12–13 hours, and to Hong Kong around 26 hours. The **Beijing Railroad Bureau Ticketing Information Office** can be reached at tel: 9510-5105.

TRANSPORT

ACCOMMODATION

A – Z

ACTIVITIES

A – Z

LANGUAGE

# ACCOMMODATION

## WHAT'S AVAILABLE, WHERE TO LOOK AND WHAT YOU'LL HAVE TO PAY

### Choosing a Hotel

In recent years, Beijing has experienced a boom in hotel construction, with some spectacular new or refurbished five-star hotels as well as an increase in the number of lower-end hotels and youth hostels. Some of the cheaper hotels are off-limits for foreigners, although this may soon change.

Many of the most palatial hotels, some with glass fronts, rotating rooftop restaurants or classical Chinese adornments, are now prominent landmarks on the city's skyline. Most are either joint ventures or wholly owned by a foreign hotel chain. They are like enclaves, small independent towns that have little connection to their surroundings, with their own restaurants, shops and other facilities that cater for homesick expats and long-stay business travellers. Some foreign firms also have offices in these hotels. Facilities are, as you would expect, comprehensive, with swimming pools, fitness centres, bars and nightclubs. The best rooms feature plasma-screen televisions hooked up to satellite/cable channels, and broadband internet access. Transport to and from the airport is also often part of the package.

There are also a large number of less grand, mid-range hotels, which can offer good value and good facilities, including business centres with internet/e-mail and fax facilities, currency exchange, shops and restaurants.

Almost all hotels above the budget category have air-conditioning and televisions in every room. Some hotels stock their own DVDs and videos. In general, all will have en suite bathrooms and shower facilities, though in some of the cheapest you may have to use a communal shower.

### Hotel Areas

Many of Beijing's luxury hotels are in the business district of Chaoyang, with several along Jianguomewnwai Dajie between the Second and Third Ring Roads. To the northeast, the area around the Lufthansa Centre at the city end of the Airport Expressway also has a cluster of top hotels. Another hotel zone, catering to tourists as well as business travellers, is in Dongcheng District, around Wangfujing and Chang'an – this is a lot closer in and within walking distance of the Forbidden City and Tiananmen Square. Other top hotels are scattered around the city, with several close to the Second and Third Ring Roads. Even the former can seem quite a

long way out of town, but bear in mind that subway Line 2 follows this Ring Road in its entirety, so access to the city centre is good.

Less expensive hotels are found all over the city, with a concentration in central tourist areas, particularly east of the Forbidden City. There is a growing number of budget options in and around Sanlitun, in northeastern Beijing. For people wanting something more traditional, courtyard hotels such as the Lusongyuan can be found in the *hutong* in the north of the city and elsewhere.

### Prices and Booking

There is quite a big difference in price between the handful of top five-star places and the many, perfectly comfortable, mid-to-upper-range hotels. Price categories are included in our listings (*see also Budgeting for your Trip, page 227*).

It's always advisable to book in advance during the peak tourist season (June to October). At other times, hotels may offer discounts or special packages – be sure to ask for a discount no matter when you are booking. Most accept reservations from abroad via internet or fax. Websites such as www.beijing-hotels.net, www.sinohotelguide.com and www.tripadvisor.com offer rooms for much less than official rates.

# WANGFUJING AND CHANG'AN AREAS

## Luxury

### Grand Hotel Beijing
35 Chang'an Dongdajie
Tel: 6513-7788
Fax: 6513-0050
www.grandhotelbeijing.com
This Hong Kong joint venture, attached to the Beijing Hotel, offers the height of luxury a stone's throw from Tiananmen Square. Its facilities include a rooftop terrace with views over the square. 217 rooms.

### Grand Hyatt Beijing
1 Chang'an Dong Lu, Oriental Plaza
Tel: 8518-1234
Fax: 6510-9508
www.beijing.grand.hyatt.com
One of Beijing's top hotels, a favourite of businessmen and short-term tourists, that includes top-notch restaurants, excellent service, and houses a museum of ancient Chinese bronzes on its basement ground floor. Great location at the southern end of Wangfujing, within the Oriental Plaza complex. 695 rooms.

### Peninsula Palace Hotel
8 Jinyu Hutong
Tel: 8516-2888
Fax: 6510-6311
www.beijing.peninsula.com
Now run by the Peninsula Group of Hong Kong fame, the modern, functional construction (with Chinese imperial flourishes) conceals a truly luxurious interior, with a complete range of facilities. The lobby is full of Chinese antiques, while designer labels compete in the shopping arcade. Located in a lively street ideal for shopping and Tiananmen. Service is impeccable. 530 rooms.

### Red Capital Residence
9 Dongsi Liutiao
Tel: 8401-8886
Fax: 8403-5303
www.redcapitalclub.com.cn
This exclusive boutique-hotel is within a Qing-dynasty courtyard house northeast of Wangfujing (past the Dongsi Mosque). Its rooms are furnished with period antiques and each has a different theme – the Chairman's Suite is dedicated to Mao Zedong and the Concubine's Private Courtyard purports to be for anyone who has ever dreamed of being – or having – a concubine. 5 rooms.

## Expensive

### Beijing Hotel
33 Chang'an Dongdajie
Tel: 6513-7766
Fax: 6523-2395
Opened in 1917, with a long list of famous guests, this is still considered one of the most prestigious hotels in Beijing. Period features give it an air of tradition, in contrast to many newer competitors. Centrally located, on the southwest corner of Wangfujing shopping street, near Tiananmen Square. 1,432 rooms.

### Beijing International Hotel
9 Jianguomenwai Dajie
Tel: 6512-6688
Fax: 6522-8777
www.bih.com.cn
With a convenient location near Beijing Zhan railway station and the Henderson and Cofco Plaza shopping centres, this huge hotel is a well known landmark. Good facilities, including booking offices for international flights and trains. 1,002 rooms.

### Lee Garden Service Apartments
18 Jinyu Hutong, Wangfujing
Tel: 6525-8855
Fax: 6525-7999
e-mail: general.manager@lgapartment.com
Good option for long-term stays or for those who like to have their own kitchen and other comforts of home. Suites range in size from studio to three room, all with kitchen and full bath. Offers usual luxury hotel facilities, plus childcare and a children's play area. Some rooms have balconies with a view of the Forbidden City. 199 rooms.

### Novotel Peace Hotel
3 Jinyu Hutong, Wangfujing Dajie
Tel: 6512-8833
Fax: 6513-3349
In the same lively street as the Peninsula Palace Hotel, close to Tiananmen and the Forbidden City, this joint venture provides spacious rooms. 344 rooms.

## Moderate

### Holiday Inn Crowne Plaza
48 Wangfujing Dajie
Tel: 6513-3388
Fax: 6513-2526
www.holiday-inn.com
Located on central Beijing's busiest shopping street, close to the Forbidden City, the Crowne Plaza has its own gallery of modern Chinese art, and a salon for performances of traditional Chinese music. 720 rooms.

### Novotel Xinqiao Hotel
2 Dongjiaomin Xiang, Chongwenmen
Tel: 6513-3366
Fax: 6512-9331
A comfortable hotel in the southeast corner of the old Legation Quarter, it is close to Tiananmen Square and Beijing Zhan railway station. Good value. 700 rooms.

## Budget

**Hademen Hotel**
A2 Chongwenmenwai Dajie
Tel: 6711-2244
Fax: 6712-1589
Good location diagonally opposite the Novotel Xinqiao Hotel, and convenient for the railway station and the Temple of Heaven. 196 rooms.

**Haoyuan Hotel**
Shijia Hutong, Dongsinan Dajie, Dongcheng
Tel: 6512-5557
Fax: 6525-3179
Hidden away in a narrow alley close to the Peninsula Palace Hotel, the Haoyuan's rooms surround two quiet courtyards. The buildings are a traditional combination of brick and red-lacquered wood, with curved tiles on the roofs. A small restaurant serves hearty traditional fare. Book well in advance. 18 rooms.

**Beijing International Youth Hostel**
9 Jianguomenwai Dajie
Tel: 6512-6688 ext. 6145

Fax: 6522-9494
Located just behind and to the east of the International Hotel, this hostel has dorm rooms that sleep 6–8 each. Amenities include a dining area, microwave, television and a reading area that has computers with internet access. 20 rooms.

# EAST OF THE SECOND RING ROAD (CHAOYANG)

## Luxury

**China World Hotel**
1 Jianguomenwai Dajie
Tel: 6505-2266
Fax: 6505-0828
www.shangri-la.com
Top-class service and accommodation, with health club, swimming pool and several Western and Asian restaurants. Well located for business. 716 rooms.

**Kerry Centre**
1 Guanghua Lu (opposite north gate of China World)
Tel: 6561-8833
Fax: 6561-2626
www.shangri-la.com
Aimed at business travellers and linked to a major new commercial and shopping complex, this hotel offers a full range of facilities, from jacuzzis to live jazz performances, and from movie channels to broadband internet access. 487 rooms.

**St Regis Hotel**
21 Jianguomenwai Dajie
Tel: 6460-6688
Fax: 6460-3299
www.stregis.com
Matching Chinese tradition with modern furniture, this luxurious hotel opened in late 1997 in a prime Chaoyang location. The hotel's Press Club Bar is a favourite of the foreign business community. 273 rooms.

## Expensive

**Gloria Plaza Hotel**
2 Jianguomen Nandajie
Tel: 6515-8855
Fax: 6515-8549
www.gphbeijing.com
A great location opposite the Ancient Observatory. The Sampan restaurant has the best dim sum in Beijing. 423 rooms.

**Jianguo Hotel**
5 Jianguomenwai Dajie
Tel: 6500-2233
Fax: 6506-7583
Convenient for the Friendship Store, Silk Market and most embassies, this is a favourite with long-term visitors. 460 rooms.

**Jinglun Hotel (Beijing-Toronto)**
3 Jianguomenwai Dajie
Tel: 6500-2266
Fax: 6500-2022
www.jinglunhotel.com

Next to the Jianguo and known for its cuisine, the Jinglun is another business person's favourite. 640 rooms.

**New Otani Changfugong Hotel**
26 Jianguomenwai Dajie
Tel: 6512-5555
Fax: 6513-9810
www.newotani.co.jp/group/beijing
A Japanese joint venture, the New Otani caters mainly for Japanese tourists and business-people. Pleasant rooms, lobbies and restaurants. 500 rooms.

**Swissotel Beijing**
Hong Kong-Macau Centre, 2 Chaoyangmen Beidajie
Tel: 6553-2288
Fax: 6501-2506
www.beijing.swissotel.com
Its semicircular, mirrored facade dominates one of Beijing's busy intersections. Popular with business travellers. The fourth floor is barrier-free for travellers with disabilities. 430 rooms.

**Traders' Hotel**
1 Jianguomenwai Dajie
Tel: 6505-2277
Fax: 6505-3144
www.shangri-la.com
Well located at the northern end of the China World Trade Centre business complex, with good service, food and accommodation, this is a

cheaper option than the neighbouring China World Hotel. 570 rooms.

**Zhaolong Hotel**
2 Gongren Tiyuchangbei Lu
Tel: 6597-2299
Fax: 6597-2266
Just north of the Workers' Stadium and convenient for the nightlife of Sanlitun, the Zhaolong has its own theatre and restaurants. 257 rooms.

## Moderate

**Jingguang New World Hotel**
Hujia Lou, Dongsanhuan Lu
Tel: 6597-8888
Fax: 6597-3333
A 53-storey building on the Third Ring Road, the New World is almost a self-contained town, with a bakery, a medical centre and a supermarket. Great views from the top floors. 446 rooms.

**Ritan Hotel**
1 Ritan Lu
Tel: 8563-5588
Fax: 8562-8671

Intimate little hotel inside Ritan Park, near the main embassy area. Good value. 151 rooms.

### Budget

**Beijing Gongti International Youth Hostel**
9 Gongren Tiyuchang

Tucked inside the Worker's Stadium, this hostel is conveniently located near Sanlitun (for nightlife). It offers such standard hotel services as ticketing and laundry, as well as access to the gardens and lake of the Workers' Stadium.

**Beijing Zhaolong Youth Hostel**
2 Gongtibei Lu, Chaoyang
Tel: 6597-2299
Fax: 6597-2288
Conveniently located with clean, air-conditioned rooms sleeping 2–6 people. Guests are entitled to use the health club and other

facilities at the adjacent Zhaolong Hotel. 35 rooms.
**Jianguomen Hotel**
12 Jianhua Road (south of Jianguomenwai Dajie)
Tel: 6568-5577
Fax: 6568-2195
Cheap hotel close to the Friendship Store. 50 rooms.

## THE NORTHEAST (AROUND THE THIRD RING ROAD)

### Luxury

**Kempinski Hotel**
Beijing Lufthansa Centre,
50 Liangmaqiao Lu
Tel: 6465-3388
Fax: 6462-2204
www.kempinski-beijing.com
Attached to Youyi (Friendship) Shopping City, with full facilities, including health club, restaurants and the authentic Paulaner Brauhaus. 526 rooms.
**Kunlun Hotel**
2 Xinyuan Nanlu (opposite Lufthansa Centre)
Tel: 6590-3388
Fax: 6590-3214
www.hotelkunlun.com
Well-established hotel which holds art auctions

and houses a popular nightclub. 767 rooms.
**Radisson SAS Royal Hotel**
6a Beisanhuan Donglu
Tel: 6466-3388
Fax: 6465-3181
www.radisson.com
Next to the China International Exhibition Centre, catering mainly to busines travellers. Full fitness and sports facilities. 362 rooms.

### Expensive

**Great Wall Sheraton**
10 Dongsanhuan Beilu
Tel: 6590-5566
Fax: 6590-5878
www.sheraton.com/beijing
This luxury US joint ven-

ture is handy for the airport and downtown areas. 850 rooms.
**Hilton Hotel**
1 Dongfang Lu, Dongsanhuan Beilu
Tel: 6466-2288
Fax: 6465-3073
www.beijing.hilton.com
Next to the airport expressway, with every comfort. 340 rooms.

### Moderate

**Holiday Inn Lido**
Jiangtai Lu
Tel: 6437-6688
Fax: 6437-8816
www.beijing-lido.holida-inn.com
A haven for foreigners, the Lido has a deli and a bakery, supermarket and

a Western pharmacy. Just 20 minutes from the airport. 430 rooms.
**Twenty-First Century Hotel**
40 Liangmaqiao Lu
Tel: 6466-3311
Fax: 6466-5735
Part of a modern complex with shops and several restaurants. Lively bars are across the road. 388 rooms.

## AROUND THE BELL AND DRUM TOWERS

### Moderate

**Lusongyuan Hotel**
22 Banchang Hutong,
Dongcheng District
Tel: 6401-1116
Fax: 6403-0418
This delightful courtyard hotel occupies a former Qing-dynasty residence. Rooms are very attractive with period furnishings, although mattresses are hard. Stone lions guard the traditional wooden gate, which leads to the pavil-

ions, trees, rockeries and potted plants that fill the courtyards. Good location south of the Bell and Drum towers. Dorms available. 50 rooms.

### Budget

**Beijing Bamboo Garden Hotel**
24 Xiaoshiqiao Hutong,
Jiugulou Dajie
Tel: 6403-2229
Fax: 6401-2633
www.bbgh.com.cn
Simple, clean rooms

open onto a classical Chinese garden, with a great location close to the Drum Tower north of the city centre. What it lacks in facilities compared with large, modern hotels, it more than makes up for in atmosphere. 40 rooms.
**Youhao Guesthouse**
7 Houyuanensi, Jiaodaokou, Dongcheng District
Tel: 6403-1114
Fax: 6401-4603
The Youhao lies behind brick walls in a tradi-

tional alley close to the Drum Tower. The rooms, part of a large compound where Chiang Kai-shek once stayed, surround Chinese courtyard gardens. 10 rooms.

# SOUTHERN AND WESTERN BEIJING

### Expensive

**Beijing New Century Hotel**
6 Shoudu Tiyuguan Nanlu
Tel: 6849-2001
Fax: 6849-1107
www.c-b-w.com/hotel/newcentury/
This five-star hotel is located near Beijing Zoo. Some rooms have views of the Western Hills. 720 rooms.

### Moderate

**Grand View Garden Hotel**
Nancaiyuan (on southwest corner of Second Ring Road)
Tel: 6353-8899
Ideal if you like classical gardens and buildings, but isolated. 300 rooms.

**Minzu Hotel**
51 Fuxingmennei Dajie
Tel: 6601-4466
Fax: 6602-2120
About 3 km (2 miles) west of Tiananmen, the Minzu is favoured by long-stay business people. It has a Turkish restaurant, with belly dancing. 400 rooms.

**Presidential Plaza (State Guest Hotel)**
9 Fuchengmenwai Dajie, Xicheng District
Tel: 6800-5588
Fax: 6800-5888
www.stateguesthotel.com
All rooms have high-speed internet access and multiple phone lines. Guests can relax in the four-storey atrium lobby. 500 rooms.

**Qianmen Jianguo Hotel**
175 Yongan Lu
Tel: 6301-6688
Fax: 6301-3883
Comfortable accommodation in the south of the city between the Temple of Heaven and Niu Jie Mosque, the Qianmen stages nightly Beijing opera performances. 403 rooms.

### Budget

**Jinghua Hotel**
Xiluoyuan Nanlu (past Yongdingmen), Fengtai
Tel: 6722-2211
Fax: 6721-1455
In the south of Beijing by the Third Ring Road, the rooms at this backpacker favourite have

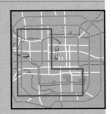

en-suite showers and air-conditioning. Dorm beds available. 140 rooms.

**Longtan Hotel**
15 Panjiayuan Nanlu, Second Ring Road South
Tel: 6778-9988
Fax: 6771-4028
Opposite Longtan Park, this backpacker favourite is a fair way out, but offers modern comfort for relatively little money. 250 rooms.

# NORTHWEST SUBURBS, WESTERN HILLS

### Expensive

**Beijing Fragrant Hills Mountain Yoga Retreat Centre**
6 Gonfuzhen, Fragrant Hills, Haidian
Tel: 8259-5335
Fax: 6259-6702
www.mountainyoga.cn
An idyllic retreat for yoga enthusiasts or others who want a unique experience in Beijing. All rooms are beautifully appointed. Meals are vegetarian, and Hatha yoga classes are offered each morning, including one session on the Great Wall.

**Shangri-La Hotel**
29 Zizhuyuan Lu, Haidian
Tel: 6841-2211
Fax: 6841-8002
www.shangri-la.com
This tasteful high-rise hotel has meeting

rooms, a ballroom, French and Asian cuisine, and a full range of other facilities. On the western edge of the city, the Shangri-La provides a shuttle-bus service to downtown areas. 650 rooms.

### Moderate

**Fragrant Hills Hotel**
inside Xiangshan Park
Tel: 6259-1166
Fax: 6259-1762
A modern sanctuary from urban noise in the Western hills. Swimming pool. 275 rooms.

**Friendship Hotel**
81 Zhonqguancun Dajie, Haidian
Tel: 6849-8888
Fax: 6849-8825
www.bjfriendshiphotel.com
Part of a huge state-run hotel in pleasant

grounds, home to many foreigners working for Chinese state employers. 300+ rooms.

### Budget

**Beijing Homestay**
Fragrant Hills, Haidian
Tel: 8259-5335
Fax: 6259-6702
Non-smoking vegetarian homestay run by the Fragrant Hill Yoga Retreat Centre. Four private rooms with courtyard and bath.

**Dragon Spring Hotel**
21 Shuizha Beilu, Mentougou
Tel: 6984-3366, 6984-3362
Fax: 6984-4377
For atmosphere and facilities, this international hotel built in classical Chinese style beats most similarly priced hotels in Beijing. But it is a little remote –

out towards the Western Hills, an hour from the city centre. 300+ rooms.

**Jimen Hotel**
Jimen Qiao, Xueyuan Lu
Tel: 6201-2211
Fax: 6201-5355
www.jimenhotel.com
Located across from the 11th-century ruins of an old city wall, north of the Third Ring Road in the northwest of the city, this functional and clean hotel has a coffee bar, vegetarian restaurant and inexpensive breakfast buffet. 160 rooms.

# FURTHER AFIELD

## Airport

### Movenpick Hotel
Xiaotianzhu Village, Shunyi County, PO Box 6913
Tel: 6456-5588
Fax: 6456-5678
Close to the airport, this hotel is a little isolated from the city, but makes up for this with excellent facilities, including summer barbecues and the chance to eat hot-pot in a real Monglian yurt. 400 rooms. **$$$**

## Chengde

### Puning Hotel
Puning Lu, West Yard of Puning Temple
Tel: (0314) 205-8888
Fax: (0314) 205-8998
This newly built, traditional-style hotel belongs to the Puning Temple. It has multiple courtyards, long corridors with painted beam ceilings, and an excellent restaurant specialising in vegetarian food. The plumbing is not perfect and the pool not particularly clean, but the serenity of the location – replete with the early-morning chanting of lamas – more than makes up for such deficits. 100 rooms. **$**

### Qianwanglou Hotel
Bifengmen Lu
Tel: (0314) 202-4385
Fax: (0314) 202-1904
For atmosphere alone this is the best option in Chengde. The small, exquisitely refurbished hotel occupies a Qing-dynasty mansion set just inside the grounds of the Imperial Resort. 61 rooms. **$$**

### Shanzhuang Hotel
127 Lizhengmen Lu
Tel: (0314) 202-3501
Good location and comfortable rooms, particularly in the older main building. **$$**

### Yunshan Hotel
6 Nanyuan Jie
Tel: (0314) 215-6171
Fax: (0314) 205-5885
This is the main tourist hotel in Chengde, close to the station with good facilities. 190 rooms. **$$**

### Mongolian Yurt Holiday Village
Tel: (0314) 216-3094
In summer, the cheapest option is a yurt (circular felt tent) inside the Imperial Resort. You don't have to rough it too much, as the yurts have washrooms and televisions. 40 yurts. **$**

## Great Wall

### Commune by the Great Wall
Tel: 8118-1888, 6567-3333
www.commune.com.cn
Twelve spectacular villas – with equally spectacular prices – designed by Asia's top architects. Each is furnished by renowned designers and comes with a personal butler. There is a restaurant in the club house. 12 villas, each with multiple bedrooms. **$$$$**

### Red Capital Ranch
28 Xiaguandi Village, Yanxi Township, Huairou
Tel: 8401-8886
www.redcapitalclub.com.cn
This is a Manchurian hunting lodge nestled in the shadow of the Great Wall. Each room is a luxuriously restored private villa filled with antiques. Guests can hike on the Wall or avail themselves of the Ranch's facilities, which include a fine restaurant and a spa. 10 rooms. **$$$$**

## Shanhaiguan and Beidaihe

### Beidaihe Friendship Hotel
1 Yongjiao Road
Tel: (0335) 404-8558
Fax: (0335) 404-1965
This beach-front, garden style hotel was reportedly built at the behest of Premier Zhou Enlai. It was renovated in 2002 and the beach is reserved for hotel guests. 250+ rooms. **$**

### Beidaihe Guesthouse for Diplomatic Missions
1 Baoean Lu, Beidaihe
Tel: (0335) 404-1807
Fax: (0335) 404-1807
Just five minutes from the main beach, this hotel has friendly staff and a good seafood restaurant. All rooms have balconies with sea views. 160 rooms. **$$**

### Jinshan Guesthouse
4 Dongsan Lu, Beidaihe
Tel: (0335) 404-1338
Fax: (0335) 404-3567
On a quiet beach, 4 km (2½ miles) north of the town centre. Full facilities include a bowling alley. 600+ rooms. **$$**

## Tianjin

### Geneva Hotel
32 Youyi Lu, Hexi
Tel: (022) 2835-2222
Fax: (022) 2835-9855
This relatively cheap hotel has four restaurants, a nightclub, a bowling centre and a health club. 240 rooms. **$**

### New World Astor Hotel
33 Tai'er Zhuang Lu
Tel: (022) 2331-1112
Fax: (022) 2331-6282
Refurbished in 1997, the Astor opened in 1863. It retains much of its 19th-century elegance and atmosphere, facing the river, while providing full facilities. 220 rooms. **$$$**

### Tianjin First Hotel
Jiefang Bei Lu
Tel: (022) 2330-3555
Fax: (022) 2312-3000
Dating from 1922, this hotel has been tastefully refurbished and offers good value. Opposite the Hyatt. 102 rooms. **$$**

### Tianjin Hyatt Hotel
219 Jiefang Beilu
Tel: (022) 2331-4222
Fax: (022) 2331-1234
Rooms are light, and the facilities, including Japanese and Western restaurants, are top-class. 300 rooms. **$$$**

### PRICE CATEGORIES

Prices are per night for two people sharing a standard double room in high season, including taxes:
**Luxury ($$$$)** over US$200
**Expensive ($$$)** $120–200
**Moderate ($$)** $60–120
**Budget ($)** under $60

TRANSPORT

ACCOMMODATION

ACTIVITIES

A – Z

LANGUAGE

# ACTIVITIES

# THE ARTS, NIGHTLIFE, FESTIVALS, SHOPPING AND SPECTATOR SPORTS

## THE ARTS

### Acrobatics

Acrobatics are a traditional form of street theatre in China, with special performances at Spring Festival fairs. It is also an important element in Beijing Opera and in many Chinese martial arts. Most regular acrobatics shows in Beijing are performed by young students, usually including children. Venues include:

**Chaoyang Theatre**, 36 Dongsanhuan Beilu, Hujialou. Tel: 6507-2421.
**Universe Theatre**, 10 Dongzhimen Nei Dajie. Tel: 6416-9893.
**Wansheng Theatre**, 95 Tianqiao Market. Tel: 6303-7449.

### Art Galleries

For an overview of the best of Chinese art, visit the newly renovated China National Art Gallery. Small commercial galleries have also flourished in Beijing since the early 1990s. These sell the work of many innovative artists, as well as masters of traditional watercolour, ceramics and sculpture techniques. Exhibitions change frequently. Several websites showcase fine art in Beijing and other Chinese cities: www.artscenechina.com, www.newchineseart.com, www.chinart-gallery.net and china-avantgarde.com.

**798 Space**, Dashanzi Art District, 4 Jiu Xian Qiao Lu. Tel: 6438-4862; www.798space.com. Open 10.30am–7.30pm daily.
**Artist Village Gallery** (Songzhuang Huajiacun Hualang), 1 Chunbei, Renzhuang, Tongxian, Songzhuang. Tel: 6959-8343; www.artistvillagegallery.com. Open 9am–noon daily.
**China Millennium Monument Gallery**, 9a Fuxing Lu. Tel: 6851-3322. Open 8.30am–6pm.
**China National Art Gallery**, 1 Wusi Dajie, Chaoyangmennei. Tel: 6401-7076. Open 9am–4pm, closed Monday.
**Red Gate Gallery**, inside Dongbianmen Watchtower. Tel: 6525-1005; www.redgate gallery.com. Open 10am–5pm.
**Wan Fung Gallery**, 136 Nanchizi Dajie. Tel: 6512-7338; www.wan-fung.com.cn. Open 9am–5pm.
**Xu Beihong Memorial Hall**, 53 Xinjiekou Beidajie. Tel: 6225-2265. Open 9am–4.30pm, closed Monday.

### Cinema

Despite the number of pirated DVDs on the streets, Beijing still has many cinemas. Most have morning, matinée and two evening showings. The latter usually start around 6.30pm and 8.30pm. Cinemas showing foreign films are especially popular, but more expensive. Hollywood is as well known in China as anywhere, and Hong Kong comedies and action films remain popular. Foreign films are usually dubbed into Chinese. You can buy tickets at each venue, but it is often not possible to book in advance by telephone. If you are travelling with a group or on a package tour, you can ask your tour guide.

### WHAT'S ON LISTINGS

Regular Beijing listing magazines *City Weekend*, *That's Beijing*, plus the China Daily publication *Beijing Weekend* and the Beijing Tourism Administration publication *Beijing This Month*, all have useful guides to entertainment, the arts and expat events. For those who read Chinese, *Beijing Youth Daily* and *Beijing Evening Post* are recommended. Or check these web listings: www.xianzai.com, www.cityweekend.com.cn, www.thatsbeijing.com

For information on the latest exhibitions at Beijing museums, see www.chineseartnet.com.

**Cherry Lane Movies**, Kent Centre, 29 Liangmaqiao Lu. Tel: 6430-1398; www.cherrylanemovies.com.cn Shows Chinese films with English subtitles. Cinemas showing both Chinese and foreign films, without subtitles, include: **Capital Times Cinema**, Times Square, Xidan. Tel: 8391-5165. **Dahua Cinema**, 82 Dongdan Bei Dajie. Tel: 6527-4420. **Oriental Plaza Multiplex**, Basement, Oriental Plaza, Wangfujing. Tel: 8518-5165.

## Classical Music

Beijing has close to a dozen orchestras, several of which maintain regular concert seasons. The China Philharmonic Orchestra generally performs at the **Poly Theatre** (14 Dongzhimen Beidajie, tel: 6506-5341). The China National Orchestra's regular venue is the **Beijing Concert Hall** (1 Beixinhua Jie, tel: 6605-5812) scheduled to open some time in 2005. In the meantime, the orchestra performs at the **National Library Concert Hall** (33 South Street, Zhongguancun, Haidian, tel: 8854-5348). The **Forbidden City Concert Hall** in Zhongshan Park (tel: 6559-8285) is also a regular venue for classical music. The Beijing International Music Festival, held each October, is a major music festival that showcases orchestras and performers from around the world.

## Dance

You can see dance and ballet at **the Beijing Exhibition Centre**, Xizhimenwai Dajie. Tel: 6835-1383; and **Capital Theatre**, 22 Wangfujing Dajie. Tel: 6524-9847.

## Theatre

Theatres generally attract larger audiences than Beijing Opera venues. Both local and foreign plays are performed. The main city theatres are:

Young people in Beijing seldom appreciate the often complex plays and style of Beijing Opera, and to counter this, some of the traditional Beijing Opera theatres have adapted to modern trends and stage pop concerts, performances of *Xiangsheng* (crosstalk, or comic dialogues) or similar pieces. But most visitors will surely want to see a typical Chinese production, and some of the best-known opera venues are: **Chang'an Theatre**, Jianguomennei Dajie (next to the International Hotel). Tel: 6510-1309. **Huguang Guildhall**, 3 Hufang Qiao, Xuanwu. Tel: 6351-8284. **Liyuan Theatre**, Qianmen Hotel, 175 Yongan Lu. Tel: 6301-6688 ext. 8860. Short performances are also held at the **Palace of Prince Gong** (Gong Wang Fu), generally available for tour groups only.

**Beijing Exhibition Centre Theatre**, Xizhimenwai Dajie. Tel: 6835-1383. **Capital Theatre**, 22 Wangfujing Dajie. Tel: 6524-9847. **Central Experimental Drama Theatre**, 45 Mao'er Hutong, Di'anmenwai Dajie. Tel: 6403-1099. **China Children's Art Theatre**, 64 Dong'anmen Dajie, Dongcheng. Tel: 6251-1425. **Tianqiao Theatre**, 30 Beiwei Lu, Xuanwu District. Tel: 8315-6300. **21st-Century Theatre**, Sino-Japanese Youth Centre, 40 Liangmaqiao Lu. Tel: 6466-0032. *For information on children's cultural activities, see page 226.*

## NIGHTLIFE

### Where to Go

Many people will tell you that Beijing is not China. The quality and quantity of entertainment available supports that claim. Karaoke no longer dominates the capital's nightlife, especially for more affluent people. Youngsters dance the night away under the laser lights of huge discos. Businessmen frequent garish clubs where hostesses offer *san pei* – three accompaniments: drinking, dancing and sex.

Once you could only find bands, dancing, foreign beer and mixed drinks in the large hotels, but now several areas popular with affluent locals or expats have whole streets full of bars.

Some bars close around 2am, though many stay open until 4 or 5am at weekends. In some, you can find live rock music or jazz; in others, DJs spin dance tunes. Discos break up the dancing and laser shows with performances by singers and cage dancers.

The main bar areas are Sanlitun, Jianguomenwai/Workers' Stadium, the back lakes, and Weigongcun in the Haidian university district. Though many Sanlitun and Chaoyang Park bars are blandly uniform attempts to recreate European or North American style, some Beijing entrepreneurs have opened bars specialising in punk rock, jazz, sportscasts, film and other entertainment. All of the music venues listed stage regular live performances on Friday and Saturday; phone or check publications for other days.

### Live Music

**The Big Easy**, Chaoyang Park South Gate. Tel: 6508-6776. Popular with affluent locals and expats, The Big Easy is a spacious New Orleans-style bar with live jazz and blues. Open 3pm–1am. **CD Café**, Dongsanhuan Lu. Tel: 6506-8288. Jazz and blues bands attract a regular crowd of aficionados; the place to enjoy jazz in Beijing. Open 4pm–late. **Cloud Nine Bar**, Shangri-La Hotel, 29 Zizhuyuan Lu, Hadian. Tel: 6841-2211, ext. 2723. Luxurious

bar with extensive drink list and a regular schedule of night-club style live music. Open 8pm–2am.
**Get Lucky Bar**, Taiyanggong Market, Huixin Dongjie. Tel: 6429-9109. Raucous punk and rock bands explore the Chinese pop fringe in suitable surroundings. Open 6.30pm–late.
**Hotline 1950**, 4–5 Liangmaqiao Lu. Tel: 6461-1950. Amidst imported Americana, the Hotline house band belts out covers of Western and Chinese standards, aided by dancers, drag acts, and comedians. Open 6pm–2am.
**Minder Café**, Dongdaqiao Xiejie. Tel: 6500-6066. A Philippine house band enlivens one of the best known expat bars, bringing a touch of Benidorm to Beijing. Open 6pm–2am.
**Nameless Highland Bar**, Building 14, Area 1, Anhuili, Yayuncun. Tel: 6489-1613. A popular bar with music from punk to folk rock. Weekend nights are crowded, with multiple bands performing. Open 5pm–2am.
**NOW Design Club** (NOW Julebu) 4 Jiuxianqiao Lu, Chaoyang (798 Factory, Dashanzi). Tel: 6438-5938. Stylish bar that showcases both art and music, located inside the 798 Space in the Dashanzi art district. Open 10am–midnight.
**Red Bar** (Zhu Chang), Sanlitun Nan Jie, Chaoyang. Tel: 139 1066-8899. This is a popular venue for the performance of rock and folk music. Open 7pm–2am.
**Sanwei Bookstore**, 60 Fuxing-

menwai Dajie. Tel: 6601-3204. At this former tea house, above a bookstore, Friday is jazz night, while Saturday is reserved for Chinese classical music played on *pipa* and *guzheng*. Open 9.30am–10.30pm.

## Clubs and discos

**Alfa**, 5 Xingfu Yicun, Chaoyang. Tel: 6413-0086. Popular club with a large outdoor patio and a reputation for wild partying, with evenings dedicated to such drinks as absinthe and martini. Open 5pm–late.
**Cloud Nine**, Building 7, Sanlitun Beijie, Chaoyang. Tel: 6417-8317. Hot Sanlitun nightspot with multiple rooms – some open, some secluded – and DJs who have loyal followings among local and foreign hipsters. Open 6pm–late.
**The Den**, Gongti Lu, next to City Hotel. Tel: 6592-6290. A fluid clientele, and an international cattle market around the crowded, sweaty dance floor, recreate Ibiza in Beijing. Open 24 hours.
**Latinos**, Chaoyang Park South Gate, Chaoyang. Tel: 6507-9898. A cavernous club with a two-storey dance floor specialising in salsa, merengue and other Latin music; dance classes are offered. Open 5.30pm–2am.
**The Loft**, 4 Gongti Bei Lu, Chaoyang District. Tel: 6586-7877. A fashionable club and restaurant opened by a prominent Beijing artist couple, The Loft serves good Mediterranean food in sleek surroundings that feel more like New York or LA than Beijing. Open 10am–2pm.
**Nightman**, 2 Xibahe Nanli. Tel: 6466-2562. Young Beijingers dance away the night to a mixed bag of sounds served up by local and imported DJs, among slightly seedy, multi-level dancing and posing areas. Open 8.30pm–5am.
**Rock 'n' Roll**, 1 Nongzhan Nanlu, south gate of Chaoyang Park. Tel: 6592-9856. A monster of dance,

this place has multiple levels in a building that resembles the inside of a power station cooling tower. Open 8pm–5am.
**Success/Dan Club**, 4 Gongti Lu, Chaoyang. Tel: 6593-9495. Billed as a cabaret, dance club and KTV lounge all rolled into one, the Success features sexy hostesses and fawning service. The Dan Club, in the basement below Success, is decorated with antiques, has inter-table phones and DJs who play dance music of all varieties. Open 7pm–3am.
**Vibes**, 4 Jiu Xian Qiao Lu (north of Beijing–Tokyo Art Project). Tel: 6437-8082. A café and bar in the trendy 798 Artspace that holds a number of themed music events. Open 2pm–late.
**Vics**, Worker's Stadium North Gate. Tel: 6593-6215. Popular venue,with DJs and theme nights including reggae and hip hop. Open 7pm–late.

## FESTIVALS

Apart from Spring Festival – New Year according to the Chinese lunar calendar – the other public holidays in modern China are observed according to the Gregorian calendar. National Day and International Workers' Day, the two most important public holidays, reflect the political changes since 1949 in China. Other important political celebrations that are not public holidays are 1 July, the day of the foundation of the Chinese Communist Party, and 1

August, the founding day of the People's Liberation Army. Several other traditional festivals have revived since the Cultural Revolution, though these are more evident in Beijing's rural areas.

The origins of these traditional festivals go back a long way, some to the Shang dynasty (16th to 11th centuries BC). Some lost their original meaning over time, changed in content or gained a religious meaning; others marked historical events or were reserved for the worship of ancestors or gods. The Spring Festival, the Qingming Festival (Day for Remembering the Dead) and the Moon Festival survive more or less intact. These form one half of the ancient six festivals: three "festivals of the living" (Spring Festival, Dragon Boat Festival and Moon Festival) and the three "festivals of the dead" (Qingming Festival, All Souls' Day and the Songhanyi Festival – for sending winter clothes to ancestors).

Traditional Western festivals such as Christmas and Valentine's Day are increasingly celebrated by young urbanites – but the celebrations have decidedly local characteristics. Christmas Eve, for instance, is a night for dining out with friends, sleeping over in a fancy hotel or going to a classical-music concert. Such celebrations have become so widespread – and profitable – that officials and culture critics have begun to call for a stronger and more commercial celebration of traditional Chinese holidays, which many fear are being out-celebrated and out-spent.

## Spring Festival

The most important traditional festival is Chinese New Year or **Spring Festival** (Chunjie). It usually falls in late January or early February. If you travel in China at that time, expect restricted and crowded public transport services, because many people return to their home towns for this festival. Trains are often fully

booked. The Chinese New Year celebrations are traditionally a family gathering, similar to Christmas in the West. On New Year's Eve, the entire family gathers for a special meal. In Beijing and the north, families make and eat *jiaozi* (pasta parcels filled with minced meat and vegetables). At midnight, they welcome the New Year with a volley of firecrackers – though officially, fireworks have been banned in Beijing since the mid-1990s.

The first day is taken up with meals and visits to relatives. The second and third days are for friends and acquaintances. People visit each other, always taking food, drink or other gifts, and offering good wishes for the New Year. During Spring Festival, many Beijing parks and temples hold fairs where you can still see stilt walkers, dragon dancers, wrestlers, jugglers, snake charmers, Yang Ge dancers and opera singers. Some of the best fairs are held in Ditan Park, the Summer Palace and Baiyunguan Temple. Longtan Park hosts a spectacular national folk arts competition.

## Lantern Festival

The **Lantern Festival** used to signify the official end of the New Year celebrations. Today, people work normally on that day. Only the meal of *yuanxiao* (sticky rice balls, usually filled with sweet red

bean or sesame paste) follows the old customs. In recent years, Beijing has again promoted Qing-style processions, inlcuding musicians, lion dancers, Yang Ge groups and banners with pictures of deities.

## Festival of Light

The **Qingming Festival** (Festival of Light) was originally a day to celebrate the renewal of life in springtime. Later it became a day to remember the dead. In the past, those who could afford it would make a pilgrimage to the graves of their ancestors, taking cooked chicken, pork, vegetables, fruit, incense and candles. They would burn paper money, often printed with the words "Bank of Hell," and sometimes paper clothes, furniture and houses to ensure their ancestors fared well in the spirit world. After the sacrifice, the cleaning of the graves would begin. Many people, especially in rural areas, have resumed the customs of sweeping graves and burning paper money. In Beijing, schoolchildren lay wreaths and flowers in Tiananmen Square in memory of those who gave their lives for the revolution.

## Moon Festival

The **Moon Festival** or Mid-Autumn Festival (Zhong qiu jie), celebrated according to the lunar calendar on the 15th day of the eighth month (usually mid-September) also remains popular in Beijing. On this day, people eat moon cakes filled with various combinations of meat, fruit, sugar, spices, seeds and nuts. The cakes are to remind people of the revolt against Mongol rule in the 14th century, when similar cakes were used to transport secret messages between Chinese leaders. According to ancient Chinese myth, the hare and toad live on the moon. Stories about the moon hare and Chang'e, the "woman in the moon", are still told. If the weather is good, people sit together outside on the day of the Moon Festival (which is a normal working day), chat, look at the moon and eat moon cakes.

## SHOPPING

### What to Buy

Beijing offers a wide variety of shopping, from table-top stalls on the street to vast new plazas full of famous brands. For visitors, silk, jade, cloisonné, lacquerware, jewellery, carpets, watercolour paintings and clothing all make popular gifts or souvenirs. Prices vary considerably, and good items can be expensive.

The city is also well known for its fake designer goods, available in many of its markets. Pirated CDs and DVDs are easy to find in the area around the Friendship Store, particularly on Jianhua Lu.

All hotels have shops, and the top hotels have elegant shopping arcades. But the most interesting and inexpensive way is to wander around one of the main shopping areas in the capital, such as Wangfujing or Qianmen. Here you will find a typical Chinese shopping atmosphere, and you will get a vivid impression of the huge number of shoppers in China. Many of the people you see shopping are not Beijing residents but visitors from other regions on holiday or business. Shops generally open from 9am–8pm every day. In department stores, chain stores and larger shops, prices are usually fixed, but bargaining is definitely expected elsewhere.

### Shopping Areas

Below are the main shopping centres and some important shops and markets.

### *Wangfujing*

Beijing's premier shopping street received a huge facelift in 1999,

in preparation for the 50th anniversary of Communist China. It is now a paved street that has two of China's biggest and glitziest shopping centres, the Sun Dongan Plaza and the Oriental Plaza, at either end. The basement of Sun Dongan Plaza houses Old Beijing Street, an indoor market and museum. Among the stores that survived the redevelopment are China Star Silk Store (No. 133), Beijing Medical Department Store (No. 153) and the refurbished Beijing Department Store (No. 255). At the northwest corner, close to a crossroads, is the Foreign Languages Bookstore, a good place to buy English books about China. Diagonally across the crossroads from the bookstore is the Luwu Jewellery and Craft Store (No. 268). Small stalls inside the Luwu store sell many craft items and souvenirs, including silk, jade, musical instruments and carved stone and wood items. Other interesting shops are the Yi Liu Chopstick Shop (No. 277) and an art shop with scroll paintings and stone rubbings (No. 265). Past the new Wangfujing Bookstore, on the east side of the street, is the famous tea shop, Wuyutai (No. 186).

### *Xidan*

Xidan is an old commercial quarter to the east of the Minzu Hotel, about a mile west of Tiananmen Square. Like Wangfujing, its main street Xidan Beidajie runs north from Chang'an Avenue and has also undergone major rebuilding, so that it is almost unrecognisable as the collection of bustling clothes markets it was in the early 1990s. Plush department stores now line Xidan Beidajie, the oldest of which is the Xidan Baihuo Shangchang. Xidan offers far less of interest to visitors than Wangfujing. Underneath Xidan is a sprawling, multi-level underground mall with shops, crowded canteens, a rock-climbing wall and an ice-skating rink. The space was dug out dur-

ing the 1950s to make part of a bomb shelter. As part of their education – lao dong ke, labour-class children, helped in the construction.

### *Qianmen*

Qianmen Dajie runs south from Qianmen Gate at the southern end of Tiananmen Square. This was part of Beijing's busiest commercial quarter during the Qing dynasty. Along Qianmen Dajie you will find the Beijing Silk Shop (Beijing Sichou Shandian, No. 5), a music shop (Xinghai Yueqi, No. 104) that specialises in traditional instruments, the Hall of Eternal Youth (Changchun Tang, No. 28), a traditional pharmacist, and the Jingdezhen Porcelain Shop (Jingdezhen Yishu Cipi Fuwubu, No. 151).

### *Dazhalan*

Just 300 metres long, Dazhalan (Large Wicker Gate) dates from the Ming dynasty and remains one of the liveliest shopping streets in Beijing. It runs southwest from the northern end of Qianmen Street. Among the highlights of the narrow lane is Ruifuxlang, an old silk shop with a marble gate and a traditional wooden interior. On the same street is the capital's best-known traditional pharmacist, Tongrentan Pharmacy, which dates from the mid-17th century.

Opposite the pharmacy and in a westerly direction is the old Shengxifu Hat Store, and a small Tibetan shop, Made in Paradise, that offers a glimpse of the distant province.

Dazhalan and the streets around it have a long history as an entertainment centre. Five of the biggest Beijing Opera houses used to be here, and you can still buy opera clothes, masks and props at the Beijing Opera Costume Shop. Two old shoe shops, Neiliansheng and Buyingzhai, make traditional handmade cotton shoes. Mao ordered his cotton shoes from Dazhalan.

If you take a right turn off Dazhalan, you can continue west to Liulichang. The walk takes under 20 minutes, not including browsing time, and takes you through some quiet, unspoilt *hutong*. Because taxis are not allowed to stop at the Dazhalan end of Qianmen it may be better to start from Liulichang. Alternatively, to start from Qianmen you can take the underground to the Qianmen stop, or walk south from Tiananmen Square.

## BUYING ANTIQUES

Although many low-quality household items are much cheaper than they are in the West, antiques and works of art often fetch surprisingly high prices. Objects dating from before 1840 cannot be exported. Most antiques date from the early 20th century, which covered the final period of the late Qing dynasty and the early republic. In recent years, factories have produced many replicas of antiques, and it is harder to find really beautiful pieces, such as woodblock prints of traditional pictures.

## *Liulichang*

This is often known as Antique Street because of the large number of antiques and art-and-craft items on sale. You can buy original paintings and woodblock print reproductions, materials for traditional Chinese painting, and old (and new) books. Be prepared to bargain.

Liulichang means glazed tile factory. The Ming dynasty tile factory that gave the street its name has long gone, but it once made the imperial yellow tiles that crown the Forbidden City. The street has been completely renovated in Qing style in recent years and has regained its splendour with even more shops. Even if you don't want to buy anything, Liullichang is fun to wander round and window-shop. The street runs east–west either side of Nanxinhua Jie, which you can cross via a footbridge. The most famous shop, Rongbaozhai, is on the western stretch. Rongbaozhai is known for its paintings, calligraphy and brilliant woodblock prints. You can find expensive, as well as many cheap, souvenirs and gifts in the shops along Liulichang, including nice stone rubbings. This is also a good place to buy artist's materials. But genuine antiques have become scarcer and are generally limited to the more expensive shops. Some of the pictures on sale here are of rather poor quality.

If you are really interested in the chance of finding genuine antiques at a bargain price, plus plenty of cheap reproductions, there are two other markets you won't want to miss: Hongqiao and Panjiayuan "Ghost Market" *(see page 224)*.

## Shopping Centres

Diagonally opposite the Friendship Store, across Jianguomenwai Dajie, is the **Scitech** shopping centre. Like several of Beijing's new upmarket malls, Scitech is full of luxury imports. Just half a mile west along

## THE FRIENDSHIP STORE

A visit to the Friendship Store (Youyi Shangdian) is definitely one of the most comfortable ways to shop in Beijing. It is located on Jianguomenwai Dajie, the eastern extension of Chang'an Dajie. You can buy most things produced in China at the store, from dried mushrooms to exquisite cloisonné. There is a large carpet section and a stock of good silk. The Friendship Store can arrange to send any goods abroad and deal with the customs formalities for you. It also has a dressmaking department, a watch repair counter, a bookshop, a tea shop, a supermarket, a Starbucks and a dry cleaner's.

Chang'an Dajie are the neighbouring **Cofco Plaza** and **Henderson Centre**. Other alternatives are the **Parkson** department store, conveniently reached from the Fuxingmen underground station, the **Sun Dongan** and **Oriental** plazas on Wangfujing, the brand-new **Full Link Plaza** by the Chaoyangmen underground station, the **New World Shopping Centre** by Chongwenmen and the **Pacific Century Plaza** on Gongti Beilu, near Sanlitun. The enormous **Golden Resources Shopping Mall** (Jinyuan Shangcheng) in Haidian District is reputedly the largest in the world; word has it that if a shopper were to spend just 10 minutes in each of the Mall's shops, it would still take 90 hours to get through it.

The **Friendship Shopping City** (usually known as Yansha), at the Lufthansa Centre, takes in a broader price range. Its five floors cover everything from ginseng to rollerblades. The basement has a small supermarket, and there are plenty of restaurants and snack bars in the **Kempinski Hotel**, which also forms part of the Lufthansa complex.

## THE SILK MARKET

The **Silk Market** was perhaps Beijing's best-known market, a tourist destination in itself, until it closed on 7 January 2005. It had stood for years in a narrow alley on Xiushui Jie, about 500 yards east of the Friendship Store. Despite the name, not much silk was sold here – instead the crowds squeezed in to bargain over misleadingly-branded outdoor gear, luggage, other clothing and footwear. Controversial plans to move it indoors, into the eight-storey building under construction next door, are now being realised, although it is not certain when the new site will open its doors – probably some time in 2005. Sky-high rents are likely to put of the less well-off vendors: one successful trader actually paid 4 million Rmb for a spot in the new building.

Many tourists, tourism authorities and even academics mourn the loss, arguing that the outdoor Silk Market was an important business and cultural site that should not have been so blithely replaced. On the opposing side is the Fire Department, which has long cited the narrow market as one of the most dangerous potential fire-traps in the city (it is for fire-safety reasons that the market closed at dusk, since no electricity is allowed). National security authorities had also joined the opposition, fearing that the crowds – as many as 20,000 per day on weekends – could have provided cover for potential terrorists wishing to target the nearby embassies.

### Markets

Once the shops and offices have closed, Beijing families hurry to the food market to find eggs or fresh vegetables for supper. Even with prices as low as a few jiao, you can still bargain. Be aware though, that foreigners buying fruit or vegetables are often quoted much higher prices than locals. If you are concerned about this, watch what someone else pays first.

Every neighbourhood has some kind of food market. Until the mid-1990s, many main roads had long rows of market stalls, often supplemented by farmers selling direct from their trucks. Many such markets sold services as well as goods. Barbers, masseurs, tailors and cobblers all offered their skills. You can still find these people plying their trades on the street, but most outdoor markets have disappeared. The municipal government now has a policy of moving all markets indoors and discouraging roadside stalls. If you see a group of vendors suddenly bundle up their wares and rush off, this probably means they have spotted a tax officer.

### Hongqiao

One of the new-style markets is **Hongqiao.** Located across the road from the Temple of Heaven,

it occupies a modern shopping centre. It sells a bewildering variety of food, electronics, clothes and antiques.

On the first floor are stalls with electronics, tools, plastic bowls and other household items. Watches, radios, CD players and cellphones can all be found here. At the eastern end is a section devoted to toys, gifts and stationery. Up on the second floor you'll find jeans, leather jackets, fur coats, furniture and luggage being sold by competing stalls. Many of these goods are fake designer brands of exceptionally poor quality, so beware.

But the third floor is the one not to miss. Here you'll find strings of pearls by the hundreds, at a fraction of their cost in the West. About 50 stalls stock antiques or reproductions, mostly selling smaller items. You can find everything from brass containers turned an "ancient" green that belies their youth, to ceramic Buddhas, wooden masks, and Red Guard alarm clocks and other Cultural Revolution kitsch. If you shop carefully, you can find some great deals. Take your time and look around before you buy. Sometimes the price at one stall can be many times that at another. Bargaining is expected.

### Panjiayuan

Close to the southeast corner of the Third Ring Road, **Panjiayuan** is one of the best places to buy genuine and reproduction antiques, as well as crafts, jewellery, furniture, old books and souvenirs of all kinds. Largely a weekend affair, Panjiayuan is already bustling by 6am, which is why some locals call it the "Ghost Market". However, the market is now so big and so established – with 3,000 fixed stalls – that any lingering ghosts have no doubt left for quieter haunts. Bargaining is expected at Panjiayuan, and patience required; it is also wise to hold on to your wallet, as pickpockets are rampant. The best time for shopping is early morning, or at lunchtime when the crowds thin out (it begins to shut down by mid-afternoon).

Just to the south is **Beijing Curio City**, a four-storey complex with a huge range of antiques. Prices are a little higher than at Panjiayun.

## Guanyuan

Another market that still offers something unique is **Guanyuan**. Specialising in wildlife, curious visitors are attracted by the colourful birds in long rows of cages, either piled on top of each other or hanging from poles and branches. On the western side of the market, which is near Fuchengmen, are brilliantly coloured ornamental fish swimming in huge glass containers or small enamel bowls.

## Ritan Office Building

This oddly named market at 15 Guanghua Lu, near the south gate of Ritan Park, is indeed a former office building that has been converted into an assemblage of small shops that sell clothing, jewellery, shoes and some knick-knacks. This is a good place to buy the works of local designers who merge Chinese and Western styles. A number of stores also sell international name-brand clothes that have been rejected for export. Bargaining is expected.

## Ya Show Sanlitun Clothing Market

Ya Show is a five-storey market on Gongtibei Lu near Sanlitun. It is full of small stalls that sell clothing, souvenirs, toys, cosmetics, silk objects, books and just about everything else a tourist in Beijing might want to buy. The fifth floor is an eatery with inexpensive snacks. Most of the name-brand clothes are undoubtedly fakes, but dedicated shoppers will find much to look at here. As always, strong bargaining is both expected and required. Open 9.30am–9pm.

## Bookstores

The state-owned Xinhua bookshop has over 100 branches in Beijing, though these usually stock few books in English, other than language textbooks. The **Xidan** bookstore is one of the largest, while Haidian, which is home to many universities, has a **Book City** full of small bookstores.

Many hotels stock good selections of books about China in English, as do several department stores, including Yansha, the Friendship Store and the China World Shopping Centre. Probably the best place to find books on Chinese history, medicine, language and culture is the **Foreign Languages Bookstore** third floor, on Wangfujing Shopping Street, or the nearby **Wangfujing Bookstore**. **The Bookworm** (10 South Building, Sanlitun Beilu, in Le Petit Gourmand) is an English-language membership lending library with over 8,000 volumes that also has a growing selection of new and used books for sale.

## SPORT

Chinese people are generally very keen on sport. Many sports halls and stadiums, some of them built to bolster Beijing's Olympic Games bids, host regular competitions and tournaments. Early each morning, the parks fill with people practising tai chi, qi gong, martial arts, badminton and table tennis. Chinese television broadcasts local and international sporting events, and stars like Ronaldo and Michael Jordan are as well known in China as Marx and Engels.

### Facilities for Visitors

All large hotels have sports facilities including gymnasia, tennis courts and swimming pools, which are available to guests at no charge; many also allow non-guests to use these facilities for a fee. There are also a number of private gyms in Beijing, including the international chains **Clark Hatch** (2F Landmark Towers Hotel, tel: 6590-7559) and **Bally Fitness** (Basement Level, Chang An Theatre, tel: 6518-1666), some of which offer daily or weekly rates for non-members. Many local gyms are located on the basement level of shopping malls.

**Dongdan Sports Centre** (Dongdan Dajie, near Chang'an Dajie, tel: 6523-1241) has a swimming pool, indoor tennis and squash courts and other facilities right in the city centre. There are two massive outdoor swimming pools just inside the south gate of the **Worker's Stadium** (Gongren Tiyuchang Nanmen).

Yoga has become extremely popular, and Beijing now has a number of yoga centres, including the **Yoga Yard** (www.yogayard.com) which offers Hatha Yoga classes in a courtyard.

**China World Hotel** (tel: 6505-2266, ext. 33) has good indoor tennis courts open from 6am to 10pm. China World Shopping Centre also has an ice-skating rink. In winter, the frozen Kunming Lake at the Summer Palace is Beijing's premier ice-skating venue.

Wealthy locals and expats dabble in horse-riding or golf at a growing number of centres in suburban Beijing. Try the **Equuleus Riding Club** (off Jingshun Lu, tel: 6438-4947) or the **Sheerwood Beijing International Equestrian Club** (off the old Airport Road, tel: 8431-1742; e-mail: sheerwood@hotmail.com). The **High Club** (tel: 6553-2228; www.highclub.cn) organises horse-riding day trips in the Kangxi Grasslands 80 km (50 miles) northwest of Beijing).

Among the golf course options are **Beijing International Golf Club** (50 km/30 miles north of Beijing near Changping, tel: 6076-2288) and **Beijing Country Golf Club** (35 km/22 miles northeast of Beijing in Shunyi County (tel: 6940-1111). Closer in is the **Beijing Willow Golf Club**, with views of the Summer Palace (Fourth Ring Road, Haidian District, tel: 8262-8899).

## Spectator Sports

Football (soccer) has overtaken basketball as the most popular spectator sport in China. Naturally, the capital has one of the top professional football teams, Beijing Guo'an. Like many Chinese teams, Guo'an regularly attract crowds of more than 50,000. They have also bought several foreign players, though the overall level of skill remains far behind that of leading European and South American teams. It is nonetheless worth watching a game to sample the unique atmosphere. Unfortunately – or perhaps fortunately – most visitors will not understand the crude chants. Professional basketball has also taken off, aided by many ex-NBA players.

Tickets for Guo'an football matches, and for basketball games featuring the Beijing Ducks in the CBA league, can be bought from the ticket office on the north side of the Workers' Stadium (Tel: 6592-1173).

## Hiking and Cycling

The Beijing area offers plenty of opportunities for **hiking** and **cycling**. The Ming Tombs, Eastern Qing Tombs, and Chengde are all set in picturesque hiking country, as are the Huairou and Miyun districts north of the city. Beijing has several active hiking clubs which arrange weekend hikes. Try **Beijing Hikers** (tel: 139-1002-5516; www. bjhikers.com) or the **High Club** (tel: 6553-2228; www.highclub.cn).

Although Beijing does not yet have Western-style campsites, wild camping is possible so long as you stay far enough away from villages and fields. Equipment can be rented from the **Sanfo Outdoor Club** (tel: 6201-5550; www.sanfo.com.cn, in Chinese only).

Cycling is a good way to see parts of Beijing; rentals and tours can be arranged through **CycleChina** (tel: 6559-3462; www.cyclechina.com). It is also possible to cycle to sights around Beijing, though some of the distances make a day trip too demanding. For cycling tours and other information about cycling in China, see www.BikeChina.com.

## Walking the Wall

An unusual place to hike – and hopefully get away from the crowds – is on one of the less visited stretches of the Great Wall, such as Jinshanling or Huanghuacheng.

You can arrange your own hike along the Wall but be warned that accommodation is rudimentary. Simatai has a modern, off-wall guesthouse and a tourist village and there are several new boutique ranches near less-visited areas of the Wall. **CNadventure** specialises in Great Wall hiking, with trips running almost daily in season (tel: 6567-4939; www.cnadventure.com). Also try www.china-hiking.com/greatwall for more information.

## CHILDREN

Beijing can be tough for kids – lots of long meals, long taxi rides and long walks through ancient sites full of staring crowds. And, as friendly as Beijingers are to children, the city itself is by no means child-friendly – the grassy areas in parks are generally off limits and playgrounds are nigh impossible to come by.

Children in need of a break can let off steam year-round at **Fundazzle**, a former Olympic-size indoor swimming pool that has been converted into a large playland in which kids can climb through tunnels, slide down slides, or plunge into the former diving pool now full of plastic balls (just inside the south gate of the Workers' Stadium, tel:

6506-9066, open Mon–Fri 9am–5.30pm, weekends 9am–7pm; entrance fee). The **Blue Zoo Aquarium** is located just a few meters away; it has a moving platform that takes viewers through tunnels that bisect the fish tanks (Workers' Stadium South Gate, tel: 6591-3397, open daily 8am–8pm, entrance fee). **Chaoyang Park**, **Ritan Park** and, further south, **Taoranting Park** all have playgrounds (fee charged) and rides for children that are open in summer. Other good outdoor destinations are the **Beijing Zoo** (open daily 7.30am–5pm) and **boating** (or skating) on one of Beijing's lakes (particularly pleasant in **Beihai Park**). Year-round ice-skating can be found at **Le Cool**, in the basement of the China World Centre.

Children who like crafts can buy items at Shengtangxuan, a shop that specialises in traditional, handcrafted toys (inside Guozijian Hutong, tel: 8404-7179). Puppet shows can sometimes be seen at the **China Puppet Theatre** (1 Anhuaxili, tel: 6425-4798). A special treat, especially popular with girls, is to dress up as a character from Chinese opera and pose for photos at **Fenmo Nong Zhuang** (29 Liangmaqiao Lu, tel: 6436-9709).

Those with a scientific bent may enjoy the **Science and Technology Museum** on the north side of the Third Ring Road (1 Beisanhuan Zhong Lu, tel: 6237-1177, open 9am–4.30pm, closed Monday) or the **Sony Explora Science Centre**, Oriental Plaza (tel: 8518-2255, open 9am–5.30pm, 10am–7pm at weekends). The **Chinese Culture Club** offers many classes and outings that are suitable for older children, including painting, calligraphy and martial arts; check their website at www.chinese cultureclub.com or call 6432-9341 to find out what's on.

If all else fails, modern toys of all sorts can be found at the **Children's Department Store** (168 Wangfujing) or on the top floor of the Lufthansa Centre.

# A-Z

## A HANDY SUMMARY OF PRACTICAL INFORMATION, ARRANGED ALPHABETICALLY

## A dmission Charges

Admission is charged to virtually every sight in Beijing – even public parks have a nominal entrance fee (usually 2 or 3 Rmb). Most museums, temples and historic sites charge around 10 Rmb, but some major sights charge more – 30 Rmb for the Temple of Heaven and 60 Rmb for the Forbidden City, for instance. Some places have different prices, depending upon how many areas or exhibitions are to be visited – an all-inclusive ticket is called a *tao piao*, and is usually worth buying unless you specifically want to visit one area only. Students and those over 55 are often entitled to discounts, but are usually

required to have identification proving their status or age. Children under certain ages are allowed in free to some sites, but this is generally determined by height – which can be verified on the spot – rather than age.

## B udgeting for your Trip

Beijing is a city that can be seen on a range of budgets. Hotel prices vary considerably, even for hotels of a similar standard, so it is always wise to shop around. Price variations will depend on the season (autumn is likely to be the most expensive), the current occupancy and any ongoing promotional events. Hotels frequented by foreign business-

people or major tour-group operators are likely to be much more expensive for individual tourists than similar hotels in less popular – but still convenient – locations. A perfectly acceptable hotel room can cost under US$50 or $60 in an area of the city less frequented by Westerners. As the hotel becomes more central, the price will rise, but there is a considerable range between US$60 and US$120. For true five- or six-star service with world-class fitness centres, plasma-screen TVs and the like, expect to pay in the range of US$200 or more per night, depending on the season.

    Food costs vary even more wildly than hotel costs – it is possible to eat a delicious and filling

## CLIMATE AND WHEN TO VISIT

The ideal time for travelling to Beijing is late spring (May to mid-June) and autumn (late August to mid-October). The week following the national holiday on 1 October, however, is not so good, as many Chinese are travelling at this time. The same applies to Chinese New Year, in January or February (date changes each year), probably the worst time to come to China.

Beijing has a continental climate, with four clearly defined seasons. Winter is cold and dry with little snow, and it is usually sunny. Sharp winds blow frequently from the northern steppes and desert regions to the west. Spring, which begins in April, is the shortest season: warm, dry and often windy. In early spring, sandstorms blow in from central Asia. These cease by mid-May at the latest. The average temperature then climbs quickly.

Summer begins around mid-June and reaches its peak in July and August. Both temperature and rainfall are highest in these two months. It is often muggy; temperatures climb to over 30°C and occasionally 35°C or more.

About 75 per cent of the annual rainfall occurs in June, July and August, when afternoon thunderstorms are common.

In autumn the sky is blue most of the time, and the air is cleaner (a noticeable cloud of smog hangs over the city much of the year). It is usually warm during the day and pleasantly cool in the evening. Early September to late October is ideal, although Beijing can be crowded at this time.

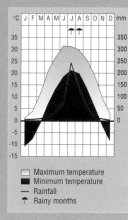

☐ Maximum temperature
■ Minimum temperature
— Rainfall
↑ Rainy months

### Tourist Sights

Many tourist sights stop selling tickets one hour before closing for the day. Closing time is generally one hour earlier from October to April. Where historic buildings are located within a public park, such as the Temple of Heaven and Beihai Park, different opening times operate for the park and the buildings.

## **C**rime and Safety

Visitors don't need to take any special precautions in Beijing, though you should never leave money and valuables unguarded. Crime in China is low, but rising. Beware of pickpockets on buses, and always keep luggage locked.

## Customs Regulations

Be aware of customs regulations when entering or leaving China as some unexpected items may be on the restricted list.

A duplicate of the customs declaration which you received on arrival should be shown on departure. Expensive jewellery, equipment and the amount of foreign exchange should all be declared, and all imported items must be taken out again. Items that are imported and not taken out of the country again are subject to customs payments.

Many books, newspaper reports, magazines and videos that are legal in the West may be deemed illegal in China, especially political or pornographic works.

Export restrictions apply to antiques. Antiques that can be exported carry a special customs sticker, which normally has a Temple of Heaven symbol. It is advisable to keep receipts for items bought, in case of spot checks.

## **D**isabled Travellers

Most major hotels have some form of ramp access, and good lifts, but it is difficult to avoid steps when visiting tourist sights. Ordinary shops and restaurants

---

meal of noodles or steamed *baozi* for less than US$1. A typical dinner of three or four dishes with beer and rice for two can be had in the US$10–15 range at most restaurants. On the other hand, meals in five-star hotels or the few truly upmarket restaurants will cost almost the same as they would at similar establishments in the West, with the bill for two people easily reaching US$50–100.

Public transport is the most economical way to get around, with subway rides costing about 35 cents and buses even less. However, since a taxi ride to most places in town is likely to be only US$2 or $3, the money saved may not always be worth the time and effort.

## Business Hours

Business hours in Beijing seem to lengthen every year. State-owned restaurants and shops still close on the early side, around 8.30 or 9pm, but private establishments stay open much later. Chain grocery stores keep long hours, from early morning until around 11pm. Major shopping malls stay open until 10pm or later, with stores closing at different times – internet cafés, bars, ice-cream parlours and the like remain open while clothing shops shut down. All stores are open every day, including weekends, and many do not even close on national holidays such as Chinese New Year,

## EMERGENCY NUMBERS

In case of emergency you can get help on the following numbers:
Police:        110
Ambulance:     120
Fire:          119

seldom provide ramp access. Some main streets have raised tracking to aid people with impaired vision.

## E lectricity

The standard for electricity in Beijing is 220 volts AC. Hotels usually have a 110-volt or 120-volt outlet for shavers.

## Embassies & Consulates

### Foreign Embassies in Beijing

**Australia**, 21 Dongzhimenwai Dajie, Chaoyang District. Tel: 6532-2331/7, fax: 6532-4605; www.austemb.org.cn
**Canada**, 19 Dongzhimenwai Dajie, Chaoyang District. Tel: 6532-3536, fax: 6532-1684; www.canada.org.cn
**Ireland**, 3 Ritan Donglu, Chaoyang District. Tel: 6532-2691, fax: 6532-6857; www.ireland-china.com.cn
**New Zealand**, Dong'er Jie, Ritan Lu. Tel: 6532-1144, fax: 6532-4317; www.nzembassy.com
**Singapore**, 1 Xiushui Beijie, Jianguomenwai. Tel: 6532-3926.
**South Africa**, 5 Dongzhimenwai

Dajie, Chaoyang District. Tel: 6532-0171, fax: 6532-0177. www.dfa.gov.za/foreign/sa_abroad/sac.htm
**United Kingdom**, 11 Guanghua Lu. Tel: 6532-1961, fax: 6532-1937; www.britishembassy.org.cn
**United States**, 2 Xiushui Dongjie, Jianguomenwai. Tel: 6532-3831 ext. 229, fax: 6532-2483; www.usembassy-china.org.cn

### Chinese Embassies in the UK and US

**UK**, Consular Section, 31 Portland Place, London, W1B 1QD. Tel: (020) 7631-1430 (visa enquiries, Mon–Fri 2–4pm), (020) 7636-5637, recorded information (premium rate) 0891-880 808; www.chinese-embassy.org.uk
**US**, Visa Office, 2201 Wisconsin Avenue, Room 110, Washington, DC 20007. Tel: (202) 338-6688, fax: (202) 588-9760; www.china-embassy.org

## Entry Requirements

A tourist visa is necessary for entering China and must be applied for in person or through an agent; mail-in applications are no longer accepted in the UK or US. If you need to extend your visa in China, contact the Public Security Bureau, Visa Section, Andingmen Dongdajie (near the Lama Temple), tel: 8401-5292. The fine for overstaying a visa is a punitive 500 Rmb per day.

On entry, a health declaration, entry card and customs declaration have to be completed. These forms are given out on the plane or at the airport.

## G ay & Lesbian Travellers

Same-sex couples can share hotel rooms and there are generally no problems for gay travellers in China. Many Chinese people, however, are either completely ignorant of homosexuality or believe that gay men and lesbians exist only in the West. Beijing has a small gay scene, which the government appears to tolerate so long as it remains low-key. Some magazines carry contact advertisements and the city has at least one gay hotline. To avoid risk of publicity-induced closure, no gay bars or clubs are identified in this guide.

## H ealth & Medical Care

No vaccinations are required for China. It may be advisable to strengthen the body's resistance to hepatitis A infection by having a gammaglobulin injection before travelling. Malaria prevention, recommended by the World Health Organisation for some areas of southern China, is not necessary for Beijing.

Anyone planning to spend more than one year in China needs a health examination, which includes an Aids test. Travellers suffering from Aids, tuberculosis and other serious illnesses are not normally allowed to enter China.

### Medical services

Getting used to a different climate and foreign food can affect your health. It is worth taking medicines for colds, diarrhoea and constipation in your medical kit, as well as a stock of any regular medication you need. While traditional Chinese remedies are often effective, language difficulties may make it hard to buy the right ones.

Most tourist hotels offer medical assistance. The Swissotel has its own pharmacy. In case of serious illness, foreigners can get treatment in special sections for foreigners at major local

## FACT FILE

**Area:** Beijing covers an area of 16,807 sq km (10,443 sq miles). The city is divided into 10 districts.
**Geography:** Beijing lies on the northern edge of the North Chinese plain at a similar latitude to Madrid and New York: 39° 56' north; longitude 116° 20' east. The city centre is 44

metres (143 ft) above sea level.
**Population:** 11.7 million. This figure does not include an estimated 2–3 million migrant workers.
**Weights and measures:** China uses a mixture of metric and more traditional weights and measures. Distances are usually in kilometres.

TRANSPORT    ACCOMMODATION    ACTIVITIES    A-Z    LANGUAGE

hospitals, but partly because of language problems, the service is not Western-style.

The best hospitals with foreigner sections are the **Sino-Japanese Friendship Hospital**, Heping Donglu, Chaoyang District. Tel: 6422-1122; and **Capital Hospital**, 53 Dongdanbei Dajie. Tel: 6529-5269, 6529-6114.

More expensive, but the best place for treatment of serious illness, is the private **Beijing United Family Health Centre**, 2 Jiangtai Lu (close to Lido Hotel). Tel: 6433-3960, fax: 6433-3963. All staff speak excellent English. **International SOS Clinic** (24hr hospital emergency facilities with English spoken), tel: 6462-9100.

You will generally be given Western medicine in the foreigner sections of hospitals, and antibiotics are readily available. If you want traditional Chinese medical treatment, whether herbs or acupuncture, you must request it. Chinese hospitals are divided into those using Western medicine and those using traditional medicine, though some use both.

### Pharmacies

Pharmacies in China are of two kinds, those that sell predominantly Chinese medicine and those that sell predominantly Western medicine. Pharmacists in both kinds will offer advice and suggest medicine, although they may not speak English. Basic cold medicines and antibiotics are inexpensive and available without prescription. Pharmacies keep varying hours, with many open until late at night. The Wangfujing Drug Store at 267 Wangfujing, and Watson's at the Holiday Inn Lido on Jiangtai Lu, both have a large range of Western medicines and toiletries.

### Internet

A fire in an internet café in 2002 led the Beijing government to exert far greater control over these popular gathering places and implement stricter operating regulations. The result is a much-improved environment for internet users. While hotel business centres generally charge 2 or 3 Rmb per **minute** for internet use, regular internet cafés charge between 10 and 20 Rmb per **hour**. Many internet cafés are open from 7am until 2am; the best time to visit is during the day, when the teenagers are in school. All are plastered with no smoking signs, but these are routinely ignored – you can complain, but be prepared for a smoky environment.

There is a centrally located internet café at "The Station" (the old railway station building just east of Qianmen Gate).

*For a list of websites on Beijing, see page 232.*

### Lost Property

Lost property that is presumed stolen should be reported to the Foreigners Section of the Beijing Public Security Bureau, tel: 6525-5486. Beijing does not have a central lost-property office, but the Beijing Tourist Hotline (tel: 6513-0828) may be able to provide some advice on where to seek help. Taxis are a common place to lose things, which is why doormen at five-star hotels sometimes hand guests a slip of paper with their taxi number on it as they board the car. If an item has been lost in a taxi, call 6835-1150; the odds of having it returned are high if the driver finds it, since there are stiff penalties for keeping lost property. For the airport lost and found, tel: 6456-4119 or 6459-8333.

### Maps

Reasonably accurate maps in English are available from most hotels. Bookshops and kiosks mainly sell Chinese maps, which usually include bus and subway routes. Some maps have street and building names in both Chinese characters and English. The Insight Fleximap to Beijing is durable, detailed and easy to use, with a full street index, and its laminated finish means that getting it wet in a Beijing summer rainstorm is not a problem.

### Media

### Newspapers and magazines

Beijing has several Chinese daily papers, including the official Party newspaper *Renmin Ribao (People's Daily)*, *Guangming Daily*, which is mainly for intellectuals, the local *Beijing Daily* and *Beijing Evening Post*. For foreign visitors, *China Daily*, which is published every day except Sunday, is a nationally distributed English-language newspaper. It includes listings of cultural events in Beijing, international news and good sports coverage. *Beijing Today* is an English-language paper from the publishers of *Beijing Youth Daily* that also carries listings. Several foreign daily papers can be bought in Beijing (a day later) from the big hotels and the Friendship Store. These include the *South China Morning Post* and *Hong Kong Standard*, which have the best coverage of China, the *International Herald Tribune* and *Financial Times*. Magazines available include *Newsweek*, *Time*, *The Economist* and *Asiaweek*.

For local listings, pick up a copy of the what's-on magazine *That's Beijing*. Published monthly, it is a comprehensive source of information and a good introduction to (Western-oriented) cultural life in the city.

### Television and radio

Chinese TV shows many foreign films, usually dubbed into Chinese but sometimes left in the original language and subtitled. CCTV broadcasts a daily English news programme at 10.30pm. CCTV-9 is an English-language news and information channel. Many large hotels carry

CNN and satellite broadcasts from Hong Kong-based Star TV. *China Daily* prints a daily television programme schedule. Bilingual Beijing radio stations Easy FM and Joy FM broadcast Western and Chinese music on 91.5 FM. More bilingual programmes can be found on Your FM at 101.8 FM and 97.4 FM.

## Money

The Chinese currency is called renminbi (Rmb; literally, "people's money"). The basic unit is the *yuan*, often called *kuai*. One *yuan* is worth 10 *jiao*, also called *mao*. Bank notes come in 100, 50, 20, 10, 5 and 1 *yuan* denominations; plus 5, 2 and 1 *jiao*. The 1 *yuan*, 5 *jiao*, 1 *jiao* coins are rarely seen in Beijing.

### Changing money

Foreign currency and Travellers' Cheques can be changed in most hotels, and at branches of the Bank of China. ATM machines that accept Western cards are located in most major shopping centres and some hotels. For credit card cash advances, there are automatic cash machines scattered throughout the city. Banks will also issue cash advances, but charge a 4 per cent commission.

When you change money, you get a receipt that allows you to change Rmb back to foreign currency within six months, but you can only change back up to 50

## PUBLIC HOLIDAYS

The following are official non-working days in China:
**1 January**
**Jan/February**: Chinese New Year (4 days; exact date varies according to lunar calendar)
**8 March**: International Women's Day (half-day for women only)
**1 May**: International Workers' Day (5 days)
**1 October**: National Day (5 days)

per cent of the original sum.

If you have problems changing money or getting a cash advance, the main branch of the Bank of China is at 1 Fuxingmen Nei Dajie (at the Second Ring Road), tel: 6659-6688. Or try the branches inside the China World Trade Centre, or at 8 Yabao Lu (Asia-Pacific Building).

### Credit cards

Major credit cards can be used in most large hotels, shops and restaurants.

### Tipping

Tips are not usually expected and are often refused, but waiters in large hotels and restaurants, as well as a few taxi drivers, do court tips. Before you tip, remember that the average wage is relatively low – about 1,000 yuan a month.

## P ostal Services

You will find postal facilities in most hotels. Letters and postcards to and from China take around six days. Parcels must be packed and sealed at the post office, to allow customs inspection. The main **International Post Office** (tel: 6512-8120) is on the Second Ring Road, just north of the Jianguomen intersection.

International express courier services, normally with free pick-up, are offered by: **DHL-Sinotrans**, 45 Xinyuan Jie, tel: 6466-5566; **Federal Express**, Rm 107, Oriental Plaza, World Service Centre, tel: 6468-5566, 800-810-2328; **UPS**, Rm 1818, China World Tower 1, tel: 6505-5005.

## R eligious Services

Greater Beijing has more than 30 Christian churches with regular services on weekdays and Sundays. Catholic mass (including Sunday mass in English) is said in **Nantang Cathedral**, 141 Qianmen Dajie (right outside Xuanwumen underground station), tel: 6602-5221, and **Beitang Cathe-**

**dral**, 33 Xishiku Dajie, near Beihai Park, tel: 6617-5198. Protestant services are held at **Gangwashi Church**, 57 Xisinan Dajie, Xicheng District, tel: 6617-6181, and **Chongwen District Church**, Hougou Hutong, Chongwenmen, tel: 6524-2193. Muslims can attend several mosques, including **Niu Jie Mosque** on Niu Jie in the south of the city, tel: 6353-2564. Buddhists have plenty of choice among Beijing's restored temples.

## S tudent Travellers

Students from outside China do not get significant travel discounts as they do in some countries, but they can generally get discounted admission to major tourist sights if they have official identification.

## T elephones

Calls within Beijing are generally free. In most hotels you can telephone direct abroad, though this is expensive and in some you still need to ask the operator to call for you. In top hotels, you can use credit cards and international telephone cards. China's IDD rates have fallen but are still higher than most Western countries; remember that costs are halved after 6pm and at weekends.

Payphones which accept phone cards can be found along most city streets and in many hotels and shopping centres.

The international code for China is **86**. The area code for Beijing is **10**, which does not need to be dialled for calls within the city, and is not included in the listed phone numbers in this guidebook.

These **"IC" cards** (30, 50 or 100 Rmb) can be bought at streetside newspaper kiosks or small shops, as well as from hotels. Small shops also sell prepaid internet phone cards called **"IP" cards**, which offer rates considerably lower than standard costs and can in theory be used from any phone – before dialling the number you wish to reach, you need to dial a local number printed on the card followed by a PIN number. US credit-phonecard codes from China can be accessed by dialling 1087901.

The International Post Office on the Second Ring Road north of the Jianguomen intersection (open 8am–7pm) handles long-distance calls, as well as money orders. The Long-Distance Telephone Building at Fuxingmen Dajie (7am–midnight) handles long-distance, conference and pre-booked calls.

Local calls can still be made from roadside booths with attendants, although as cellphones become ever more commonplace, these are disappearing. They generally cost four jiao. These booths can also be used for long-distance calls but charges can be high.

Dial 115 for operator assistance with long-distance calls, and 114 for directory enquiries.

**Fax:** Almost all hotels have fax services, although rates vary widely. Expect to pay about 10 Rmb per page to send or receive.

## Time Zone

Beijing time, which applies across China, is GMT +8 hours

(EST +13 hours). There is no daylight savings time, so from early April to late October, Beijing is 7 hours ahead of London and 12 hours ahead of New York.

## Toilets

All public toilets are now free, and their standards are much higher than in the past. The city government has allocated 100 million Rmb per year for further upgrading in the run-up to the Olympics. But many are best avoided except in cases of dire need (for which it is wise to carry a packet of tissues, as they do not yet have paper). When nature calls, the best option is to go to a hotel or restaurant.

## Tourist Information

Beijing's tourist information offices are not especially helpful, and mainly exist to sell tours. The state-run **China International Travel Service** (CITS), 1 Dongdan, tel: 8522-8888, fax: 6522-6866, www.cits.com.cn, has offices in several hotels and at some tourist venues. Most hotels offer guided tours to sights inside and outside Beijing. Larger hotels organise their own tours, others arrange trips through CITS or smaller travel companies.
**Beijing Hutong Tourist Agency**, Dianmenxi Dajie near the north gate of Beihai Park, tel: 6615-9097 or ask your hotel, runs guided pedicab tours through the old *hutong* of what used to be one of Beijing's wealthiest areas, with stops at the Drum and Bell towers. From the same area, starting at the southwest corner of Qianhai Lake, you can take boat tours as far as the Summer Palace.

Complaints or specific enquiries are handled by the Beijing Tourism Administration hotline on 6513-0828. If you want to book direct with a travel agency, several are listed below, divided into national travel agencies, which deal mainly with tours

booked outside China or travel to other provinces, and agencies which deal specifically with the Beijing area.

### Travel Agents

**Beijing CITIC Guo'an International Travel Service**, Rm 304, Guo'an Hotel, 1 Guangdongdian Beijie.Tel: 6501-0841, fax: 6501-0887.
**Beijing Hutong Tourist Agency** North gate of Beihai Park, Houhai. Tel: 6615-9097.
**China International Travel Service (CITS)**, Beijing Tourism Building, 28 Jianguomenwai Dajie. Tel: 6515-8562, 6515-0515, fax: 6512-9193, tlx: 22047 CITSB. www.cits.com.cn
**Panda Tours**, Holiday Inn Crowne Plaza, 48 Wangfujing Dajie. Tel: 6513-3388, ext.1212/13, fax: 6513-2513.
**Tour-beijing**, Jia 23 Fuxin Lu. Tel: 8775-7080, fax: 8775-7110 Besides the main travel agencies, Beijing has many small-scale, sometimes unlicensed tour operators. On some of the organised tours, as in many countries, the operators take tourists to shops and restaurants that pay the guides a commission. Others charge double for entrance tickets that you can buy yourself. But most tour companies are reasonably trustworthy, and usually cheap.

## **W**ebsites

Official websites on Beijing: www.beijing-tour.com, www.bjta.gov.cn, www.cbw.com, and www.cits.com.cn.

### Women Travellers

Women travelling alone generally experience few problems in China. Travelling by public transport or bicycle is usually safe, but there have been occasional reports of Beijing taxi drivers harassing foreign women. When taking taxis, especially at night, or visiting smaller bars and clubs, it may be better to join other tourists.

# LANGUAGE

## UNDERSTANDING MANDARIN CHINESE

### Mandarin and Dialects

People in Beijing speak *putonghua*, or "common language", known in the West as Mandarin Chinese. Based on the northern dialect, one of the eight dialects of China, putonghua is taught throughout the country. It is promoted as standard Chinese across the country, though most people also, or only, speak a local dialect. In most Beijing hotels you will find someone who can speak at least some English, and in the top hotels good English is spoken. You can generally get by without Chinese in tourist areas; however, taxi drivers speak little English.

*Putonghua* or other Chinese dialects such as Cantonese is the first language of 93 per cent of the population of China. There is considerable difference in the pronunciation of different dialects, though written forms are the same everywhere. Many ethnic minorities, such as Tibetans and Mongolians, have their own written and spoken language. In Beijing, a slightly different dialect is spoken.

Although the pronunciation in Beijing is very close to standard Chinese, it also has some distinctive characteristics, particularly the "er" sound added to the end of many syllables.

### The Pinyin System

Since 1958, the *pinyin* system has been used to represent Chinese characters phonetically in the Latin alphabet. Pinyin has become internationally accepted, so that Peking is today written Beijing (pronounced Bay-jing), Canton is Guangzhou, and Mao Tse-tung is Mao Zedong.

At first this may seem confusing to Westerners, but it is a useful, practical, if imperfect system that is increasingly popular in China. You will find many shop names written in pinyin above the entrance, and the names at railway stations are written in pinyin, so it is helpful to learn the basic rules of the system.

Most modern dictionaries use pinyin. (Taiwan, however, usually uses the older Wade-Giles system.) This transcription may at first appear confusing if one doesn't see the words as they are pronounced. The city of Qingdao, for example, is pronounced *chingdow*.

It would definitely be useful, particularly for individual travellers, to familiarise yourself a little with the pronunciation of pinyin. Even when asking for a place or street name, you need to know how it is pronounced, otherwise you won't be understood. This guide uses the pinyin system

throughout for Chinese names and expressions on occasion.

### Written Chinese

Written Chinese uses thousands of characters, many of which are based on ancient pictograms, or picture-like symbols. Some characters used today go back more than 3,000 years. There are strict rules in the method of writing, as the stroke order affects the overall appearance of the characters. Because of the slowness of formal calligraphy, ordinary people develop their own simplified handwriting for everyday use. In the past the script was written from right to left and top to bottom, but today it is usually written from left to right.

Some 6,000 characters are in regular use; 3,000 characters are sufficient for reading a newspaper. Mainland China has reformed written Chinese several times since 1949, and simplified characters are now used. In Hong Kong and Taiwan the old characters remain standard.

### Tones

It is sometimes said that Chinese is a monosyllabic language. At first sight, this seems to be true, since each character represents a single syllable that generally indicates a specific concept. However, in modern Chinese, most words are made up of two or three syllables, sometimes more. In the Western sense, spoken Chinese has only 420 single-syllable root words, but tones are used to differentiate these basic sounds. Tones make it difficult for foreigners to learn Chinese, since different tones give the same syllable a completely different meaning. For instance, *mai* with a falling fourth tone *(mài)* means to sell; if it is pronounced with a falling-rising third tone *(măi)*, it means to buy. If you pay attention to these tones, you can soon tell the difference, though correct pronunciation requires much practice. Taking another example, the four tones of the syllable ma: first tone, *mā* means mother; second tone, *má* means hemp; third tone, *mă* means horse; and fourth tone *mà* means to complain.

The first tone is pitched high and even, the second rising, the third falling and then rising, and the fourth falling. There is also a fifth, "neutral" tone. The individual tones are marked above the main vowel in the syllable.

## Grammar

Chinese sentence structure is simple: subject, predicate, object. Many Chinese words serve as nouns, adjectives and verbs without altering their written or spoken forms. Verbs have single forms and do not change with the subject. There are no plural forms for verbs or nouns. All of these have to be inferred

from the context. The easiest way to form a question is to add the interrogative particle *ma* (neutral tone) to the end of a statement.

## Names and Forms of Address

Chinese names usually consist of three, or sometimes two, syllables, each with its own meaning. Traditionally, the first syllable is the family name, the second or two others are personal names. For instance, in Deng Xiaoping, Deng is the family name, Xiaoping the personal name. The same is true for Fu Hao, where Fu is the family name, Hao the personal name. Until the 1980s, the address *tongzhi* (comrade) was common, but today *xiansheng* and *furen*, the Chinese equivalents of Mr and Mrs, are more usual. A young woman, as well as female staff in hotels and restaurants, can be addressed as *xiaojie* (Miss). Address older men, especially those in important positions, as *xiansheng* or *shifu* (Master).

## Language Guide

There are a standard set of diacritical marks to indicate which of the four tones is used:
mā = high and even tone
má = rising tone
mă = falling then rising tone
mà = falling tone

## Pronunciation

The pronunciation of the consonants is similar to those in English: b, p, d, t, g, k are all

voiceless; p, t, k are aspirated, b, d, g are not aspirated. The i after the consonants ch, c, r, sh, s, z, zh is not pronounced: it indicates that the preceding sound is lengthened.

**Pinyin/Phonetic/Sound**
a/a/f**a**r
an /un/r**un**
ang/ung /l**ung**
ao/ou/l**oud**
b/b/**b**ath
c/ts/ra**ts**
ch/ch/**ch**ange
d/d/**d**ay
e/er/di**r**t
e (after i, u, y)/a/tr**a**m
ei/ay/m**ay**
en/en/wh**en**
eng/eong/**ng** has a nasal sound
er/or/hon**our**
f/f/**f**ast
g/g/**g**o
h/ch/lo**ch**
i/ee/k**ee**n
j/j/**j**eep
k/k/ca**k**e
l/l/**l**ittle
m/m/**m**onth
n/n/**n**ame
o/o/b**o**nd
p/p/tra**pp**ed
q/ch/**ch**eer
r/r/**r**ight
s/s/me**ss**
sh/sh/**sh**ade
t/t/**t**on
u/oo/sh**oo**t
ü (after j, q, x, y)/as German ü (midway between "ee" and "oo"
w/w/**w**ater
x/sh/as in **sh**eep
y/y/**y**ogi
z/ds/re**ds**
zh/dj/**j**ungle

### GREETINGS

| | | |
|---|---|---|
| Hello | Nĭ hăo | 你好 |
| How are you? | Nĭ hăo ma? | 你好吗? |
| Thank you | Xièxie | 谢谢 |
| Goodbye | Zài jiàn | 再见 |
| My name is... | Wŏ jiào... | 我叫... |
| My last name is... | Wŏ xìng... | 我姓... |
| What is your name? | Nín jiào shénme míngzi? | 您叫什么名字? |
| What is your last name? | Nín guìxìng? | 您贵姓? |
| I am very happy... | Wŏ hěn gāoxìng... | 我很高兴... |
| All right | Hăo | 好 |

| Not all right | Bù hǎo | 不好 |
|---|---|---|
| Can you speak English? | Nín huì shuō Yīngyǔ ma? | 您会说英语吗？ |
| Can you speak Chinese? | Nín huì shuō Hànyǔ ma? | 您会说汉语吗？ |
| I cannot speak Chinese | Wǒ bù huì Hànyǔ | 我不会汉语 |
| I do not understand | Wǒ bù dǒng | 我不懂 |
| Do you understand? | Nín dǒng ma? | 您懂吗？ |
| Please speak a little slower | Qǐng nín shuō màn yìdiǎnr | 请您说慢一点儿 |
| What is this called? | Zhège jiào shénme? | 这个叫什么？ |
| How do you say... | ... zěnme shuō? | ...怎么说？ |
| Please | Qǐng | 请/谢谢 |
| Never mind | Méi guānxi | 没关系 |
| Sorry | Duìbùqǐ | 对不起 |

**PRONOUNS**

| Who/who is it? | Shéi? | 谁？ |
|---|---|---|
| My/mine | Wǒ/wǒde | 我/我的 |
| You/yours (singular) | Nǐ/nǐde | 你/你的 |
| He/his | Tā/tāde | 他/他的 |
| She/hers | Tā/tāde | 她/她的 |
| We/ours | Wǒmen/wǒmende | 我们/我们的 |
| You/yours (plural) | Nǐmen/nǐmende | 你们/你们的 |
| They/theirs | Tāmen/tāmende | 他们/他们的 |
| You/yours (respectful) | Nín/nínde | 您/您的 |

**TRAVEL**

| Where is it? | zài nǎr? | ...在哪儿？ |
|---|---|---|
| Do you have it here? | Zhèr... yǒu ma? | 这儿有...吗？ |
| No/it's not here/there aren't any | Méi yǒu | 没有 |
| Hotel | Fàndiàn/bīnguǎn | 饭店/宾馆 |
| Restaurant | Fànguǎnr | 饭馆 |
| Bank | Yínháng | 银行 |
| Post Office | Yóujú | 邮局 |
| Toilet | Cèsuǒ | 厕所 |
| Railway station | Huǒchē zhàn | 火车站 |
| Bus station | Qìchē zhàn | 汽车站 |
| Embassy | Dàshǐguǎn | 大使馆 |
| Consulate | Lǐngshìguǎn | 领事馆 |
| Passport | Hùzhào | 护照 |
| Visa | Qiānzhèng | 签证 |
| Pharmacy | Yàodiàn | 药店 |
| Hospital | Yīyuàn | 医院 |
| Doctor | Dàifu/yīshēng | 大夫/医生 |
| Translate | Fānyì | 翻译 |
| Bar | Jiǔbā | 酒吧 |
| Do you have...? | Nín yǒu... ma? | 您有...吗？ |
| I want/I would like | Wǒ yào/wǒ xiǎng yào | 我要/我想要 |
| I want to buy,... | Wǒ xiǎng mǎi... | 我想买... |
| Where can I buy it? | Nǎr néng mǎi... ma? | 哪儿能买吗？ |
| This/that | Zhège/nèige | 这个/那个 |
| Green tea/black tea | Lǜchá/hóngchá | 绿茶/红茶 |
| Coffee | Kāfēi | 咖啡 |
| Cigarette | Xiāngyān | 香烟 |
| Film (for camera) | Jiāojuǎnr | 胶卷儿 |
| Ticket | Piào | 票 |
| Postcard | Míngxìnpiàn | 明信片 |
| Letter | Yì fēng xìn | 一封信 |
| Air mail | Hángkōng xìn | 航空信 |
| Postage stamp | Yóupiào | 邮票 |

TRANSPORT
ACCOMMODATION
ACTIVITIES
A – Z
LANGUAGE

## SHOPPING

| | | |
|---|---|---|
| How much? | Duōshǎo? | 多少 |
| How much does it cost? | Zhège duōshǎo qián? | 这个多少钱? |
| Too expensive, thank you | Tài guì le, xièxie | 太贵了，谢谢 |
| Very expensive | Hěn guì | 很贵 |
| A little (bit) | Yìdiǎnr | 一点儿 |
| Too much/too many | Tài duō le | 太多了 |
| A lot | Duō | 多 |
| Few | Shǎo | 少 |

## MONEY MATTERS, HOTELS, TRANSPORT, COMMUNICATIONS

| | | |
|---|---|---|
| Money | Qián | 钱 |
| Chinese currency | Rénmínbì | 人民币 |
| One yuan/one kuai (10 jiao) | Yì yuán/yì kuài | 一元/一块 |
| One jiao/one mao (10 fen) | Yì jiǎo/yì mǎo | 一角/一毛 |
| One fen | Yì fēn | 一分 |
| Traveller's cheque | Lǚxíng zhīpiào | 旅行支票 |
| Credit card | Xìnyòngkǎ | 信用卡 |
| Foreign currency | Wàihuìquàn | 外汇券 |
| Where can I change money? | Zài nǎr kěyǐ huàn qián? | 在哪儿可以换钱? |
| I want to change money | Wǒ xiǎng huàn qián | 我想换钱 |
| What is the exchange rate? | Bǐjià shì duōshǎo? | 比价是多少? |
| We want to stay for one (two/three) nights | Wǒmen xiǎng zhù yì (liǎng/sān) tiān | 我们想住一(两、三 |
| How much is the room per day? | Fángjiān duōshǎo qián yì tiān? | 房间多少钱一天? |

## TIME

| | | |
|---|---|---|
| When? | Shénme shíhou? | 什么时候? |
| What time is it now? | Xiànzài jídiǎn zhōng? | 现在几点种? |
| How long? | Duōcháng shíjiān? | 多长时间? |
| One/two/three o'clock | Yì diǎn/liǎng diǎn/sān diǎn zhōng | 一点/两点/三点种 |
| Early morning/morning | Zǎoshang/shàngwǔ | 早上/上午 |
| Midday/afternoon/evening | Zhōngwǔ/xiàwǔ/wǎnshang | 中午/下午/晚上 |
| Monday | Xīngqīyì | 星期一 |
| Tuesday | Xīngqīèr | 星期二 |
| Wednesday | Xīngqīsān | 星期三 |
| Thursday | Xīngqīsì | 星期四 |
| Friday | Xīngqīwǔ | 星期五 |
| Saturday | Xīngqīliù | 星期六 |
| Sunday | Xīngqītiān/xīngqīrì | 星期天/星期日 |
| Weekend | Zhōumò | 周末 |
| Yesterday/today/tomorrow | Zuótiān/jīntiān/míngtiān | 昨天/今天/明天 |
| This week/last week/ next week | Zhègexīngqī/shàngxīngqī/ xiàxīngqī | 这个星期/上星期/ 下星期 |

## EATING OUT

| | | |
|---|---|---|
| Restaurant | Cāntīng/fànguǎn'r | 餐厅/饭馆儿 |
| Attendant/waiter | Fúwúyuán | 服务员 |
| Waitress | Xiǎojiě | 小姐 |
| Eat | Chī fàn | 吃饭 |
| Breakfast | Zǎofàn | 早饭 |
| Lunch | Wǔfàn | 午饭 |
| Dinner | Wǎnfàn | 晚饭 |
| Menu | Càidān | 菜单 |
| Chopsticks | Kuàizi | 筷子 |
| I want... | Wǒ yào... | 我要 |
| I do not want... | Wǒ bú yào... | 我不要 |
| I did not order this | Zhège wǒ méi diǎn | 这个我没点 |
| I am a vegetarian | Wǒ shì chī sù de rén | 我是吃素的人 |
| I do not eat any meat | Wǒ suǒyǒude ròu dōu bù chī | 我所有的肉都不 |

# FURTHER READING

## Beijing

***On a Chinese Screen*** by Somerset Maugham. Oxford University Press, 1997. Maugham, who first published this travelogue in 1922, wrote brief but engaging sketches of some of the local and foreign characters he met in Beijing.

***The Forbidden City: Centre of Imperial China*** by Gilles Beguin and Dominique Morel. Abrams, 1997. A brief account details the daily lives of Ming and Qing emperors in the former imperial palace.

***Hiking on History*** by William Lindesay. Oxford University Press, 2000. Indispensable for hikers, this is a guide to walking on unrestored, less-visited sections of the Great Wall near Beijing.

***Old Peking: City of the Ruler of the World*** by Chris Elder (Editor). Oxford University Press, 1997. A collection of passages written by foreigners who visited Beijing at various times during its long history as China's imperial capital.

***The Private Life of Chairman Mao: The Memoirs of Mao's Personal Physician*** by Li Zhisui. Random House, 1996. As the Great Helmsman loses control, Dr Li chronicles the degeneration of the revolutionary leader into a callous, drug-dependent tyrant, and gives an insight into life in Zhongnanhai, Beijing's new "Forbidden City".

## General

***Behind the Forbidden Door*** by Tiziano Terzani. Unwin Counterpoint, 1985. This correspondent's book gives a personal and very readable insight into the early, not always smooth processes of reform and opening up to the outside world.

***China Wakes: The Struggle for the Soul of a Rising Power*** by Nicholas Kristof and Sheryl Wudunn. Random House, 1995. Another Beijing correspondent and his wife detail personal experiences in China.

***Real China: From Cannibalism to Karaoke*** by John Gittings. Pocket Books, 1997. In an attempt to portray life beyond Beijing, one of China's longest-serving foreign correspondents travels through several provinces to examine the problems faced by 800 million rural Chinese.

***Understanding China: A Guide to China's Economy, History, and Political Culture*** by John Bryan Starr, Hill and Wang, 2001. A general, comprehensive survey of China's past and present.

## History

***China Remembers*** by Zhang Lijia and Calum MacLeod. Oxford University Press, 1999. A fascinating and accessible look at New China through the eyes of 33 people who have vivid memories of five decades.

***Dragon Lady: The Life and Legend of the Last Empress of China*** by Sterling and Peggy Seagrave. Vintage Books, 1993. Blaming the fabrications of the "Hermit of Peking", Edmund Backhouse, for the myth of the "evil" Empress Dowager Cixi, this book shows how Cixi was herself manipulated by princes and eunuchs.

***From Emperor to Citizen*** by Aisin-Gioro Puyi. Foreign Languages Press, 1989. The quite readable autobiography of the last emperor, Puyi, covers his progress from a childhood in the confines of the imperial throne, to an adult life as a puppet of the

Japanese, prisoner of the communists, and comrade of new Beijing.

***Hungry Ghosts***, Jasper Becker. John Murray, 1996. Using meticulous research, Becker tells the grim truth about the darkest period of post-1949 China: the death of some 30 million in the famines of the Great Leap Forward.

***Red Star over China*** by Edgar R. Snow. Grove Press, 1973. A classic first-hand account of the years of guerilla war leading up to the 1949 revolution, when Snow followed Mao and other communist leaders.

***The Search for Modern China*** by Jonathan Spence. Norton, 1990. Bringing to life Chinese society and politics over the past 400 years, this has become a standard text for students of Chinese history.

***Wild Swans: Three Daughters of China*** by Jung Chang. Anchor Books, 1991. Adding plenty of historical detail, Wild Swans records 20th-century China through the lives of three generations of women, starting with the author's concubine grandmother.

## Politics

***The Era of Jiang Zemin*** by Willy Wo-lap Lam. Prentice Hall, 1999.

***China after Deng Xiaoping*** by Willy Wo-lap Lam. Wiley, 1995. Often considered the leading political commentator on China, Lam explains the inner workings of Beijing politics as well as any outsider can.

***Mandate of Heaven: The Legacy of Tiananmen Square and the Next Generation of China's Leaders*** by Orville Schell. Touchstone Books, 1995. Schell explores the

issues facing China's political leaders from the perspective of writers, artists, musicians, dissidents, underground publishers and venture capitalists. Slightly out of date but still fascinating.
**Mao, A Life** by Philip Short. John Murray Publishers, 2004. A masterful, authoritative biography of China's iconic leader.

## Culture

***China Pop: How Soap Operas, Tabloids, and Bestsellers Are Transforming a Culture*** by Zha Jianying. New Press, 1995. Zha takes an offbeat look at the explosion of Chinese popular culture in the 1980s and 1990s.
***The Chinese*** by Jasper Becker. Free Press, 2001. After 20 years of touring through China and living in Beijing, Becker offers his observations of the Chinese people, from peasant to politician.
***In the Red*** by Geremie Barme, Columbia University Press, 1999. An examination of literary trends in China since 1989, especially the role of dissenting voices.
***Mr China*** by Tim Clissold, Constable and Robinson, 2004. A wonderful insight into Westerners' business (ad)ventures in China.
***Rhapsody in Red: How Western Classical Music Became Chinese***. Algora Publishing, 2004. In this engaging book, classical music is a lens for viewing four centuries of China's cultural exchange with the West. The authors' approach is novelistic rather than academic, and the story they tell is at heart one of the battle between art and politics.
***River Town: Two Years on the Yangtze*** by Peter Hessler. Harper Perrenial, 2001. Hessler writes about his time in the Peace Corps teaching English in a remote part of China, a rich account that reveals what life is like outside major cities.
***Travels Through Sacred China*** by Martin Palmer. Thorsons, 1996. After brief but helpful introductions to the main religious beliefs and practices, the rest of this book is devoted to detailing the most important among hundreds of temples and sacred sites in China.

## Other Insight Guides

Over 200 titles in the acclaimed *Insight Guides* series cover every continent. Those highlighting destinations in the East Asian region include guides to *China, Hong Kong, Taiwan, Korea, Japan, Shanghai* and *Tokyo*. The entire region is detailed in *Insight Guide East Asia*.

There are also over 100 *Insight Pocket Guides*, with an itinerary-based approach designed to assist the traveller with a limited amount of time to spend in a destination. Titles include *Beijing, Canton (Guangzhou), Shanghai, Hong Kong, Macau* and *Tibet*.

*Insight Compact Guides* offer the traveller a highly portable encyclopedic travel guide packed with carefully cross-referenced text, photographs and maps. Titles include *Beijing, Shanghai* and *Hong Kong*.

*Insight Fleximaps* combine clear, detailed cartography with essential travel information. The laminated finish makes the maps durable, weatherproof and easy to fold. Titles include *Beijing, Shanghai* and *Hong Kong*.

### FEEDBACK

We do our best to ensure the information in our books is as accurate and up-to-date as possible. The books are updated on a regular basis, using local contacts who painstakingly add, amend and correct as required. However, some mistakes and omissions are inevitable and we are ultimately reliant on our readers to put us in the picture.
We would welcome your feedback on any details related to your experiences using the book "on the road". We will acknowledge all contributions, and we'll offer an Insight Guide to the best letters received.

Please write to us at:
Insight Guides
PO Box 7910
London SE1 1WE
United Kingdom
Or send e-mail to:
insight@apaguide.co.uk

# BEIJING STREET ATLAS

The key map shows the area of Beijing covered by the atlas section. An index of street names and places of interest shown on the maps can be found on the following pages. For each entry there is a page number and grid reference.

## Map Legend

| | | | |
|---|---|---|---|
| Motorway with Junction | ✈ Airport | Motorway | Ⓜ Subway |
| Motorway (under construction) | ✝ Church (ruins) | Dual Carriageway | 🚌 Bus Station |
| Dual Carriageway | ✝ Monastery | } Main Roads | ❶ Tourist Information |
| Main Road | Castle (ruins) | | ✉ Post Office |
| Secondary Road | ∴ Archaeological Site | } Minor Roads | ✝ Cathedral/Church |
| Minor road | ∩ Cave | | ☾ Mosque |
| Track | ★ Place of Interest | Footpath | ✡ Synagogue |
| International Boundary | 🏠 Mansion/Stately Home | Railway | Statue/Monument |
| Province/State Boundary | ※ Viewpoint | Pedestrian Area | Tower |
| National Park/Reserve | ⚑ Beach | Important Building | Lighthouse |
| Ferry Route | | Park | |

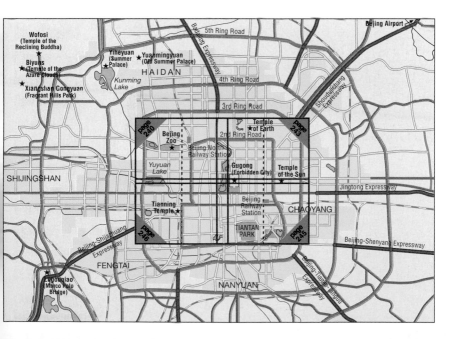

WEIGONGCUN

Xisanhuan Beilu

Beilu

Dahuishu Lu

North China

Gaoliangqiao Lu

Jiaotong University

Dahuisi Lu

Central College of Nationalities

Nanlu

Beijing College of Meteorology

**China Grand Theatre**

National Bureau of Meteorology

Minzuxueyuan

Baishiqiao Lu

**Wutasi**
**(Temple of Five Pagodas)**

National Library

**Shouduliyuguan**
**(Sports Hall of the Capital)**

ZIZHUYUAN GONGYUAN
(PURPLE BAMBOO PARK)

**Beijing Dongwuyuan**
**(Beijing Zoo)**

Beijing Zhanlanguan
(Beijing Exhibition Centre)

Zizhuyuan Lu

Xizhimenwai Dajie

Xizhimenv

**Beijing Planetarium**

BAISHIQIAO

Xizhimenwai Nanlu

Xizhimenwai Nanlu

Yushug

Wenxing Jie

**Beijing College of Architectural Engineering**

Zhanlanguan Lu

Xisanhuan Beilu

Wenxing Xijie

Wenxing Dongjie

Sanlihe Lu

Chegongzhuang Xidajie

Chegongzhuang Dajie

Beij Comm Party S

Lu

Baiwanzhuang Beijie

Baiwanzhuang Xilu

Baiwanzhuang Jie

Colleg of Fore Affai

Baiwanzhuang Nanjie

Kouzhong Hutong

GANJIAKOU

Luyuan 10 Tiao

Zhanlanguan

Nanfuyuan Hutong

Fucheng Lu

Fucheng Lu

Fuchengmenwai D

Xisanhuan Zhonglu

YUYUANTAN GONGYUAN

(SONG QINGLING CHILDREN'S SCIENCE PARK)

Sanlihe Lu

Yuetan Beijie

Sanlihe Donglu

Yuetan Beixiaojie

*Yuyuan* Lake

0 _____ 800 m

0 _____ 800 yards

Yuetan Nanjie

A                                    B

D
E

1

2

3

4

D
E

Rendinghu
Lake

RENDINGHU
GONGTUAN

DESHENGMEN

Xiaocun Lu
Xinde
Deshengli Xijie
Jie
Tayuan
Jie
Jiaochangkou
Deshengli
Hutong
Andeli
Nanjie
Jie
Hongji
Andeli

Xizhimen Beidajie

Wenhuiyuan Beilu

Ande Lu

Libaisi
Hutong
Linglu
Hutong
Dejing
Hutong

White Peacock
Art World

Deshengmen Xibinhelu
Xiao    Hutong

Wenhuiyuan Jie

Wenhuiyuan Nanlu

Xiaocun Lu

Xinjiekouwai Dajie

Dewaxihou

JISHUITAN

Huifeng Temple

Xihai Beiyan
Banqiao
7 Tiao
Banqiaotou
Tiao

Xihai Lake

Xihai Dongyan

Houhai Beiyan

Former Home
of Song Qingling

Deshengmen Xidajie (Second Ring Road)

Putaoyuan
Hutong
Houtaoyuan
Hutong
Qiantaoyuan
Hutong

Xijiaochangxiao
7 Tiao
Xinjiekou
7 Tiao

Xinjiekou
4 Tiao

Gulou Xidajie

Xizhimen
Railway
Station

Xinjiekou

Xu Beihong
Memorial Hall

Jishuitan
Hospital

Houhai

Lake

Heita
Hutong

Xinjiekou

Dongxinkai
Hutong

Yangfang Hutong

Maojiawan
Hutong

Beicaochang
Hutong

Xinjiekou Dongjie

Shichahai
Hutong

Gaolianqiao Lu

xing
xiang
Lu

Xitang
(West Cathedral)

Xizhimennei Dajie

Sihuan
Hutong

Xinjiekou

Gong Wang Fu
(Palace of Prince
Gong)

XIZHIMEN

Houbanbi Jie

Dahoucang Hutong

Qianbanbi Jie

Liu Xiang

Beiwei Hutong

Dongguanying
Hutong

Hougangping
Hutong

Zhengjue H.

Hangkong
Hutong

Boqicang H.

Sanbulao
Hutong

Hongshan
Hutong

Dashihu
Hutong

Daxinkai

Nandajie

Lu

Qiangongyong
Hutong

Baitasi

Liuhai H.

Hutong

Music
Conservatory
of China

IMEN

Beilishi Lu

Huguo Temple

Mei
Lanfang
Memorial

Yannian

Lu

Dingfu Lu

Dacheng

Xiang

Nanxiaojie

Guoying H.

Ancheng H.

Baochan Hutong

Huguosi Jie

Xinghua

Hutong

Longtouqing

Ping'anli Xidajie

Yujiao Hutong

People's
Theatre

Di'anmen Xidajie

Jingxinzhai
(Place of the
Quiet Heart)

GONGZHUANG

Zhongxiucai
Hutong

Dayu H.

Qianche    Hutong

Xisibei 8 Tiao

Taipingcang
Hutong

Beijie

Jiulongbi
(Nine Dragon Screen)

zhuang Jie

Xigongliang
Hutong

Fusujiing

Xiangxia Hutong

Fuguo Jie

Houshaluo
Hutong

Xisibei 7 Tiao

Xisibei 6 Tiao

Zhongmaojiawan

Aimin 4
Xiang

Wulongting
(Five-Dragon Pavilion)

Cuihuaheng Jie

Culhua Jie

Xisibei 5 Tiao

Aimin 7
Xiang

Beihai
Lake

Jinguo
Hutong

ngzhuang
Dajie

Former Residence
of Lu Xun

Dongjiangxia H.

Dachaye H.

Xisibei 4 Tiao
Xisibei 3 Tiao

Dahongluochang

Jie

Tianhong Hutong

Fenliang
Tower

ngfang
jie
Fuwai
Hospital

Gongmenkou 3 Tiao

Anping Xiang

Guangjisi
(Temple of
Universal Rescue)

Beitang
(North
Cathedral)

Guanganmen H.

Duanwang H.

Caohong Hutong

Baita
(White Dagoba)

Gongmenkoutou Tiao

Baistasi
(Temple of the
White Pagoda)

Ministry
of Geology

Xisi
Dongdajie

XISI

Yong'ansi
(Temple of Eternal Peace)

HENGMEN

Bank
of China

Minkang Hutong

Fuchengmennei Dajie

Wangfucang Hutong

Yangrou Hutong

Zhuanta Hutong

Xi'anmen Dajie

Wenjin Jie

FUCHENGMEN

Geological
Museum

Bansang

Zhonghai
Lake

Beijie

Daxi
Hutong

Huajia H.

Jinsheng
Hutong

Sandaozhalan
Hutong

Dayuan H.

Xixin H.

Guangning Hutong

Furun

Dacheng Hutong

Wuding Hutong

Bingmasi Hutong

Fengsheng Hutong

Nanjie

Xixin H.

Fuyou Jie

Yuetan
Gymnasium

Mengduan Hutong

Houliwa H.

Fenzi Hutong

Dajiangfang
Hutong

Xuanchengmen

Xuanchengcheng

Yuetan

Shifangxiao

Hongmiao Hutong

N GONGYUAN
TER OF THE
ON PARK)

Zhenjif H.

Qianjian H.

Taipingqiao Dajie

Yuejun Hutong

Jie

Dongnie_Jie

XI CHENG

D
E

D     E

**ZUOJIAZHUANG SHANGCHANG**

Hepinglidongjie
Jiaolinjiadao
Zuojiazhuang
Jing'an Dongjie
Zhonglü Building
Dongjie
International Telecommunications Office

1

Minwang
Beihutong
Xbahe Nanlu
Zuojiazhuang Nanjie
Zuojiazhuang Zhongjie
Liufang Jie
Jingxin Building
Dongsanhuan Beilu

Minwang Nanhutong
Zuojiazhuang Nanxiejie
Xinyuan Jie
Shunyuan Jie

Public Security Building Visa Office
Xiangheyuan Lu
Dongzhimenyi Xiejie
Xin Donglu
**Forture Building**

Beiguanting Hutong Beixiajie
Xinyuan Nanlu

**XINQIAO**
**Liangma**
Liangmahe Nanlu

Zhimennei Dajie
**NANGUAN GONGYUAN**
Xianggguanlou Hutong
Minran Hutong
**DONGZHIMEN**
Xiangheyuan Lu
**DONGZHIMEN**
Sanlitunxi 6 Jie
Sanlitundong 6 Jie
Sanlitundong 5 Jie

2

Dongshoupa Hutong
**Dongzhimen Bus Terminal**
Dongzhimenwai Xiaojie
Xin Donglu
Sanlitunxi 5 Jie
**District of Embassies (North)**

Beixincang Hutong
Dongzhimen Beidajie
Dongzhimenwai Dajie
Sanlitundong 4 Jie

**Dongzhimen Hospital (Traditional Chinese Medicine)**
Dong Huan Plaza
Dong Zhongjie
Dongzhimenwai Dajie
Sanlitundong 3 Jie

Haiyuncang Hutong
Songnian Hutong
Dong Zhongjie
Tongchangzi Hutong
Sixiang
Sanlitundong 2 Jie

Beimencang Hutong
Beigongmen Hutong
Xinzhongjie 4 Tiao
Xin Donglu
Sanlitundong 1 Jie

angsi 10 Tiao
Blandian Hutong
**DONGSISHITIAO**
Xingfucun Zhonglu
**Yashow Market**

**College of Chinese Medicine**
Dongmencang Hutong
**Poly Plaza**
Xinzhongjie 4 Tiao
Xinzhongjie
Xingfucun 4 Xiang
Chumen
Sanlitun
Sanlitundong 1 Jie

Dongcuiya Hutong
**Gongren Tiyuchang Beilu**
**Gongren Tiyuchang Beilu**

3

**General Hospital**
Beixiajie
Nanmencang Hutong
Xi Zhongjie
Zhuo Zhongjie Dong Zhongjie
Xinzhong Jie
**Workers Gymnasium**
**Workers Stadium**
Gongren Tiyuchang Donglu
Nansanlitun Lu

Chaoyangmen Beidajie
Doufaji Hutong
Nandouya Hutong
Chaoyangmen Beiheyan
Panliapo Hutong
**Ministry of Culture**
Jishikou 7 Tiao
Gongren Tiyuchang Xilu
Gongren Tiyuchang Nanlu
Baijiazhuang Lu
Dongdaqiaoxie

Yuanfu Jie
**CHAOYANGMEN**
Chaoyangmen Beiheyan 2 Tiao
Santiao
Gongren Tiyuchang Nanlu
Dongdaqiaoxie

haoyangmennei Dajie
Chaoyangmen Nandajie
Chaoyangmenwai Dajie
**Dongyuemiao (Temple of the God of Tai Mountain)**
**Chaoyang Hospital**

Beizhuan Hutong
Zhugan Hutong
**Ministry of Foreign Affairs**
Nanheyan 2 Tiao
Sanfeng Hutong
Rongsheng Hutong
Gongren Tiyuchang Nanlu
Guandongdian Beijie

Nanzhugan Hutong
Xinxian Hutong
Fangjiayuan Hutong
Nanyingfang Hutong
Fangcaodi Xijie
Dongdaqiao Lu
**Chaoyang Dajie**

Chaoyangmen Nanxiaojie
Dafangjia Hutong
**Zhihuaisi (Temple of Perfect Wisdom)**
Chaowai
Fangcaodi
**CHAOYANG**

Lumicangnou Xiang
Xiaoputang
Chaowaitou
Xiushuihe Hutong
Chaowaichang Jie
Shenti
Ritan Beixiang
Ritan Beixiang

Lumicang Hutong
Ritan
**Ritan (Alter of the Sun)**
Beilu

0      800 m
0      800 yards

D     E

**A**

**B**

## 1

Nanhai Lake

Wumen
(Meridian Gate)

Donghuamen Dajie

Xila Hutong

Ganyu Hutong

DONGCHEN

Donghuamen
Night Market

Dong'anmen
Dajie

Jinyi Hutong

Imperial
Ancestral
Temple

Pudu
Temple

Nanchizi Dajie

Caichang
Hutong

Jixiang Theatre

DONG

Daruanfu H.

Central Meizha Hutong

Nanheyan

Xiehe
Hospital

Xinhuamen
(Xinhua Gate)

ZHONGSHAN
GONGYUAN

PARK OF
THE PEOPLE'S
CULTURE

Datianshuijing
Hutong

Central
Fine Arts
Institute

Wangfujing Dajie

Union
Medical
University
of China

Waijiaobu
Xizongbu H.

Xinkaifu

DONG

Tian'anmen
(Gate of Heavenly Peace)

DONG
TIAN'ANMEN

Changpuheyan

Dongdan
3 Tiao

Dongdan

Xitang H.

Chang'an Jie

Fengsheng Hutong

WANGFUJING

Beijing Hotel

Oriental
Plaza

Xifenglou H.

Xichang'an Jie

XI TIAN'ANMEN

Tian'anmen
Square

DONGDAN

Xibiaobei H.

Zhongguo
Guojia Dajuyuan
(China National
Grand Theatre)

Renmin
Dahuitang
(Great Hall of
the People)

Zhongguo Guojia
Bowuguan
(National Museum
of China)

The People's
Government
of Beijing
Municipality

Beijing
Hospital

Dongda
Shango

Suzhou Hu

Dongrongxian Hutong

Dongliufanzi
Hutong

Gao Beihutong

Renmin Yingxiong
Jinian Bei
(Monument to the People's
Heros)

Mao Zhuxi
Jinian Tang
(Mao's Mausoleum)

Supreme
People's Court

Zhengyi Lu

Taijichangtou Tiao

DONGDAN
GONGYUAN

Nanbaca
Hutong

Beijingzh

Xijiaomin

Xiang

Bank of
China
Touring Car
Terminal

Zhengyangmen
(Gate facing the Sun)

Zhengyi Lu

Tongren
Hospital

Dongzhong
Hutong

HEPINGMEN

Qianmen

**2**

QIANMEN

Qianmen (Qian Gate)

Qianmen Dongdajie

Qianmen Xidajie

Chongwenmen
Xidajie

CHONGWENME

Chongwenmen

Beixinhua Jie

Dongjiaomin

Dajie

Taijichang

Chongwenmenwai Dajie

Bingbuwa H.

Qianmen
Jie

Qianmen Xihouheyanjie
Xiheyanjie

Jianlou (Arrow Tower)

Chongwenmen Xiheyan

Xin

Dongdamochang Jie

Chongwe
dongh

Shella H.

Paizi Hutong

Daqiao
Hutong

Jinmao Hutong

Shang 2

Sanjing Hutong

QIANMEN

Xianyukou Jie

Xixingtong Jie

Langfangtou Tiao

Dongxingtong Jie

Huashisha

Xihuashi

Liulichang
Dongjie

Yangwei H.
Yangmeizhuxie Jie

Baotoushi Jie

Dongmen

Caochangheng
Hutong

Shoupa Hut

Dazhalan
Jie

Dongchashi Hutong

Wutiao

People
Hospita
Beijing

Nanxinhua

Dazhalan Xijie

Xiang

Meishi Jie

Binggiaoxie H.

Kuejiawan H.

Dongdajie

Maweimao H.

Balshou H.

Zongshuxie

Shijing Hutong

Daxi
Hutong

Jinxiutou Tiao

Qinghua Jie

Xitang H.

Zhushikou Xidajie

Peiying Hutong

Dongbanbi Jie

CIQIK

**3**

ZHUSHIKOU

Xixiaoshi

Dongxiaoshi Jie

Qianmen Dajie

Banzhang
Hutong

Yao'e H.

Zhuanzhizi
Hutong

Shanjiankou
Jie

Xiyuanzi Jie

Liyuan Theatre

Xiangchang Lu

Chuziying
Hutong

Tiantan Lu

Tiantan Lu

Fahuas

HUFANGQIAO

Yong'an Lu

North Heavenly
Gate

Hongqiao
Market
(Pearl Marke

Friendship
Hospital

Fuchangjietou Tiao

Double Ring,
Longevity Pavillion

TIANTAN GONGYUAN

72 Long
Corridor

Beiwei Lu

Xibei Lu

Tianqiao
Bus Terminal

Tianqiao
Theatre

Ziran Bowuguan
(Beijing Natural
History Museum)

Qi'niandian
(Hall of Prayer
for Good Harvests)

Qinianmen
(Gate of Prayer
for Good Harvests)

★ Seven-Star
Rock

East Heavenly
Gate

Nanwei Lu

Wutiao

Zhaigong
(Hall of
Abstinence)

Chengzhenmen
(Chenzhen Gate)

Tiantan
Stadium

**4**

East Gate

Xiannongtan
(Altar of Agriculture and
Museum of Chinese
Architecture)

West Heavenly
Gate

Fukangli

Fukang Nanli

Huangqiongyu
(Hall of Heaven)

Echo Wall

Sanyinshi
(Echo Stones)

Yuanqiu
(Altar of Heaven)

0 _____ 800 m

Guanglimen
(Guangli Gate)

Zhaohengmen
(South Heavenly Gate)

(TEMPLE OF HEAVEN PARK)

Taiyuanmen
(Taiyuan Gate)

0 _____ 800 yards

Taiping Lu

Yongdingmennei Dajie

Yongdingmen

Yongdingmen

Dongjie

**A**

**B**

YUYUANTAN GONGYUAN
(SONG QINGLING CHILDREN'S SCIENCE PARK)

**WEIGONGCUN**

China
Millennium
Monument

Renmin Geming Junshi Bowguan
(People's Liberation Army Museum)

Ministry
of Finance

Yuetan Nanjie

Yue

Sanlihenanheng Jie

China
Academy
of Sciences

GONGZHUFEN

Ministry
of Defense

Sanlihe Donglu

Nanlish

Ⓓ Fuxing Lu  Ⓓ  Fuxing Lu  Ⓓ  Fuxingmenwai Dajie

**JUNSHIBOWUGUAN**

Sanlihe Lu

Sanlihenan 7 Xiang

Sanlihenan 6 Xiang

MUXIDI

Fuxing
Hospital

**MUXIDI**

Zhenwumiao Lu

Zhenw
2 T

Beifengwo Lu

Yangfangdian Lu

Beijing
Public Security
University

Baiyun Lu

Zhenw

Baiyunguan
(Temple of the
White Cloud)

Beifengwo Lu

Lianhuachi Donglu

Lianhuachi Donglu

Sanlihenan Nanli

Tianning Si
(Temple of
Heavenly
Tranquillity)

Maliandao Beilu

Lianhuachi Donglu

Nanfengwo Lu

Beijing Xi Zhan
(West Railway Station)

Xiaomachang Nanli

Machang Lu

Shoupakou Xijie

Shoupakou

Tianningsiqian Jie

Yongju
Hutong

Ahmenwai
Beilie

Guang'anmen Nanbinhelu

Lianhua-Lotus
Pond

Lianhuahe Hutong

**SHIJING-
SHAN**

Guang'anmenwai  Dajie

Beilie

Shoupakou Nanjie

Lianhua

Maliandao Lu

Beijie

Hongju Jie

Hongju
Dongjie

Guang'anmenwai Nanjie

Guang'an Lu

Maliandao

Maliandao 3 Xiang

Maliandao Zhongxiang

Maliandao Zhongjie

Lu

Hongjue

Hongju 2 Xiang

Nanxinh 2  Xiang
Jie

Guang'anmen Nanbinhelu

Maliandao Nanjie

Maliandao Nanjie

Maliandao Dongjie

Hongjian

Hongjue

Hongju Nanjie

Guang'anmen
Railway Station

Maliandao
Hutong

Lianhua

Guang'anmenchezhan Xijie

Xuanwu

Hongjian Nanlu

Yaziqiao Lu

(Second Ring Road)

(Third Ring Road)
Xisanhuan Zhonglu

Xisanhuan Nanlu

0 ⟼⟼⟼⟼ 800 m

0 ⟼⟼⟼⟼ 800 yards

Sanluju Lu

Sanluju Lu

A  B

A  B

1

2

3

4

**1**

Children's Hospital
Ledao Xiang
Namishi Lu

Exhibition Hall of Chinese Arts and Crafts
FUXINGMEN
Duchenghuangmiao Temple
Zhongjingjidao
China International Travel Service
Zhongguo Gongyishuguan (National Treasures Museum)

Guangningbo Hutong
Tunjuan Hutong
Xueyuan Hutong
Anyuan Hutong
Naoshikou Beijie
Pical
Longfu Xijie
Damucang Hutong
Piku Hutong
Dazi Hutong
Minfeng H.

Shibanfang 3 Tiao
Lingling Hutong
Belyin Hutong
Talpusi Jie
Bei'anti
XIDAN
Xidan Beidajie
Heng 2 Tiao
Zhongsheng Hutong
Fuyou Jie

Nanhai Lake
Xinhuamen (Xinhua Gate)

Fuxingmennei Dajie
XIDAN
Xichang'an Jie

**Fuxingmennei Dajie**

Chayuan Hutong
Xidanshoupa H.
Dongtiejiang Hutong
Jiaoyu Jie
Wenhua
Xinwenhua Jie
Yongning H.
Toufa Hutong
Yuetai Hutong
Wenjia Jie

**FUXINGMEN**

Capital Cinema
Xi'anfu Hutong
Beixinping Hutong
Xirongxian Hutong
Xijiulianzi
Xixinlianzi Hutong
Xinbi Jie

Beijing Concert Hall
Dongrongxian Hutong
Dongjiufianzi Hutong
Dongzhong Xiang
Xijiaomin Hutong
Bongzhong Hutong

Nantang (South Cathedral)

Xuanwumen Xidajie
Xuanwumen Dongdajie
Qianmen

**XUANWUMEN**
CHANGCHUNJIE
**HEPINGMEN**
Qianmen Xidajie

Xuanwumen Xiheyanjie
Shangkle Jie
Sanmiao Jie
Chukuying
Dazhiqiao Hutong
Xuanwumen Dongheyanjie
Qianmen Xiheyanjie
Sheila H.

**XIBIANMEN**
XUANWU ART GARDEN
Hualbalshuhou Jie
Changchun Jie
Laoqiangen Jie
Jiaochangkou Hutong
Jiaoochangxiao 8 Tiao
Haibal Hutong
Qiangdingchang H.
Chunshu-shangtou Tiao
Liufichang Xijie
Liufichang Dongjie

Xuanwu Hospital
Baoguo Si (Temple)
Xicaochang Jie
Qiahsungongyuan Hutong
Mianhuaxia 7 Tiao
Dingliu Hutong
Jiadajiu Hutong
Baishun H.
Shanxi Xixiang

**Guang'anmennei Dajie**
Luomashi Dajie

**3**

Danglai Hutong
Dequan Hutong
Madao H.
Cuzhang Hutong
Beldaji Xiang
Bao'ansi Hutong
Huguang Guild Hall and Opera Museum
Fuzhouguan
Liyuan Theatre

**NG'ANMEN**
Niujie Qingzhensi (Niu Jie Mosque)
Fayuansi (Temple of the Source of the Buddhist Doctrine)
**HUFANGQIAO**
Fayuansiqian
Nanheng Xijie
Nanheng Dongjie
Beiwei Lu

Xuanwu Stadium
Zaolinxie Jie
Shalan H.

**CAISHIKOU**

Chongxiao Hutong
Yingtao 3 Tiao
Baizhifang Xijie
WANSHOU GONGYUAN
Baizhifang Dongjie

Jiangong Dongli Xin'an Zhongli
Central Academy of Traditional Opera
Liren Jie

**YOU'ANMEN**

Taoranting
North Gate
**TAORANTING GONGYUAN (HAPPY PAVILION PARK)**
West Gate
Taoranting Lake
Central Isle
Temple of Mercy
Cloud-Depicting Tower
Waterside Pavilion
East Gate
Xiannongtan Stadium
Yongdingmen Xijie

**XUANWU**
You'anmennei Dajie

**DAGUANYUAN (GRAND VIEW GARDEN)**

**4**

D   E

# STREET INDEX

# ART & PHOTO CREDITS

# GENERAL INDEX